Teacher Learning that Matters

Routledge Research in Education

For a full list of titles in this series please visit www.routledge.com

Teacher Learning that Matters

International Perspectives

Edited by Mary Kooy and Klaas van Veen

Routledge
Taylor & Francis Group

NEW YORK   LONDON

First published 2012
by Routledge
711 Third Avenue, New York, NY 10017

Simultaneously published in the UK
by Routledge
2 Park Square, Milton Park, Abingdon, Oxon OX14 4RN

*Routledge is an imprint of the Taylor & Francis Group,
an informa business*

Typeset in Sabon by IBT Global.
Printed and bound in the United States of America on acid-free paper by
IBT Global.

Library of Congress Cataloging-in-Publication Data
Teacher learning that matters : international perspectives / [edited by]
  Mary Kooy, Klaas van Veen.
    p. cm. — (Routledge research in education ; 62)
  Includes bibliographical references and index.
    1. Teachers—In-service training—Cross-cultural studies. 2. Teachers—
Professional relationships—Cross-cultural studies. 3. Professional learning
communities—Cross-cultural studies. 4. School improvement programs—
Cross-cultural studies. I. Kooy, Mary. II. Veen, Klaas van, 1970–
  LB1731.T4187 2012
  370.71'1—dc22
  2011010545

ISBN13: 978-0-415-88880-6 (hbk)
ISBN13: 978-0-203-80587-9 (ebk)

For the teachers in Ontario, Canada, whose commitment to teaching and learning in community continues to build their knowledge, skill, and expertise and taken me on a transformative research journey since 2000. For the students whose collaborative dialogues and keen insights have been reshaping my visions and views of teaching and learning since 2006.

Mary Kooy

To Willem, a 4 year old student, who learned from me, his pre-service student teacher in 1988, how to use scissors, and proudly and promptly, cut paper all that afternoon. It was Willem who opened a window to the fascinating and puzzling process of learning and teaching. I also dedicate this work to all those teachers who, every school day, dedicate themselves to inviting their students on the never-ending learning journey.

Klaas van Veen

Contents

PART I
Orienting the Way on the Landscape

PART II
Perspectives for Teacher Learning in Multiple Contexts

PART III
Foundations for Developing the Self in Teacher Learning

PART IV
Professional Learning for Teacher Practice

Figures

Tables

Preface
Introducing the Landscapes of Teacher Learning that Matters

The study of teacher learning and development has exponentially evolved in the last 20 years. This can be attributed, in significant part, to ongoing reforms and changes characterizing educational contexts around the globe. We call on researchers from divergent nationalities, disciplines and fields, who share our questions and issues on teacher learning that matters. This offers an unusual opportunity to bring together multinational, multiple and complex conversations with and from a range of experts and expertise in the field.

The increase in studies focusing on the effects of teacher learning on classroom teaching, however, are often small-scale; found in a range of journals, disciplines and national contexts; and lack cohesion and connection. In this book, we bring together a complex network of research, though we do not claim to connect or bring the cohesion desired. Yet, the research stories cumulatively provide glimpses into teacher learning and development that matter insofar as they inform and shape student learning. As such, we present theoretical, social and contextual (e.g., workplace) international research and theory of effective teacher learning with a focus on how teachers build their capacities as learners and teachers. To that end, we entitle the book: *Teacher Learning that Matters: International Perspectives.*

The focus in education has been to raise standards, improve achievement and make students more competitive in an increasingly market-driven world. Impositions of mandates, policies and programs have cleared the way to recognizing the key role of teachers, regardless of national context and educational system, in implementing and instantiating reforms and change. The increasing awareness has led to a focus on preparing teachers to develop skills and strategies reflecting the changes required to improve student learning. This is particularly true in light of the fact that highly qualified and skilled teachers affect the performance and learning of their students.

The critical knowledge that a highly skilled teaching force is needed for actualizing student achievement and educational change has resulted in increased calls for "professional development" for teachers. While, on the surface, this appears promising, the typical "one-shot workshop," the persistent mainstay model of teacher learning, fails to sufficiently affect teacher knowledge or make way for professional learning that is teacher driven and in social contexts (see Borko, 2004; Desimone, 2009; Kooy, 2006; Little, this volume; van Veen, Zwart and Meirink, this volume, for example).

Yet, breaking with what Dewey called "the crust of convention" remains a complex challenge. This is complicated by research suggesting that more highly skilled teachers effectively improve student learning. Since change depends on teachers, and effective teacher learning leads to improved knowledge and skill, then it becomes imperative to develop sustained teacher learning as the portal through which change and reforms can be realized across national and cultural boundaries.

This is not to say that we fuse such knowledge. Indeed, we assiduously avoid essentializing or assuming that the part in any way represents the whole (country, educational systems, teachers and students). There is no "thereby hangs a tale" sensibility that veers toward conclusions or finite results. What we present, instead, are instances of knowledge development that challenge existing conventional wisdom and practices around teacher development and learning.

The structure of the volume evolved organically and intentionally, simultaneously. We agreed early in the process, for instance, on a bookend frame: an introduction, which James Britton coined as an "assisted invitation," a "come with me into multiple worlds and ways research is being developed in eight different nations." The gesture is dialogic, inviting the reader to engage with the knowledge (re)presented. How does this challenge, shape, reframe my conception of teacher learning? How does that affect or how is it affected by change—in context, content, educational system, researcher, reform agendas? Is this important, even critical, to my developing knowledge? How does this affect teacher learning that matters where I am?

The book is divided into five parts moving from a macro-position (establishing the landscapes of teacher learning) to a micro-position (applied research on teacher learning). Part I contains a chapter by Klaas van Veen, Rosanne Zwart and Jacobiene Meirink entitled "What Makes Teacher Professional Development Effective? A Literature Review." They create a literature review examining empirical studies conducted over the last 25 years that focus on the relationships between forms of in-service teacher learning and development. Judith Warren Little's chapter, "Professional Community and Professional Development in the Learning-Centered School," brings life to the literature review as it creates a portrait of developing a culture of continuous learning. She portrays the effective professional community as one rooted in local problems; linked to external sources of knowledge and support; and nurtured by leadership for critical, collegial and improvement-oriented practice. The chapters set the stage as they characterize the context for and diverse voices of the research that follows.

Part II consists of studies conducted by researchers in Australia, Canada and the United States as they explore teacher knowledge and learning by focusing lenses on the conditions, metaphors, voices and curriculum. In Loughran's chapter (Chapter 3), two rich examples are described of teachers learning about their own practice, and becoming more aware of the knowledge, skills and abilities as pedagogues. In their 10-year longitudinal study, Wallace and Mullholland (Chapter 4) explore the learning processes of five science teachers to gain deep understanding of and insights into complexities and nuances of teacher learning in the divergent contexts of their daily work lives. In Chapter 5, Kooy and Colarusso investigate teacher learning through reframing teacher and student voices to transform teaching and learning in schools. To demonstrate, they explore how site-based book clubs that include students and parents create a powerful learning environment for the teachers involved. Students informing the teachers about what and how they learn and experience teaching pedagogies and practices provide the teachers with insights into learning and teaching that matters. Cheryl Craig in Chapter 6 provides a framework for teacher learning and development through a metaphor of teacher as curriculum maker. Acknowledging the value of personal practical knowledge of teaching, Craig argues that teachers are uniquely situated at the interstices of the curricular exchange and hence active agents in curriculum making.

Part III includes studies conducted by researchers in the Netherlands, China and Australia detailing the perspectives and practices that inform and shape the ways teacher professional learning develops both individually and socially. The research looks introspectively, through discourse and critical moments, to call on teacher knowledge and know-how as a heuristic for professional learning and development. In Chapter 7, Attema-Noordewier, Korthagen and Zwart describe an approach that engages teachers to look inward to build awareness of personal qualities, potential and inspiration. They found that teachers grew in their awareness of their personal, collegial and student strengths that, in turn, affected relationships and curriculum development. Meijer and Oolbekkink (Chapter 8) investigate forms of transformative learning that affect teachers' identity and how these forms inform learning processes and reconstruction of commitment and passion to teaching. Chapter 9 documents research conducted by Parr and Doecke, who describe in detail a rich example of how two teacher educators and two teachers use reflective writing about learning processes to create dialogue resulting in powerful and transforming learning. Ying (Chapter 10) expands the social context to include educators from a broad range of contexts as they meet in professional learning communities using writing and reflections to destabilize conventional thinking about teacher learning and develop and strengthen the contexts for collaboration construction of professional knowledge.

Part IV consists of studies conducted in the United Kingdom, Cyprus and Sweden. Each aims to enact research and practice as expressed in a new master's program for teachers, and two research inquiries into science education and professional learning. Mitchell and Alexandrou (Chapter 11) explore a master's program for teacher learning in a context of increasing political pressures and economically deprived urban schools to successfully support teachers to identify and challenge their existing practices by focusing on the fundamental and personal core of teaching and pupil learning. In Chapter 12, Hadjiachilleos and Avraamidou investigate the learning processes of elementary teachers actively involved in an open-ended science inquiry in an outdoor setting that led to new understanding of the subject matter and pedagogy. Nilsson (Chapter 13), also located in science education, aims to gain a deeper understanding of identifying the qualities of a local professional development program based framed in the research of Desimone (2009) revealing how features such as engagement, shared vision, a community of learners and subject matter knowledge materialize in a local context.

Part V's chapter shares a focus on teacher learning that really matters for both teachers and their students. The teacher as learner is a significant stakeholder in each educational context and culture. The divergent national, cultural and political backgrounds of the researchers and research provide landscapes of teacher learning that bring alternative perspectives and insights to life. As such, it seeks to expand and extend the discourse to open the way for interactive dialogue and mutual explorations. For those of us interested in knowing more about teacher learning, we acquire more to work with for informed decision-making and continuing the inquiries.

The volume etches landscapes worth exploring for those critically interested in and aware of the changing texts, contexts and commitment to teacher learning that matters.

Mary Kooy and Klaas van Veen

REFERENCES

Borko, H. (2004). Professional development and teacher learning: Mapping the terrain. *Educational Researcher*, 33(8), 3–15.

Desimone, L. M. (2009). Improving impact studies of teachers' professional development: Toward better conceptualizations and measures. *Educational Researcher*, 38(3), 181–199.

Kooy, M. (2006). *Telling stories in book clubs: Women teachers and professional development*. New York: Springer.

Part I

Orienting the Way on the Landscape

1 What Makes Teacher Professional Development Effective?

A Literature Review

Klaas van Veen, Rosanne Zwart and Jacobiene Meirink

INTRODUCTION

This chapter aims to explore what is currently known about the effectiveness of teachers' professional development (PD) programs or PD interventions on the quality of teachers, their teaching and student learning. *PD activities* refer to a wide range of activities in which teachers participate, such as information meetings, study days, 1-day workshops and training sessions; coaching and intervision; mentoring, classroom observations, participation in a network, offsite team training sessions, book and study clubs; and research projects. Most of the current PD activities can be characterized as traditional forms of PD. *Traditional* refers to the way PD was organized for the last decades: mainly through lectures, 1-day workshops, seminars and conferences, which were not situated at the workplace, in which teachers played a passive role, and in which the content was not adjusted to the problems and issues in the daily teaching practice. *Innovative forms* refer to all those interventions in which teachers do play an active role, and the issues in their own teaching practice determine the content. Some examples are collaboration of colleagues, study and book clubs, mentoring, coaching, intervision and research by teachers. It also includes the discourse on professional learning communities in which the emphasis is on the collective responsibility of teachers for the learning of their students and insights on teaching and PD (see also the chapter of Judith Warren Little in this volume; Borko, Jacobs & Koellner, 2010).

The distinction between traditional and innovative is rather normative in the sense that innovative would be better than traditional, even although empirical evidence for this assumption is still missing, as will be shown in this review. Besides, traditional forms are still used on a large scale, although there is also an increase of mixed forms. The current discourse views PD as more effective if the teacher has an active role in constructing knowledge and collaborates with colleagues, the content relates and is situated in the daily teaching practice and the possibilities and limitations of the workplace are taken into account. However likely, these assumptions lack empirical evidence. Therefore, it is relevant to review what is currently known empirically on effective features of divergent PD interventions and on the school organizational conditions to successfully implement these interventions. So, the following questions guide the review study:

1. What is known about the effective features of interventions for PD?
2. What is known about the school organizational conditions of these PD interventions?

THEORETICAL FRAMEWORK

Teacher PD in this chapter refers to those processes and activities designed to enhance the professional knowledge, skills and attitudes of educators so that they might, in turn, improve the learning of students (Guskey, 2000). The focus of the review are those activities explicitly designed for PD of teachers, which we describe as interventions for PD. More specifically, the focus is on those studies that report about effective features of PD.

When, however, is PD effective? Assuming the only relevant indication is increased student results, studies should focus on the relationships between the intervention and student results. If improving teacher behavior or teacher knowledge is the main goal of PD, then the focus should be relationships between the intervention and teachers' behavior or knowledge. However, if the assumption is that a change in behavior is always the result of a change in cognition, the focus should be the relationships between the intervention and the cognition, and perhaps also on teacher behavior. The same applies to the assumption that student results are the result of a change in teacher behavior or teacher cognition. Given different aims and assumptions behind concepts of PD effectiveness, it is essential to formulate the model this review uses to understand the effectiveness of PD.

As a main theoretical and organizing frame, this study applies Desimone's (2009) conceptual model for studying the effects of PD on teachers and students, based on an extended literature review. The model demonstrates interactive, nonrecursive relationships between (a) the critical features of PD, (b) teacher knowledge and beliefs, (c) classroom practice and (d) student outcomes (see Figure 1.1).

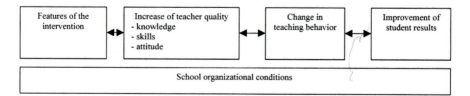

Figure 1.1   Analytical framework for the study (based on Desimone, 2009).

The relationships between these elements are not linear per se, as often is the case, rather as integrated and dynamic (cf. Clarke & Hollingsworth, 2002). For instance, research shows that a change in teaching behavior can be caused as much by a change in teacher knowledge as a change in student behavior (Guskey & Sparks, 2004). Rather, it is essential to articulate the relationships between the different elements, which can be described as the 'theory of improvement' (Wayne, Yoon, Zhu, Cronen & Garet, 2008; Desimone, 2009). What is the intervention supposed to do? Who has to learn what, how and why? And what elements will result in an effective PD intervention? This theory of improvement can refer to three aspects: theory of change, theory of instruction and theory of context.

Theory of change refers to the assumed relationships between the features of the PD intervention and the change in teacher knowledge and/or change in instruction. Theory of instruction focuses on student results and refers to the relationships between the features of the PD intervention, the intended changes in teacher knowledge and instruction and the expected changes in student outcomes. Theory of context refers to the school organizational conditions necessary to implement and sustain successful PD in the school or in the classrooms. As Smylie (1995) observed, and more recently Little (2006) and Imants and van Veen (2010) confirm, most PD research hardly takes the conditions of the daily workplace into account, while these conditions strongly determine the opportunities and limitations of PD interventions.

Measurement is another important factor in effective PD interventions. Despite the recent focus on evidence-based practices, interventions that are hardly explored for their effect still dominate PD practice. As Hattie (2009, p. 2) summarized the general state of educational research on these topics: "[T]he research evidence relating to 'what works' is burgeoning, even groaning, under a weight of such beautiful 'try me' ideas." One of the reasons for this lack of evidence is the discussion about what is considered to be evidence.

Some argue that conclusions about causality and effectiveness can only be based on randomized controlled trials (cf. Slavin, 2008; Raudenbush, 2005; Wayne et al., 2008). Others argue that this approach is limited due to the underlying technocratic assumption, in which the effectiveness of the features of the intervention is the only relevant focus. Educational goals, which can strongly differ per school and teacher, can also determine effectiveness (Biesta, 2007). Others, while supporting the evidence-based approach, point to the risk of constructing lists of what works because it might "provide yet another set of recommendations devoid of underlying theory and messages" (Hattie, 2009, p. 3) or neglecting the specific features of the context.

These last issues seem to complicate the debate on effectiveness: Often it is only known what works in general, or only in very specific situations. So Raudenbush (2005) argues that randomized controlled trials are actually the only valid way to explore effectiveness, but it is not sufficient to understand why what works. Qualitative, small-scale case studies are therefore needed (cf. Little, 2006). And, as Raudenbush (2005) adds, (multiple) case studies are needed to provide working assumptions that can be tested in large-scale studies.

In addition, Verloop (2003, p. 208) notes that besides effectiveness studies, there are all kinds of educational and subject pedagogical theories and notions providing clear and insightful descriptions of educational processes that are the result of systematic thinking and research into teaching and learning. Although this body of knowledge provides no rigid empirical evidence about what works, it can be very relevant for teachers. So, to get an overview of what is known, this review will include both large-scale effectiveness studies and small-scale qualitative studies. The combination of both research approaches enables us to understand when and why and for whom an intervention is effective.

METHOD

This review focuses on those activities that are explicitly designed for PD of teachers (referred to as PD interventions). An important criterion for inclusion of studies in this review is that researchers examined the effect of the intervention. As described earlier in the theoretical framework, effectiveness can refer to different elements of the analytical framework: teacher quality, teacher classroom behavior and/or student learning.

Search Strategies and Criteria

Several search strategies were used to accomplish an extended overview of studies on the effect of PD interventions. We conducted literature searches with the use of ERIC, PsychINFO, Dissertation Abstracts, Sociological Collection, PiCarta and Google Scholar. Furthermore, we examined references of previous reviews. For this process of searching and analyzing a protocol was developed. This protocol included a list of search terms, which was partly based on previous reviews. The most important search terms were: teacher PD, teacher learning, in-service program, learning in the workplace, effects of PD, effective PD and more specific terms referring to learning activities and formats as coaching, mentoring, workshops, seminars, etc.

After an extensive exploration, it appeared that many studies conducted in the past 25 years have been summarized in a large number of review studies. Therefore, we decided to take these review studies as a starting point for the analysis. Next, we researched PD interventions conducted in the past 10 years (2000–2010) in addition to the existing overviews.

For the selection of the additional studies, the following criteria were used:

- The study needs to report on a PD intervention.
- The study needs to report on outcomes with respect to teacher learning or student learning, outcomes for teacher learning as well as student learning or even on the relation between teacher learning and student learning.
- The study has to be published in a peer-reviewed journal, in a dissertation or in a report commissioned by a renowned institute or government agency.
- Both quasi-experimental case studies and quantitative and qualitative studies are included as long as the method was elaborate and transparent enough in order to draw some conclusions about effective features. We based this decision on weighing the methodology and the 'impact' of the results. Studies were scored on: (a) soundness/rigidity of methodology and (b) substantial qualitative or quantitative results.
- The study needs to add to previous studies in such a way that it concerns an intervention that has not been examined yet or it concerns a new design or method.

Content Analysis of Additional Studies

Based on this first selection, we selected 11 reviews and 95 additional studies on PD interventions. We summarized all studies according to 22 aspects, such as: type of study, context, the content of the intervention, learning goals, 'theory of improvement,' the results, school conditions and how it can be placed in the 'conceptual framework.' Of the 95 additional studies it appeared that some studies did not offer enough information to learn more about effective features of the PD interventions. In the end, 34 studies on PD interventions remained for the more detailed analysis.

Input of Experts in the Field of Teacher Learning

The aim of consulting various (international) experts in this field was to make sure that no important, not (yet) published or published reports were excluded in this review. In addition, the researchers used these consults to identify the most relevant studies and to discuss the results and conclusions.

RESULTS

A General Overview

The review brings together 11 major reviews and texts and 34 additional empirical studies on effective PD that cover the last 25 years of research on PD interventions. The 11 review texts are: Blank and de las Alas (2009); Borko et al. (2010); Desimone (2009); Hawley and Valli (1999); Kennedy

(1998); Knapp (2003); Little (2006); Smith and Gillespie (2007); Timperley, Wilson, Barrar and Fung (2007); Vescio, Ross and Adams (2008); and Yoon, Duncan, Lee, Scarloss and Shapley (2007). Some of these reviews refer to each other or are based on some of the same studies, but some differ strongly in focus, and also in studies they chose to include. For instance, Timperley et al. includes studies from Australia, New Zealand and Europe, which are not mentioned in the other texts. Regarding the difference in focus, Yoon et al. selected only studies that are in line with the Clearinghouse Standards, while others are less concerned with these strict criteria and more focused on understanding the effectiveness of features (for instance, Kennedy, 1998; Little, 2006). Together they provide an impressive collection of the theoretical and empirical body of research of the last 25 years.

Furthermore, as a result of intensive research, we include 34 empirical studies of the last 10 years. Some of these studies comprise large-scale surveys, aiming at exploring general effects of PD interventions on teachers and students. The majority of the studies, however, explore the effects of one PD intervention. The interventions differ in duration from 3 months to 5 years, in composition from interdisciplinary teams to individual approaches and in type of education, from primary to vocational education. The topics for PD also differ strongly. Most interventions, however, have a duration of about 1 (school) year and aim at primary education in the United States. Other countries are France (Morge, Toczek & Chakroun, 2010), Switzerland (Vogt & Rogalla, 2009), Canada (Butler, Lauscher, Jarvis-Sellinger & Beckingham, 2004), Australia (Ingvarson, Meiers & Beavis, 2005) and the United Kingdom (James & McCormick, 2009; Stark, 2006). Four studies were conducted in the Netherlands (Bakkenes, Vermunt & Wubbels, 2010; Hofman & Dijkstra, 2010; Ponte, Ax, Beijaard & Wubbels, 2004; Zwart, Wubbels, Bergen & Bolhuis, 2009).

The interventions emphasize subject matter, curriculum design, instructional strategies and student learning in a subject area and they often concern science subjects (like math and natural sciences) (Buczynski & Hansen, 2010; Chamberlin, 2005: Cohen & Hill, 2000; Desimone, Porter, Garet, Yoon & Birman, 2002; Doppelt et al. 2009; Ermeling, 2010; Fishman, Marx, Best & Tal, 2003; Franke, Carpenter, Levi & Fennema, 2001; Garet, Porter, Desimone, Birman & Yoon, 2001; Holmlund Nelson & Slavit, 2007; Kazemi & Franke, 2004; Lee, Hart, Cuevas & Enders, 2004; Lee, Lewis, Adamson, Maerten-Rivera & Secada, 2007; Morge et al., 2010; Norton & McCloskey, 2008; Saxe, Gearhart & Nasir, 2001; Supovitz & Turner, 2000; Telese, 2008; Vogt & Rogalla, 2009; Wallace, 2009).

Studies related to language education were less represented. The few studies concern language education in primary schools (Garet et al., 2008; Lee et al., 2007; Tienken & Achilles, 2003; Wilson, 2008), language education in secondary schools (Wallace, 2009) and language education in kindergarten (Domitrovich et al., 2009; Bierman et al., 2008; McCutchen et al., 2002). Two studies concern teacher networks (Hofman & Dijkstra, 2010; James & McCormich, 2009); one study pertains to an intervention with highly structured subject matter content and curricula (Domitrovich et al.; Bierman et al.). One study was conducted in special education (Butler et al., 2004).

The interventions that were studied are usually subject-matter-oriented summer schools or series of subject-matter-oriented workshops followed by a transfer to teachers' teaching practices. They come to light through teacher research (Buczynski & Hansen, 2010; Butler et al., 2004; Chamberlin, 2005; Desimone et al., 2002; Doppelt et al., 2009; Ermeling, 2010; Fishman et al., 2003; Hofman & Dijkstra, 2010; Holmlund Nelson & Slavit, 2007; James & McCormich, 2009; Kazemi & Franke, 2004; Lee et al., 2004; Levine & Marcus, 2010; Morge et al., 2010; Norton & McCloskey, 2008; Ponte et al., 2004; Saxe et al., 2001; Supovitz & Turner, 2000; Wilson, 2008), participation in learning communities (Butler, et al.; Desimone, et al.), observing and experimenting in the classroom (Chamberlin, 2005; Zwart et al., 2009), coaching by in-service trainers in the classroom (Domitrovich et al., 2009), but also other forms. During this process, follow-up meetings are regularly organized. The amount of involvement of the in-service trainers (which are also often researchers) varies from a coach with a fair amount of distance from participants on the one end to a participating member of a learning community on the other end. Although most programs claim to be based on issues and concerns of teachers, it is striking that the idea of an expert trainer who determines what teachers should know or do and how they should learn is still dominant. Exceptions are forms of action research (e.g., Ponte et al., 2004; Stark, 2006) and working in professional learning communities as described in the review study of Little (2006; see also her chapter in this volume). More specifically, it concerns teacher networks, research teams in schools, lesson study groups, meetings on student work using a reflection protocol, collegial observation and video clubs. The discussion on professional learning communities and teacher research goes beyond 'deficit thinking' to provide guidelines for unraveling and solving daily recurrent problems in practice.

In general, there is a strong focus on subject matter, active and inquiry-oriented learning and professional learning communities. Nevertheless, (elements of the) traditional forms of PD are still in use.

Methodological Problems

One of the results refers to the nature of the current research on effective teacher PD. Various factors complicate conclusions on what works. Assumptions about what constitutes valid research will determine whether these problems are classified as minor or major dilemmas. The problems are:

Teacher Quality As Primary Effect Size

The analytical framework of this review distinguishes factors that can be affected by the intervention such as teacher quality, teacher behavior and/or student learning. In research on effective PD interventions it appears that the majority of the studies concern the relation between the intervention and teacher quality. To a lesser degree there are studies that examine the relation between the intervention and the quality of classroom behavior. Only a limited number of studies focused on the relation between PD interventions and student results (cf. Borko, 2004; Little, 2006; Loucks-Horsley & Matsumoto, 1999; Smith & Gillespie, 2007; Supovitz, 2001). Recently, studies on the relation between interventions, teacher and student outcomes are increasing (for example, Garet et al., 2008; Timperley et al., 2007; Yoon et al., 2007).

Effect Size

Another problem is that most studies rely on self-reports of teachers (teachers' perceptions on possible effects and not more [quasi-] objective effect sizes like assessments, observations and student test scores). Well-known examples of studies that rely on self-reports are the large-scale studies of Cohen & Hill (2000), Garet et al. (2001) and Kennedy (1998). These studies are cited in many reviews as empirical evidence for the positive effect of PD interventions on teacher quality (cf. Borko, 2004; Little, 2006). A recent exception is the large-scale study of Garet et al. (2008), which includes a 'teacher knowledge assessment' and also extended observations and student-scores (cf. for the limited amount of studies that incorporate student outcomes, Timperley et al., 2007; Yoon, 2007).

Furthermore, in many studies the effect size is too general to define the effects of the PD interventions (Hattie, 2009). In other words, there is incongruence between the goal of the intervention and the effect that is measured. However, studies aimed at measuring more specific effect sizes for a PD intervention are also increasing (as the majority of the 34 additional studies found in this review show).

Lacking a 'Theory of Improvement'

In PD interventions the 'theory of improvement' often remains implicit. It often lacks a well-thought-out idea of how the form and content of intervention influence teacher learning ('theory of change') or student learning ('theory of instruction'). This is problematic since research on PD intervention does offer lists of effective features but it is not clear in what way these features contribute to the effect of an intervention on teacher or student learning.

Dominance of Research into 'Traditional' Forms of PD

Another problem is that studies are lacking on the effectiveness of many innovative forms of PD. Most research concerns more traditional forms of PD like workshops, conferences and courses (cf. Borko, 2004; Timperley et al., 2007; Wayne et al., 2008). Studies into forms of PD at the workplace, like coaching and mentoring, action research, study groups and teacher networks, often focus on the processes that take place during these interventions rather than on their effects.

Size of Studies

Finally, in research on teacher learning a more general problem can be detected, which was identified by Borko (2004; Borko et al., 2010). There is an overload of (mostly qualitative) studies that examine one program or intervention in one specific setting (type 1 studies in terms of Borko). Fewer studies examine one specific intervention and features in several settings with several coaches (type 2 studies). Largely missing is research in studies featuring several interventions in more than one setting, with several coaches (type 3 studies). The latter two types of research are necessary to draw valid, reliable and generalizable conclusions.

In type 1 studies it is impossible to define which features of an intervention are relevant and in what way. For example, many studies argue that coaching can be effective, but often it is not clear how many hours should be invested in the coaching. The number of hours is important since they require a financial investment that affects the number of hours that are available for working with students.

The general problem, which Borko (2004) and Wayne et al. (2008) point out, is that most of the research on PD interventions is not complete, generalizable, precise or valid enough. In this respect, Wayne et al. discuss the distinction between 'efficacy trials' and 'effectiveness trials.' With 'efficacy trials' they refer to studies that focus on one PD intervention aimed at contributing to the PD of teachers, whereas 'effectiveness trials' comprise studies where PD interventions are tested in numerous diverse settings. The latter type of studies can be highly relevant for developing knowledge about features and effects of PD. In their review of studies on the relation between teacher PD and student results, Yoon et al. (2007) found that only 9 studies of 1,300 studies in total meet these criteria. Regarding the 34 additional studies found in the current review, most are type 1 studies, except for Desimone et al. (2002); Ingvarson et al. (2005); James & McCormich (2009); McCutchen et al. (2002); Saxe et al. (2001); Supovitz & Turner (2000); and Telese (2008).

Apparently, it is impossible to draw rigid conclusions about 'what works' in PD interventions. Nevertheless, Borko et al. (2010, pp. 548–549) argue that there is "a growing consensus within the field regarding the central features of PD that are effective in improving teaching practice" (cf. Wayne et al., 2008). This makes a review on the effects of the different PD interventions less significant compared to a review of what is known about features of effective PD in general. Those features should be regarded as *indications* for what works. This list of features can be used to design, implement and evaluate specific forms of PD.

Effective Features

In the following, we present an overview of effective features based on an analysis of 11 review studies and 34 intervention studies. Features described by Kennedy (1998) form the starting point of the analysis. We then compared the list of these features to other review texts and additional studies and adjusted or complemented.

Design: Traditional Versus Innovative

The distinction between more traditional and more innovative designs of a PD program does not necessarily seem meaningful when distinguishing between effective and ineffective PD programs. This is because empirical research underpinning that one design is more effective than the other design is still lacking. Although there is a growing consensus that PD programs situated at the workplace are more fruitful, there is (still) no empirical evidence that supports this consensus. Also, the research into individual PD interventions does not show specific designs to be more effective than others (Garet et al., 2001; Smith & Gillespie, 2007). Teacher effects are found for both more traditional designs (e.g., 1-day courses and visiting lectures at conferences) as well as for more innovative designs (e.g., coaching and study groups).

What seems to be more relevant is the perceived relevance and usefulness of the program with respect to teachers' daily work: "Quality professional development engages teachers in inquiry about the concrete tasks of teaching, assessment, observation, and reflection, and provides them with the opportunity to make connections between their learning and their classroom instruction" (Borko et al., 2010, p. 549). There is hardly any research that demonstrates that this qualitative PD can only be realized 'on-site' or only within innovative designs of PD programs.

Content Focus

An effective feature of PD programs that appears in many studies—and is even considered most relevant in some studies—is the content focus of the program. The content of the intervention should be related to classroom practice, more specifically to subject content, pedagogical content knowledge and student learning processes of a specific subject. When teachers develop with respect to these aspects of content, an increase in teacher quality and student learning results. This is in line with findings from research into features of effective teachers. Effective teachers master the subject content and are capable of explaining this content to students in a way that students do understand and learn (Scheerens & Bosker, 1997).

In addition, understanding the processes of student learning increases the quality of education and student achievement. For instance, in a more recent form of PD teachers together analyze student work and student test results in order to get more insights into how their students learned and understood the content.

Quality of the Content Provided

Multiple studies underpin the need for the provision of theory-based content and well-researched (evidence-based or evidence-informed) methods and practices (Buczynski & Hansen, 2010; Bierman et al., 2008; Domitrovich et al., 2009; Yoon et al., 2007). Examples of learning and teaching in a PD program should be powerful and clear, intellectually challenging, and exceptional (not a routine example) (Knapp, 2003). Furthermore, there should be a provision of permanent access to newly developed knowledge and expertise of colleagues within and outside the teacher's own school (Little, 2006).

Active and Inquiry-Based Learning

Another critical feature has to do with the actual activities teachers should undertake in PD programs. In almost all studies, opportunities for teachers to take part in active learning link to effective PD. Active learning, as opposed to passive learning (e.g., listening to a lecture), takes form in observing expert teachers or being observed by other teachers followed by feedback and discussion, or reviewing student work. Nowadays, active learning is more and more understood as similar to inquiry-based learning. Almost all studies report on 'inquiry-based' elements incorporated in the design of the PD program. Those elements range from analyzing student data, performing research activities with respect to practice-related content such as student work, learning problems of students or innovative curricula. In these studies, inquiry-based activities do not necessarily mean that teachers are actually performing research themselves—as is the case in developments as the 'teacher as researcher.' Rather, teachers are actively engaged in order to learn in the context of the PD program.

Collective Participation

A feature closely connected to active learning is collective participation and collaborative teacher learning. It concerns collaborations between teachers from the same school, grade or department. "Such arrangements set up potential interaction and discourse, which can be a powerful form of teacher learning" (Desimone, 2009, p. 184). Another aspect of collective participation emphasized in literature on professional learning communities is the importance of a shared responsibility of the teachers for their own PD (Little, 2006). Teachers need to be involved in setting the goals of a PD program but also in choosing content and design of the PD intervention (Hawley & Valli, 1999) in order to increase both the effectiveness as well as the usefulness of the PD program.

Duration and Sustainability

Another feature often mentioned with respect to effective PD is duration: "Research shows that intellectual and pedagogical change requires PD activities to be of sufficient duration, including both span of time over which the activity is spread (e.g. 1 day or one semester) and the number of hours spent in the activity" (Desimone, 2009, p. 184). It is difficult to identify an exact 'tipping point' since it always depends on the type of activity. Findings from the review of Yoon and colleagues (2007) show support for at least 14 hours of training. Desimone (2009) comes up with a minimum of 20 hours, but Supovitz and Turner (2000) indicate a minimum of 80 hours of training for teacher behavioral change to occur. On the other hand, research from Telese (2008) shows that too many hours of PD can be ineffective. What all these studies bring to the fore is that a substantial amount of time (both span of time and actual hours) is necessary in order for PD to be effective.

In many studies work pressure is a frequently mentioned problem related to PD. Often there seems to be too little time for development. There will be further discussion of this problem in the section on school organizational conditions. A different aspect of duration has to do with the notion of sustainability of the intervention (cf. Desimone, 2009; Yoon et al., 2007). This means that one-shot, short-term interventions might be less effective than long-term interventions combined with enduring follow-up support (i.e., follow-up interventions, permanent support of group collaboration and ongoing facilitation of teacher learning).

Coherence

A feature increasingly emphasized in the literature is coherence: "the consistency of school, district and state reforms and policies, with what is taught in PD" (Desimone, 2009, p. 184). This might prevent the PD program from becoming perceived as an isolated endeavor in the school and therefore help to improve the sustainability of the effects of the program. Another important aspect of coherence is the extent to which the goals, content and design of the PD program are consistent with teachers' knowledge and beliefs. Knapp (2003) advises linking PD to ongoing innovations, but also to specific problems the teachers experience in their daily work, including external pressure most innovations bring along (cf. Blank & de las Alas, 2009; Borko et al., 2010; Desimone, 2009; Hawley & Valli, 1999; Little, 2006; Smith & Gillespie, 2007; Timperley et al., 2007).

Theory of Improvement

Recent research shows more and more support for the necessity of a well-defined and explicit understanding of the relation between specific features of the intervention and the intended learning goals, the 'theory of improvement.' This understanding must comprise both teacher learning ('theory of change') as well as student learning ('theory of instruction') (Desimone, 2009; Yoon et al., 2007).

Organizational Conditions

In a limited number of studies on teacher learning, school organizational conditions that contribute to the success and sustainability of a PD intervention are included. In most studies on effective teacher PD this is not the central focus. They merely focus on the relation between features of the intervention and the effectiveness in terms of teacher or student learning. The school organizational dimension was also neglected in most studies on teacher PD. The same applies, however, for school organizational research on learning in the workplace, organizational learning and professional learning communities, in which insights from research on teacher PD are hardly used. Recently, this seems to be changing (e.g., Smylie, 1995; Imants & van Veen, 2010).

Some studies point to the importance of leadership or creating a professional learning community in general (cf. Desimone, 2009; Ermeling, 2010; James & McCormick, 2009; Timperley et al., 2007). Other studies argue that a sufficient amount of time is important (Buczynski & Hansen, 2010; Lee et al., 2004; Norton & McCloskey, 2008; Stark, 2006; Vogt & Rogalla, 2009; Wilson, 2008), but they almost never elaborate on the implications of such conditions for the daily schedule of a school and teachers' workload.

The feature that an intervention should be consistent with the school, district or state policy should also be incorporated with school organizational conditions.

A few studies discuss school organizational conditions in more detail. For example, Smith and Gillespie (2007) extensively describe the culture and structure of the organization, the working conditions for teachers and schoolwide expectations and incentives to use new teaching practices. Also, Little (2006) discusses rather extensively the importance of a culture in which teachers themselves and school management consider teacher learning relevant. Little also stresses the importance of leadership and a shared focus of teachers on vision, responsibility, decisions, working and learning.

Other examples are Zwart et al. (2009), who in the context of peer-coaching interventions point to the significance of a safe learning culture in the school and the problem of relatively short periods in a year that teachers have time to learn. Holmlund Nelson and Slavit (2007) also refer to this problem when they point out that executing a research cycle often does not coincide with the duration of a school year. In this context, Ermeling (2010) stresses the importance of "dedicated and protected times to meet on a regular basis to get important work done."

In research on professional learning communities, developing and having a shared vision, shared responsibility, shared approach, shared reflection and shared influence are emphasized. This requires a focus on learning, mutual trust and shared norms for giving peer feedback (Little, 2006).

In general, it can be argued that organizing teacher learning in a school needs to be well thought out. Many initiatives in this domain are not successful. Projects are often temporary and not sustainable. Furthermore, they often take place in isolation with only a limited number of teachers involved instead of an entire school team.

Another, perhaps more important, reason for a well-thought-out plan for teacher learning is that most schools are not set for teacher learning. They are established for student learning and teacher work. Teacher learning requires a different design, culturally and structurally. The majority of a week at school is filled with lesson hours, time to prepare lessons or to work on student-related matters. The time that remains for PD activities is scarce and often not ideal for learning. For example, there are schools where teachers have time for PD activities on Friday afternoons after the final lesson hour. Or most schools consist of mainly classrooms, one staff room and maybe department workspaces—a structure more aimed at student learning than teacher learning.

In general, school culture and structure place less emphasis on teacher learning simply because student learning and achievement are the primary concern. School organization literature and research on learning at the workplace, organizational learning and professional learning communities provide some valuable suggestions and ideas for this purpose. In research on organizational learning, for example, concepts like leadership, organizational climate, teacher collaboration and agency are elaborated (Sleegers & Leithwood, 2010). In research on learning at the workplace five factors are distinguished:

1. the learning potential of the task
2. possibilities for feedback, evaluation and reflection on activities
3. formalizing work processes
4. teacher participation in dealing with problems and designing and developing work processes
5. learning resources (Ellström, 2001; Imants & van Veen, 2010)

It is important to note that these organizational features are not objective facts, but they are defined by the way in which teachers and school leaders make sense of these conditions (Imants & van Veen, 2010; Sleegers & Leithwood, 2010).

These organizational conditions primarily show that attending to teacher learning in schools requires a different way of thinking, namely, taking the structural and cultural possibilities and constraints for teacher learning in the entire organization into consideration. This can have far-reaching implications, which if not taken into consideration, may explain the failures of many initiatives. A relevant example in this respect is a recent study into the development of about 200 schools in Chicago, revealing that teacher learning can be organized successfully if it occurs consistently and is supported by committed leadership, a student-centered learning climate and professional learning capacity of the schools: "[I]t entails coherent, orchestrated action across all essential supports" (Bryk, 2010, p. 25; Bryk, Sebring, Allensworth, Luppescu & Easton, 2010).

CONCLUSIONS

The central aim of this chapter was to provide an overview of what is currently known about the effectiveness of teachers' PD programs or PD interventions on the effectiveness of teachers, the quality of their teaching and student learning. The chapter is based on a systematic exploration of empirical studies on the effects of divergent PD interventions.

A first set of conclusions refers to the nature of the current research on effective teacher PD. Some problems exist that complicate the conclusions on what works. Besides some methodological and conceptual issues, the most urgent problem is the overload of (mostly qualitative) studies that examine one program or intervention in one specific setting. Fewer studies examine one specific intervention in several settings or several interventions in several settings, with different coaches. Such studies are necessary to draw valid, reliable and generalizable conclusions. Apparently, no rigid conclusions can be drawn on 'what works' in PD interventions or on specific interventions. What remains possible, however, is to describe what is known about effective features of PD in general, which should be regarded as *indications* for what works.

A second set of conclusions refers to the effective features of teacher PD. The most relevant and striking feature refers to the content: It is important to focus on the daily teaching practice, more specifically, the subject content, the subject pedagogical content knowledge and the students' learning processes of a specific subject. Furthermore, there is still hardly any research showing that PD situated in the workplace would be more effective than offsite PD. Other relevant features are active and inquiry-based learning, collegial learning, a substantial amount of time, cohesion with the school policy and or national policy and at the same time a congruence with the problems teachers experience in their daily teaching practice. In the case of all of these features, a theory of improvement is relevant: knowing how the specific features stimulate the learning of teachers and/ or their students. Finally, it is relevant to consider the school organizational implications to ensure that the PD is relevant, successful and sustainable. Schools are mainly designed for student learning and for teachers to work, rather than for teachers to learn.

To conclude, there seems to be a large degree of conceptual saturation regarding the effective features in general. What is lacking is a more precise operationalization of these effective features in specific situations and contexts. Furthermore, the set of effective features described in this chapter shows a need for well-designed PD interventions, in which teachers' learning goals and their daily teaching practice are central, teachers are actively involved in the learning process and are sustainable over time. In other words, there is a strong need for teacher learning that matters. The following chapters provide examples of such interventions.

REFERENCES

Bakkenes, I., Vermunt, J. D. & Wubbels, T. (2010). Teacher learning in the context of educational innovation: Learning activities and learning outcomes of experienced teachers. *Learning and Instruction, 20, 533–548.*

Bierman, K. L., Domitrovich, C. E., Nix, R .L., Gest, S. D., Welsh, J. A., Greenberg, M. T., Blair, C., Nelson, K. E. & Gill, S. (2008). Promoting academic and social-emotional school readiness: The Head Start REDI Program. *Child Development, 79*(6), 1802–1817.

Biesta, G. (2007). Why 'what works' won't work: Evidence-based practice and the democratic deficit in educational research. *Educational Theory, 57*(1), 122.

Blank, R. K., & de las Alas, N. (2009). *Effects of teacher professional development on gains in student achievement: How meta analysis provides scientific evidence useful to education leaders.* Washington, DC: Council of Chief State School Officers.

Borko, H. (2004). Professional development and teacher learning: Mapping the terrain. *Educational Researcher, 33*(8), 3–15.

Borko, H., Jacobs, J. & Koellner, K. (2010). Contemporary approaches to teacher professional development. In E. Baker, B. McGaw & P. Peterson (Eds.), *International encyclopedia of education* (3rd ed.) (pp. 548–555). Oxford: Elsevier Scientific Publishers.

Bryk, A. S. (2010). Organizing schools for improvement. *Phi Delta Kappa, 91*(7), 23–30.

Bryk, A. S., Sebring, P. B., Allensworth, E., Luppescu, S. & Easton, J. Q. (2010). *Organizing schools for improvement. Lessons from Chicago.* Chicago / London: University of Chicago Press.

Buczynski, S., & Hansen, C. B. (2010). Impact of professional development on teacher practice: Uncovering connections. *Teaching and Teacher Education, 26, 599–607.*

Butler, D. L., Lauscher, H. N., Jarvis-Sellinger, S. & Beckingham, B. (2004). Collaboration and self-regulation in teachers' professional development. *Teaching and Teacher Education, 20, 435–455.*

Chamberlin, M. T. (2005). Teachers' discussions of students' thinking: Meeting the challenge of attending to students' thinking. *Journal of Mathematics Teacher Education, 8, 141–170.*

Clarke, & Hollingsworth. (2002). Elaborating a model of teacher professional growth. *Teaching and Teacher Education, 18*(8), 947–967.

Cohen, D., & Hill, H. C. (2000). Instructional policy and classroom performance: The mathematics reform in California. *Teachers College Record, 102, 296–345.*

Cohen, D., Raudenbush, S., & Ball, D. (2003). Resources, instruction, and research. *Educational Evaluation and Policy Analysis, 25*(2), 1–24.

Desimone, L. M. (2009). Improving impact studies of teachers' professional development: Toward better conceptualizations and measures. *Educational Researcher, 38*(3), 181–199.

Desimone, L. M., Porter, A. C., Garet, M. S., Yoon, K. S. & Birman, B. F. (2002). Effects of professional development on teachers' instruction: results from a three-year longitudinal study. *Educational Evaluation and Policy Analysis, 24,* 81–112.

Domitrovich, C. E., Gest, S. D., Gill, S., Bierman, K. L., Welsh, J. A. & Jones, D. (2009). Fostering high-quality teaching with an enriched curriculum and professional development support: The Head Start REDI Program. *American Education Research Journal, 46*(2), 567–597.

Doppelt, Y., Schunn, C. D., Silk, E. M., Mehalik, M. M., Reynolds, B. & Ward, E. (2009). Evaluating the impact of a facilitated learning community approach to professional development on teacher practice and student achievement. *Research in Science & Technological Education, 27*(3), 339–354.

Ellström, P. E. (2001). Integrating learning and work: Problems and prospects. *Human Resource Development Quarterly, 12,* 421–435.

Elmore, R. F. (2005). Building new knowledge: School improvement requires new knowledge, not just good will. *American Educator, 29*(1), 20–27.

Ermeling, B. A. (2010). Tracing the effects of teacher inquiry on classroom practice. *Teaching and Teacher Education, 26,* 377–388.

Fishman, B. J., Marx, R.W., Best, S. & Tal, R. T. (2003). Linking teacher and student learning to improve professional development in systemic reform. *Teaching and Teacher Education, 19,* 643–658.

Franke, M. L., Carpenter, T. P., Levi, L. & Fennema, E. (2001). Capturing teachers' generative change: A follow-up study of professional development in mathematics. *American Educational Research Journal, 38*(3), 653–689.

Garet, M. S., Cronen, S., Eaton, M., Kurki, A., Ludwig, M., Jones, W., Uekawa, W., Falk, A., Bloom, H. S., Doolittle, F., Zhu, P., Sztejnberg, L., & Silverberg, M. (2008). *The impact of two professional development interventions on early reading instruction and achievement.* Washington, DC: National Center for Educational Evaluation and Regional Assistance, Institute of Education Science, U.S. Department of Education.

Garet, M. S., Porter, A., Desimone, L., Birman, B. & Yoon, K. S. (2001). What makes a professional development effective? Results from a national sample of teachers. *American Education Research Journal, 38*(4), 915–945.

Guskey, T. R. (2000). What makes professional development effective? *Phi Delta Kappan, 80,* 748–750.

Guskey, T. R., & Sparks, D. (2004). Linking professional development to improvements in student learning. In E. M. Guyton, J.R. Dangel & I. A. Dubuque (Eds.), *Teacher education yearbook XII: Research linking teacher preparation and student performance* (pp. 11–22). Dubuque, IA: Kendall/Hunt.

Hattie, J. (2009). *Visible learning: A synthesis of over 800 meta-analyses relating to achievement.* New York: Routledge.

Hawley, W., & Valli, L. (1999). The essentials of effective professional development: A new consensus. In L. Darling-Hammond & G. Sykes (Eds.), *Teaching as the learning profession: Handbook of policy and practice* (pp. 127–150). San Francisco: Jossey-Bass.

Hofman, R. H., & Dijkstra, B. J. (2010). Effective teacher professionalization in networks? *Teaching and Teacher Education, 26,* 1031–1040.

Holmlund Nelson, T., & Slavit, D. (2007). Collaborative inquiry among science and mathematics teachers in the USA: Professional learning experiences through cross-grade, cross-discipline dialogue. *Journal of In-service Education, 33*(1), 23–39.

Imants, J., & van Veen, K. (2010). Teacher learning as workplace learning. In E. Baker, B. McGaw & P. Peterson (Eds.), *International Encyclopedia of Education* (3rd ed.) (pp. 569–574). Oxford: Elsevier Scientific Publishers.

Ingvarson, L., Meiers, M. & Beavis, A. (2005). Factors affecting the impact of professional development programs on teachers' knowledge, practice, student outcomes & efficacy. *Education Policy Analysis Archives, 13*(10), 1–28.

James, M., & McCormick, R. (2009). Teachers learning how to teach. *Teaching and Teacher Education, 25,* 973–982.

Kazemi, E., & Franke, M. L. (2004). Teacher learning in mathematics: Using student work to promote collective inquiry. *Journal of Mathematics Teacher Education, 7,* 201–235.

Kennedy, M. (1998). *Form and substance of in-service teacher education.* Madison: University of Wisconsin-Madison, National Institute for Science Education.

√ Knapp, M. S. (2003). Professional development as a policy pathway. *Review of Research in Education, 27,* 109–157.

Lee, O., Hart, J. E., Cuevas, P. & Enders, C. (2004). Professional development in inquiry-based science for elementary teachers of diverse student groups. *Journal of Research in Science Teaching, 41*(10), 1021–1043.

Lee, O., Lewis, S., Adamson, K., Maerten-Rivera, J. & Secada, W. G. (2007). Urban elementary school teachers' knowledge and practices in teaching science to English language learners. *Journal of Research in Science Teaching, 41*(10), 1021–1043.

√ Levine, T. H., & Marcus, A. S. (2010). How the structure and focus of teachers' collaborative activities facilitate and constrain teacher learning. *Teaching and Teacher Education, 26,* 389–398.

√ Little, J. W. (2006). *Professional community and professional development in the learning- centered school.* Arlington, VA: Education Association National.

Loucks-Horsley, S., & Matsumoto, C. (1999). Research on professional development for teachers of mathematics and science: The state of the scene. *School Science and Mathematics, 99*(5), 258–271.

McCutchen, D., Abbott, R. D., Green, L. B., Beretvas, S. N., Cox, S., Potter, N. S., Quiroga, T. & Gray, A. L. (2002). Beginning literacy: Links among teacher knowledge, teacher practice, and student learning. *Journal of Learning Disabilities, 35*(1), 69–86.

Morge, L., Toczek, M. & Chakroun, N. (2010). A training programme on managing science class interactions: Its impact on teachers' practices and on their pupils' achievement. *Teaching and Teacher Education, 26,* 415–426.

√ Norton, A. H., & McCloskey, A. (2008). Teaching experiments and professional development. *Journal of Mathematics Teacher Education, 11*(4), 285–305.

√ Ponte, P., Ax, J., Beijaard, W. & Wubbels, T. (2004). Teachers' development of professional knowledge trough action research and the facilitation of this by teacher educators. *Teaching and Teacher Education, 20,* 571–588.

Raudenbush, S. W. (2005). Learning from attempts to improve schooling: The contribution of methodological diversity. *Educational Researcher, 34*(25), 25–31.

Saxe, G. B., Gearhart, M. & Nasir, N. S. (2001). Enhancing students' understanding of mathematics: A study of three contrasting approaches to professional support. *Journal of Mathematics Teacher Education, 4,* 55–79.

Scheerens, J., & Bosker, R. J. (1997). *The foundations of educational effectiveness.* Oxford: Elsevier Science Publishers.

Secada, W. G., & Adajian, L. B. (1997). Mathematics teachers' change in the context of their professional communities. In E. Fennema & B. S. Nelson (Eds.), *Mathematics Teachers in Transition* (pp. 193–219). Mahwah, New Jersey: Lawrence Erlbaum Associates.

Slavin, R. (2008). Perspectives on evidence-based research in education—What works? Issues in synthesizing educational program evaluations. *Educational Researcher, 37*(1), 5–14.

√ Sleegers, P., & Leithwood, K. (2010). School development for teacher learning and change. In E. Baker, B. McGaw & P. Peterson (Eds.), *International Encyclopedia of Education* (3rd ed.) (pp. 557–561). Oxford: Elsevier Scientific Publishers.

Smith, C., & Gillepsie, M. (2007). Research on professional development and teacher change: Implications for adult basic education. *Review of Adult Learning and Literacy, 7,* 205–244.

Smylie, M. A. (1995). Teacher learning in the workplace: Implications for school reform. In T. R. Guskey & M. Huberman (Eds.), *Professional development in education: New paradigms and practices* (pp. 92–113). New York: Teachers College Press.

Stark, S. (2006). Using action learning for professional development. *Educational Action Research, 14*(1), 23–43.

Supovitz, J. A. (2001). *Translating teaching practice into improved student achievement.* Chicago: University of Chicago Press.

Supovitz, J. A., & Turner, H. M. (2000). The effects of professional development on science teaching practices and classroom culture. *Journal of Research in Science Teaching, 37*(9), 963–980.

Telese, J. A. (2008). Teacher professional development in mathematics and student achievement: A NAEP 2005 analysis. Paper presented at the annual meeting of the school science and mathematics association.

Tienken, C. H., & Achilles, C. M. (2003). Changing teacher behavior and improving student writing achievement. *Planning and Changing, 34,* 153–168.

Timperley, H., Wilson, A., Barrar, H. & Fung, I. (2007). *Teacher professional learning and development. Best evidence synthesis iteration (BES).* Wellington: Ministry of Education.

Verloop, N. (2003). De leraar [The teacher]. In N. Verloop & J. Lowyck (Eds.), *Onderwijskunde, een kennisbasis voor professionals* [Educational studies, a knowledge base for professionals] (pp. 194–249). Groningen/Houten: Wolters-Noordhoff.

Vescio, V., Ross, D. & Adams, A. (2008). A review of research on the impact of professional learning communities on teaching practice and student learning. *Teaching and Teacher Education, 24,* 80–91.

Vogt, F., & Rogalla, M. (2009). Developing adaptive teaching competency through coaching. *Teaching and Teacher Education, 25,* 1051–1060.

Wallace, M. R. (2009). Making sense of the links: Professional development, teacher practices, and student achievement. *Teachers College Record, 111*(2), 573–596.

Wayne, A. J., Yoon, K. S., Zhu, P., Cronen, S. & Garet, M. S. (2008). Experimenting with teacher professional development: Motives & methods. *Educational Researcher, 37*(8), 469–479.

Wilson, N. S. (2008). Teachers expanding pedagogical content knowledge: Learning about formative assessment together. *Journal of In-service Education, 34*(3), 283–289.

Yoon, K. S., Duncan, T., Lee, S. W. Y., Scarloss, B. & Shapley, K. (2007). *Reviewing the evidence on how teacher professional development affects student achievement* (Issues & Answers Report, REL 2007–No.033). Washington, DC: Department of Education, Institute of Education Sciences, National Center for Education Evaluation and Regional Assistance, Regional Educational Laboratory Southwest.

Zwart, R. C., Wubbels, T., Bergen, Th. & Bolhuis, B. (2009). Which characteristics of a reciprocal peer coaching context affect teacher learning as perceived by teachers and their students? *Journal of Teacher Education, 60*(3), 243–257.

2 Professional Community and Professional Development in the Learning-Centered School

Judith Warren Little

INTRODUCTION

For more than two decades, research has shown that teachers who experience frequent, rich learning opportunities have in turn been helped to teach in more ambitious and effective ways. Yet few teachers gain access to such intensive professional learning opportunities.[1] More typically, teachers experience professional development (PD) as episodic, superficial and disconnected from their own teaching interests or recurring problems of practice. This prevailing pattern—a few rich opportunities, many disappointing ones—speaks both to the promise and to the limitations of PD as it is typically organized. An important part of this enduring story centers on the schools and districts where teachers work and whether they are positioned well to foster professional learning opportunities that enhance the quality of teaching and learning.

This chapter focuses on PD and professional community as foundations of the learning-centered school. Its purpose is to marshal research evidence that can be used productively to enhance professional learning and thereby to nourish such a school. To establish benchmarks for best practice, the chapter begins with an overview of the goals that professional learning serves, then suggests strategic content priorities and ends with a discussion of effective approaches or means. It is addressed to school leaders—especially teachers and administrators—who must identify priorities for PD and allocate scarce PD resources in ways that will improve instruction and enhance children's success in school.

As will become apparent, the research is uneven (Borko, 2004; van Veen, Zwart & Meirink, this volume). We know more about the characteristics of high-quality formal PD (typically outside the school) than we do about the content, processes and outcomes of ongoing, informal workplace learning. We know a substantial amount about how to help teachers become effective in helping students learn core academic subjects (especially math and science), but our knowledge tends to come up short when those students are also learning English (or any other language of instruction) as a second language. We know more about the benefits of strong student assessment practices than we do about how to help teachers incorporate such practices into daily instruction. We have begun to assemble rich portraits of teaching that responds to and builds on student diversity in ways that support student learning, but we have little in the way of research on related programs of PD. The research provides more guidance for schools in some areas than in others—or, put another way, the lessons from research do not map neatly or completely onto the professional learning needs or interests of a given school. Nonetheless, it provides a worthy starting point.

THE SCHOOL'S STAKE IN TEACHER LEARNING

The basic premise of this chapter is that a school is more likely to be effective in supporting high levels of student learning and well-being where it also plays a powerful, deliberate and consequential role in teacher learning. As the context most directly connected to the daily enterprise of teaching and learning, the school has a stake in pursuing PD purposes that together build the individual and collective expertise and commitment of the staff, sustain professional growth for both novice and veteran teachers and equip the school to tackle its most central goals, priorities and problems.

Four Goals for Teacher Learning

The school's stake in teacher learning may be expressed in terms of a set of four broad, ambitious goals that join the needs and interests of individual teachers to the collective needs and interests of the school.

Making Headway on the School's Central Goals, Priorities or Problems

A key test of PD lies in its capacity to mount a strong collective response to schoolwide problems or goals. Some of these problems and goals arise out of a broad policy agenda affecting all schools—raising the bar of educational achievement and closing the achievement gap. Other problems and goals arise from teachers' and parents' interest in educational benefits that go beyond measured academic achievement in tested subjects: students' overall intellectual growth; their social, moral and political development; their independence and self-confidence; their aesthetic sensitivity; and more. Finally, some problems and goals arise out of the specific circumstances of each school. For example, schools in some areas have experienced a flood of non-English-speaking immigrants over the past two decades and reasonably expect that all or most teachers will acquire expertise in teaching second-language learners. A well-wrought school plan would show evidence that PD forms one part of a larger strategy for pursuing ambitious levels of teaching and learning in this school, with these students, in this community and with these resources.

Building the Knowledge, Skill and Disposition to Teach to High Standards

The quality of a school's teaching staff can be judged by the depth and breadth of knowledge, skill and judgment that teachers bring to their work, both individually and collectively. Sound hiring practices offer one resource in this respect, but hiring well-qualified teachers will not be sufficient to meet this goal. Insights into teachers' expertise and their learning trajectories have multiplied as researchers have uncovered the complexities of teaching and the cognitive and social demands associated with learning to teach well. Thus, one test of effective PD is whether teachers and other educators come to know more over time about their subjects, students and practice and to make informed use of what they know.

Cultivating Strong Professional Community Conducive to Learning and Improvement

Research has steadily converged on the importance of strong teacher learning communities for teacher growth and commitment, suggesting as well their potential contribution to favorable student outcomes. Schools whose staff members espouse a shared responsibility for student learning and are organized to sustain a focus on instructional improvement are more likely to yield higher levels of student learning. Creating and sustaining robust professional learning communities is difficult, but research provides examples of what such communities look like and helps illuminate the conditions that place them within reach. Effective PD might thus be judged by its capacity for building (and building on) the structures and values, as well as the intellectual and leadership resources, of professional community.

Sustaining Teachers' Commitment to Teaching

Individuals experience PD at particular points in a teaching career and in conditions that bolster or erode commitment to teaching over time. Here, the test of PD lies in teachers' access to professional opportunities that afford them satisfaction, support and stimulation appropriate to their stage of career and that make good use of their acquired expertise and experience. Recent studies of teaching careers, derived primarily from in-depth biographical interviews, emphasize the meanings that individuals attach to their work, the kinds of professional responsibilities they seek and the identities and relationships they form. These studies draw attention to overlooked intersections of professional career and PD (e.g., how particular teaching assignments build on, stimulate or frustrate teacher learning). Such studies seem particularly consistent with recent initiatives in the support and assessment of beginning teachers and the cultivation of networks, teacher research groups and other manifestations of professional community.

Why Focus on the School?

Despite talk of "site-based staff development", most organized PD activity takes place outside the school. Furthermore, in an era of heightened accountability pressures, more districts are exercising control over PD, thus constraining funds and staff time at the school level. Yet an alternative vision of teacher learning is emerging from the research. School-based professional communities are the core of the system; these are purposefully and coherently linked with external PD opportunities. Why focus on the school?

First, and most simply, the school is where the work of teaching and learning resides. It is where the problems of practice take on a particular face, where pressures for achievement are most directly felt and where investments in professional learning pay off or do not. To focus on the school is to sustain attention to improvements in teaching and learning and to signal a broad conception of PD encompassing "the full range of activities, formal and informal, that engage teachers or administrators in new learning about their professional practice" (Knapp, 2003, p. 112). The school looms large not because it is the site of formal PD activity (although it may be) but because its staff have a stake in thinking wisely and strategically about whether and how the school is organized to invest in professional learning.

Second, the school is important because a school's failure to create an environment conducive to professional learning has high costs. Students bear those costs in the form of inadequate instruction and high teacher turnover. Teachers bear the costs in the form of weak instructional support and personal stress. In contrast, schools that are well organized for professional learning stand to reap the benefits of demonstrable student gains and enduring teacher commitment. Over the past two decades, evidence has accumulated that the workplace learning environment matters. Schools that support teacher learning and foster a culture of collegiality and continuous improvement are better able to support and retain new teachers, pursue innovation, respond effectively to external changes and secure teacher commitment (Johnson et al., 2004; Little, 1982, 2003; Little & Bartlett, 2002; Louis & Kruse, 1995; McLaughlin & Talbert, 1994, 2001; Rosenholtz, 1989; Bryk et al., 2010).

Corresponding to the four goals for teacher learning outlined earlier, conceptions of PD in education have both broadened and deepened over the past two decades. We have moved from a model that emphasized the acquisition of discrete skills and behaviors to a more complex vision of teacher thinking, learning and practice in particular subject domains. We have moved increasingly away from an individualistic view of teacher growth and toward a view that emphasizes a school's collective capacity and that credits the potential power of strong professional community. We have acknowledged the ways in which teachers' career experience and teaching commitments are shaped by the quality of the workplace environment and by the nature and extent of their professional ties. In addition, in many schools and districts, PD planning has matured. Plans that were once a laundry list of activities are more often framed in terms of explicit links between student learning goals and expenditure of PD resources.

It is true that school-level changes emerging from these bodies of research have been slow in developing. The most ambitious examples of powerful teacher learning remain relatively rare and modest in scale. Not all practitioners can say that they have frequent and meaningful contacts with colleagues or consultants or that they have been richly supplied with stimulating ideas, materials and experiences. Indeed, many would readily report being "in-serviced" in ways that do little justice to their experience, interests and circumstances. Patterns of local resource allocation at both the school and district levels have tended to favor traditional training models over promising but unfamiliar alternatives. Large districts are more likely than smaller ones to offer intensive, sustained PD. Few schools or districts conduct meaningful evaluation of the benefits derived from PD activity. Yet meaningful shifts are evident. Table 2.1 summarizes the direction of these shifts in the form of strategic benchmarks for PD and professional community at the school level.

Of course, no school exists in a vacuum. Schools are embedded in relationships that directly or indirectly affect teachers' work and PD—relationships with school districts, the state, professional associations, reform organizations and various PD providers or partners. In particular, school districts have assumed growing importance as a context for professional learning and as a source of both resources and requirements for teaching. Although this chapter centers on the school, it does so with the understanding that the school's ability to support teachers' professional learning depends both on its internal resources and on its external connections and relationships.

PROFESSIONAL DEVELOPMENT ROOTED IN THE GOALS AND PROBLEMS OF TEACHING AND LEARNING

Educators and researchers alike have lambasted the scattered, shallow, fragmented array of activity that so often makes up the PD landscape, with

Table 2.1   Benchmarks for Professional Community and Professional Development

Benchmarks for . . .	Moving from . . .	Moving toward . . .
Purposes for professional development	Individual knowledge or change	Individual, collective and school goals: • Making headway on school goals and problems • Building knowledge and skill to teach to high standards • Cultivating a strong professional community • Sustaining professional commitment
Content focus of professional development	Unfocused "laundry list" of topics not related to school improvement goals Relationship to student learning unclear, unexamined or left up to teachers to figure out	Focus on the "instructional triangle": • Pedagogical content knowledge • Student thinking, learning and assessment • Understanding and responding to student diversity
Strategy for professional development	Episodic training events on topics often disconnected from practice Strategies poorly designed to achieve effect	School-based professional communities are the core; these are coherently linked with external professional development opportunities Strategies have characteristics associated with effectiveness: collective participation, active learning, coherence, sustained duration
Professional community as resource for professional learning	Professional community a weak resource for professional learning Little attention by school leaders to building strong professional community Working conditions weakly or unevenly conducive to professional learning	Continuous learning is a schoolwide norm; learning is embedded in the professional community Cultivating professional community is a focus for school leaders Working conditions are conducive to professional learning (teaching assignment, time, space, materials and access to colleagues)

(continued)

Table 2.1   (continued)

Benchmarks for . . .	Moving from . . .	Moving toward . . .
External professional development supports	Insufficient external support for teacher learning and school capacity building	Multiple external professional development opportunities link school professional communities with:
		• New advances in knowledge about subject content, learning and teaching • Opportunities to understand students and their diverse communities • Externally developed tools and materials

special criticism reserved for activities that seem remote from teachers' priorities and problems of practice. In a paper commissioned for the National Commission on Teaching and America's Future, Ball and Cohen (1999) acknowledged this long-standing problem and offered a remedy: designing PD more persuasively "in and from practice" (p. 10):

> Rarely do . . . in-services seem based on a curricular view of teachers' learning. Teachers are thought to need updating rather than opportunities for serious and sustained learning of curriculum, students, and teaching. . . . Hence, we propose new ways to *understand and use practice as a site for professional learning*, as well as ways to cultivate the sorts of inquiry into practice from which many teachers could learn. (pp. 3–4, 6; emphasis added)

Problems of Practice and the Instructional Triangle

When Ball and Cohen (1999) urge more opportunities for teachers to learn in and from professional practice, they focus PD squarely on what many now term the instructional triangle: the relationships between teacher, students and content. The instructional triangle encompasses the dynamic, fluid and complex interactions by which teachers help children learn challenging subject content and pursue other important intellectual and social goals.

Lampert's *Teaching Problems and the Problems of Teaching* (2001) provides a compelling illumination of the instructional triangle. Drawing from her fifth-grade classroom, Lampert showed how teaching mathematics required that she solve problems related not only to her goals for students' content learning but also—and simultaneously—to her goals for building a classroom culture in which children can reason and argue about mathematics, learn how to work both independently and collaboratively, build up "intellectual courage" and develop a sense of their own growing understanding and accomplishment. In working toward those ambitious ends, she had to find ways to "cover the curriculum" without compromising "the complex character of content" while contending with "the complexities of human character." Throughout the book, the children's encounters with problems in mathematics helped Lampert, as teacher, expose and work on the problems of teaching.

Lampert's (2001) book embodies the kind of teaching knowledge required if teachers are to help all children meet ambitious standards. It also suggests the crucial importance of professional learning opportunities that are rooted firmly and specifically in problems of practice. Finally, it demonstrates the way in which the large, seemingly intractable problems of student achievement and achievement gaps—the problems that pervade policy debates and that stimulate waves of reform—take on a local and arguably more tractable face in each classroom and each school.

Consistent with the principle of organizing PD in and from practice, then, a school organized for teacher learning would promote systematic attention to teaching and learning in multiple ways. School leaders would support teachers in acquiring a deep understanding of what it means for children to learn core concepts and skills in particular subject domains. School staff would develop the habit of collectively examining evidence of student learning and investigating the sources of students' progress or difficulties. Teachers would be helped to locate and participate in the best of external PD opportunities and helped to parlay what they learn into collective capacity in the school. Partnerships with organizations or groups outside the school would be strategically chosen for their contributions to PD and professional community.

From Problems of Practice to Professional Development

Working from the image of the instructional triangle, the following sections take up three entry points for professional learning. As Figure 2.1 shows, each represents one of three principal relationships in the instructional triangle; each offers a potential focus for activity within the school and for strategic participation in programs and partnerships beyond the school. The instructional triangle is useful as a strategic guide that provides a clear focus for the content of PD.

The first relationship centers on teachers' understanding of subject domains for purposes of teaching. A substantial body of research now supplies evidence that teachers benefit from in-depth understanding of subject-specific concepts and from an understanding of how to help students learn them (for example, Saxe, Geahart & Nasir, 2001; Cohen & Hill, 2001; Desimone, Porter, Garet, Yoon & Birman, 2002; Garet et al., 2001).

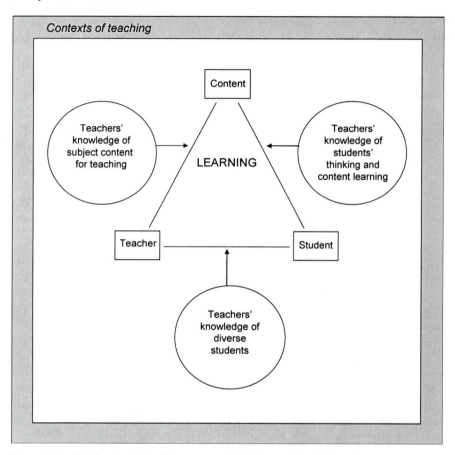

Figure 2.1 Professional development and the instructional triangle.
Source: Adapted by the author from Cohen, Raudenbush, and Ball (2003).

Research on subject-specific PD programs, sometimes in conjunction with innovative curricula, shows the power of intensive PD to deepen teachers' understanding, alter teaching practice and promote student learning. In particular, these programs may help teachers transform basic subject knowledge into the practical knowledge required for teaching, or what Shulman (1986) termed pedagogical *content knowledge*.

The second area of PD activity and research centers on teachers' grasp of students' thinking and learning (for example, Kazemi & Franke, 2004; Black & Wiliam, 1998; Shepard et al., 2005). This relationship puts students' interaction with the content of the curriculum into the foreground. It encompasses efforts to expand teachers' facility with formative assessment as well as other initiatives that involve close, collective examination of students' thinking by means of what students say and do and the work they produce. In all of these activities, an underlying assumption is that systematic attention to student learning—and to students' responses to the instructional activities intended to promote that learning—will foster teacher learning and improve instructional decision-making.

The final relationship focuses on teachers' understanding of and responsiveness to the students they teach, with special emphasis on understanding the nature and significance of student diversity (Banks et al., 2005). Of the three starting points for PD, this relationship presents the broadest terrain by encompassing the many sources of student diversity—cultural, linguistic, cognitive and more—that present resources and challenges for teaching and learning. Further, it offers a particular reminder that the instructional triangle of classroom life resides in—and reflects—multiple contexts beyond the classroom.

As Figure 2.1 suggests, these three relationships intersect and intertwine in practice. However, each relationship places a different aspect of the instructional triangle at the center, and each tends to emphasize a different central purpose for PD activity. Subject-specific PD focuses principally on the depth of teachers' subject teaching expertise and how it might serve as a scaffold for children's learning, aided by well-designed curricula and instructional resources. PD focused on children's thinking and student work turns attention to the nature and progression of children's learning (in general and in particular subject areas) and the meaning they make of instructional activities and materials. Finally, PD focused on student characteristics and conditions highlights teachers' knowledge of how those characteristics and conditions affect students' success in learning and how teachers' response matters. Together, the three suggest a broad set of foundational concerns and priorities for PD.

Everything we know about the nature of ambitious and successful classroom teaching points toward taking the instructional triangle seriously as the point of departure for professional learning. In doing so, however, schools take on a task of considerable magnitude. The sheer magnitude of the task, and the fact that it is never ending, points our attention toward the way in which the school itself is organized to facilitate teachers' individual and collective efforts to deepen their teaching knowledge, foster inquiry into student learning and develop meaningful supports for all students.

PROFESSIONAL COMMUNITY IN SUPPORT
OF TEACHING AND LEARNING

At the very least, one must imagine schools in which teachers are in frequent conversation with each other about their work, have easy and necessary access to each other's classrooms, take it for granted that they should comment on each other's work, and have the time to develop common standards for student work. (Meier, 1992, p. 602)

It does not take a newcomer long to take stock of whether the school's professional environment is consistent with professional learning. Although multiple workplace conditions play a part,[2] vigorous professional communities occupy a particularly central role in schools conducive to teacher learning. Ideally, professional communities within schools are fundamentally oriented to problems of classroom practice and linked to a variety of external sources of knowledge and support for teacher learning. As we turn from the content of PD to consider the process or the means, Figure 2.2 provides a schematic overview that places school-based professional learning communities focused on problems of classroom teaching and learning at the center of a larger constellation of learning opportunities.

As commonly used, the phrase *professional community* refers to close relationships among teachers as professional colleagues, usually with the implication that these relationships are oriented toward teacher learning and PD. Although there are some variations from study to study in how researchers define and characterize professional community, most definitions encompass the elements shown in Table 2.2.

The image of professional community has its origins in research on teachers' workplace relationships and their relationship to school improvement. In one early example of such research, Little (1982) found that schools with "norms of collegiality and experimentation" were more likely to adapt

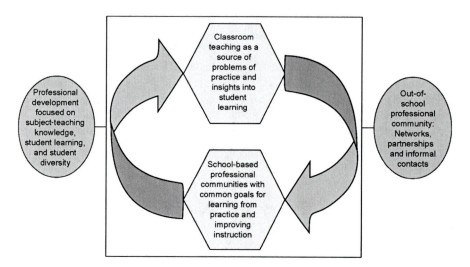

Figure 2.2   Linking professional community and professional development.
Source: Author.

Table 2.2   Defining Elements of Professional Community

- Shared values and purposes, including shared orientations to the teaching of particular subjects

- Collective focus on and responsibility for student learning, sometimes described as a "service ethic," with regard to students' learning and well-being

- Collaborative and coordinated efforts to improve student learning

- Practices supportive of teacher learning, including observation, problem solving, mutual support and advice giving—sometimes summed up as "deprivatized practice and reflective dialogue"

- Collective control over important decisions affecting curriculum.

Source: Grodsky and Gamoran (2003); Louis and Kruse (1995); McLaughlin and Talbert (2001); Secada and Adajian (1997).

successfully to a major change (court-ordered desegregation) and to record higher levels of student achievement than schools where teachers worked in isolation and where norms of privacy and noninterference prevailed. In the highly collegial and improvement-oriented schools, teachers talked frequently with each other about their teaching and how to improve it. They spoke in focused, specific ways about classroom practice and student learning; worked with each other to develop and share classroom materials; observed each other teach when possible; were open to giving and receiving advice; and participated together in PD, helping one another learn new ways of teaching.

Other studies produced similar results, showing that schools benefited when teachers achieved high levels of collaboration and adopted a norm of "continuous improvement." Rosenholtz (1989) concluded that her sample of 78 elementary schools could be divided into "learning enriched" and "learning impoverished" schools based on the level of collaboration, professional sharing and advice giving among teachers. Those in the learning enriched category—with robust learning environments for teachers—were also more likely to have strong profiles of student achievement. Schools engaged in whole-school restructuring during the 1990s were also found to produce higher levels of student achievement where teachers formed a professional community oriented toward learning (Newmann & Wehlage, 1995; Newmann & Associates, 1996).[3]

Over a decade or so, educators and researchers have gradually shifted from a language of "collegiality" and "collaboration" toward language centered on notions of "community," linking a "community of learners" in the classroom and "professional community" among teachers. Of those who write about professional community, many have referred to Wenger's (1998) work on "communities of practice." As Wenger defined it, a community of practice exists when individuals are mutually engaged in a joint enterprise and over time develop a "shared repertoire of ways of doing things" (p. 49). Wenger described local communities of practice, but he also envisioned "constellations" of professional communities that link local communities together with broader networks in shared enterprises. An example might be a school professional community that is linked with a professional association and a university partner—all working together on a more challenging mathematics curriculum for the school.

Cultivating Professional Community for Teacher Learning and School Improvement

As the research on teachers' professional community has evolved and matured, it has tackled a series of questions of importance to school leaders: Are all forms of "professional community" beneficial for teachers, students and schools? What conditions enable professional communities to form and be productive? What goes on inside teacher communities that provide resources for teacher learning? Each of these questions yields insights for cultivating professional community.

Distinguishing Strong "Traditional Community" from "Teacher Learning Community"

Much of the early research distinguished between collegial (strong) and isolating (weak) professional cultures and offered compelling portraits of how some collegial schools or groups successfully pursued improvement. However, in schools, as in other organizations or in society more generally, strong cultures are not necessarily innovative cultures. That is, groups or schools may prove to be "strong" from a social and political perspective (cohesive and adept at securing resources), but "weak" as sources of improvement in teaching and learning.

Based on extensive research in public and private secondary schools, researchers at Stanford's Center for Research on the Contexts of Teaching (CRC) found that professional communities vary in significant ways. McLaughlin and Talbert (2001) differentiated between a weak professional culture, where classroom work remains private and teachers "pass like ships in the night," and a strong professional culture in which teachers share a set of commitments regarding teaching and learning. They further distinguish between two types of strong professional community. In *tradition-oriented strong communities* teachers unite to preserve their preferred conceptions of subject and pedagogy even in the face of student failure. Teachers in these groups are held together by conservative views of a subject discipline, school curriculum and instruction, but display little in the way of collective responsibility for student learning. Teachers in *teacher learning communities* also share certain core views and commitments but take a more dynamic and flexible stance toward subject teaching and routinely question and challenge teaching routines when they prove ineffective with students. Such communities embrace collective obligations for student success and well-being, and develop collective expertise by employing problem solving, critique, reflection and debate (see also Gutierrez, 1996; Horn, 2005; Louis & Kruse, 1995; Talbert, 1995).

The CRC studies, other studies of whole-school reform (Newmann & Wehlage, 1995; Louis & Kruse, 1995) and analyses of large-scale data sets all point to a high standard for the kind of teacher learning community that is likely to boost student learning. In one analysis of a national data set, Lee and Smith (1996) found measures of staff cooperation to be unrelated to student achievement, even though a spirit of cooperation is no doubt desirable from a workplace perspective. However, student achievement in math and science was significantly higher in schools where teachers expressed what the authors termed *collective responsibility for student learning*. Collective responsibility was defined in terms of teachers' expressed view that it was their responsibility to ensure that students learned and to help prevent them from dropping out or failing.[4]

Moving from a Culture of Privacy to Teacher Learning Community

Creating and sustaining such a robust teacher learning community is no small matter. The available research, although relatively small in quantity, points consistently to certain perspectives and practices that must develop over time and to the leadership required to nurture them.

First, portraits of robust teacher communities show teachers at ease with disclosing their teaching dilemmas, discussing them in depth and helping one another craft solutions to problems of teaching practice and student learning. In one recent study of teacher study groups ("critical friends groups"), looking closely at examples of student work became the means by which teachers gained a deeper appreciation for dilemmas that they and their students faced (Little, Gearhart, Curry & Kafka, 2003).

Second, teachers move toward more robust forms of teacher community if and when they find ways to air and explore disagreement, acknowledge their differences and tolerate conflict. Grossman et al. (2001), reporting on a 3-year study of a project involving high school English and history teachers, considered this "navigation of fault lines" pivotal in the teachers' gradual shift from what they termed *pseudo-community* to authentic community. In its initial stages, the authors said:

> A group may deny differences and proclaim a false sense of unity. . . . With the formation of community, differences among participants can be acknowledged and understood. With such recognition comes the ability to use diverse views to enlarge the understanding of the group as a whole. (2001, p. 989)

Finally, case study research suggests that teacher groups benefit from the kinds of leadership or facilitation that help build the conditions outlined above—the ease in disclosing problems and the disposition to dig into them as well as a growing acceptance of teacher-to-teacher initiative on matters of practice. Grossman et al. (2001) noted that teacher communities become venues for cultivating teacher leadership. A comparable finding emerges from the study of critical friends groups cited earlier:

> Where we saw evidence of group norms built on open discussion, constructive questioning and critique, it was where individuals took the initiative to establish a different kind of conversation—one in which people could push on ideas and practice while still being respectful of one another. (Little et al., 2003, p. 190)

Creating Resources for Learning inside Teacher Community

Not all schools or groups that are committed to learning and improvement necessarily possess or create resources sufficient to act productively on those commitments. Research that probes "inside teacher community" concentrates on trying to uncover the kinds of distinctive processes that characterize vigorous and effective teacher communities—those that demonstrably influence the quality of teaching and learning. Although this research remains in its early stages, it has begun to illuminate how even "collaborative" groups vary in the variety and density of resources that teachers marshal in their interaction with one another, and thus vary in their ability to sustain their focus on teaching practice and student learning. In one recent comparison among highly collaborative groups (Horn, 2005; Little & Horn, 2007), one group consistently emerged as a powerful site for teacher learning. What stood out in this group of math teachers—all teaching algebra in detracked classrooms—was the sheer density of human and material resources on which the teachers relied to focus their attention productively on teaching and learning. In their once-a-week after-school meetings, the teachers routinely drew on three kinds of resources that distinguished them from other collaborative groups of math and English teachers.

Expectations and routines for extended talk about teaching, or what Horn (2005) has called "episodes of pedagogical reasoning." In particular, a routine called "check-in" served not only as a coordination function (where are we in the semester's curriculum?) but also more importantly, as a problem-raising and problem-solving function for novice and veteran teachers alike (Little & Horn, 2007). Problems raised by individuals ("I started the geo-boards today and it felt like mayhem. It felt like no one understood.") became the focus of further "unpacking" questions and extended talk about possible interpretations of the problem and approaches to solving it.

Frequent and purposeful use of curricular resources. Teachers made active use of texts, binders of sample problems, manipulatives and reference books as they talked with one another about what and how they were teaching core concepts and how students responded. With a pile of transparencies ready at hand, they used the overhead projector to display problems and map out approaches to teaching them ("So this graphic up here sort of illustrates . . ."). They recorded and referred back to their own thinking about their goals for particular problems and their instructional strategies.

Plentiful, detailed examples of student work and teaching practice. The face of the classroom was constantly present in the form of lesson plans, samples of student work, demonstrations and simulations of classroom teaching, teachers' accounts of student response in the classroom, teachers' thinking aloud in detail about future classes and even references to their observations of one another's teaching.

Fostering Professional Community at Multiple Levels and Locations

Where might teacher community best be constituted if it is to foster professional learning and influence student learning? Huberman (1993) has speculated that professional community seems most likely to take root in grade levels, departments or teams "where people have concrete things to tell one another and concrete instructional help to provide one another—where the contexts of instruction actually overlap" (p. 45). Yet schoolwide improvement teams have also become widespread. One recent study suggests that the most productive stance might be to foster professional community at multiple levels, with different expectations about what it might accomplish at each level.

In a 2-year study of one innovative elementary school, Stokes (2001) showed how the staff structured opportunities to offer precisely such multilevel inquiries. Each form of inquiry worked well to enable some kinds of learning or to tackle some kinds of problems but was less well suited to others. The entire school staff engaged in what Stokes described as "whole-school assessment of learning outcomes," developing common benchmark assessments of students' literacy learning and devoting a full week in midyear to examining the data. Inquiry at this level enabled the teachers not only to develop a common understanding of student progress in reading and writing, but also to see that a gap remained in race-based patterns of differential achievement and opportunity. This form of inquiry had an important motivational effect but could not supply teachers with sufficient insight to attack the gap and gauge their effectiveness. For this, smaller groups of teachers designed action research projects that afforded an opportunity to experiment with changes in curriculum and instruction at grade level and to assemble evidence regarding the nature and extent of any change in student performance. This form of activity provided the kind of mutual support and peer pressure needed to persist with a difficult task. However, it also tended to expose teachers' own uncertainties and to reveal differences in teachers' beliefs about teaching and learning. It was within a third inquiry context, which Stokes characterized as "individual reflection with small-group support," that individual teachers created a more private, voluntary forum in which they took up their individual concerns and problems. This was the forum, Stokes reported, that "enabled teachers to 'say things you wouldn't say' in other settings" (p. 148).

Stokes (2001) emphasized that no one strategy for introducing and organizing inquiry satisfies all interests. No one approach encompasses all of the work of teacher learning and instructional improvement. Further, to develop this constellation of activities required that the staff develop both normative capacity ("the staff's collective embrace and enactment of values that support self-study as an important kind of learning") and technical capacity ("the structures, processes, knowledge, and activities by which the school staff does the actual work of inquiring into their practices") (pp. 150–151). These in turn required serious leadership work on the part of both the principal and the teachers. As Stokes observed, "inquiry generates powerful learning—but also guilt and conflict." (p. 153). Staff continually navigated a tension familiar to observers of (or participants in) professional community—the tension between individuality and the common good (Hargreaves 1993), or, put another way, between individual and collective autonomy (Little & McLaughlin 1993). The Stokes study suggests the kinds of benefit that might be realized by cultivating professional community in ways that promote sustained attention to student learning and teaching practice at multiple levels and locations in the school.

Making the Most of External Ties

Schools are busy places that easily become insular places. Individuals, organizations and groups outside the school sometimes provide the stimulation and intellectual push needed to consider possibilities beyond those a school would come up with independently. The strongest and most generative professional communities appear to benefit from ties to external sources of ideas, material and assistance. These include teacher-to-teacher networks, university–school partnerships, school networks and special projects that join teachers with knowledgeable colleagues and inform them about new possibilities of import to their teaching.

The growing pressure on schools to reduce the persistent achievement gap heightens the significance of external ties. Elmore (2005) described two schools that most lay observers would say are good schools. The teachers worked hard and students appeared engaged in learning. There was a sense of internal accountability, and a great deal of emphasis was placed on improving student performance and closing achievement gaps. The school staffs did everything they knew how to do. Yet, despite their efforts, after some initial gains, student performance went flat and the schools were designated as "failing." To continue moving to higher levels of performance, according to Elmore, these schools needed external help and support for capacity building commensurate with the demands being placed on them. They needed help diagnosing and addressing crucial issues, such as raising the level of cognitive demand in lessons and improving program coherence.

In sum, robust teacher learning communities stand out for their relentless focus on student learning, student experience and student success; their willingness to take (and tolerate) initiative on matters of teaching practice; and the value they place on the ideas, feedback and resources they derive from ties to individuals, groups and organizations outside the school. Such communities are well positioned as sites of ongoing teacher learning—and to seek and benefit from participation in well-designed PD.

Linking Professional Development and Professional Community

At their best, high-quality PD and vibrant teacher community intersect to form strong foundations for the learning-centered school. In one of the earliest studies of PD and school-based professional culture, schools with strong, improvement-oriented professional communities were more likely to value and make use of coherent, long-term PD offered by the district (Little, 1984). This and other studies suggest that no matter how well designed a structured program of PD, its track record of success in the classroom owes a debt to the quality of professional community and other supports at the school level (Wilson & Berne, 1999; Stein, Silver & Smith, 1998; Little, 1984).

At the same time, there is some indication that when a school supports teachers' participation in high-quality PD, it may also strengthen professional community. In one recent summary of survey-based research (Grodsky & Gamoran, 2003), the authors concluded:

> Positive effects of school-sponsored professional development on professional community obtain at both the school and individual teacher levels, suggesting that teachers who participate in school-sponsored professional develop benefit not only from their own participation, but from the participation of their colleagues as well. (p. 1)

The authors also acknowledged that the relationship may be the other way around (i.e., professional community has an effect on participation in PD).

Overall, then, both case study and survey research suggest that the relationships between PD and professional community are likely to be reciprocal, with good PD stimulating or strengthening professional community and professional community providing fertile ground for participation in PD. Schools might more deliberately and profitably link PD and professional community by taking a two-part strategic approach. One element of the strategy focuses on investing time and money in teachers' access to high-quality PD both inside and outside the school. Such investments represent a departure from the conventional stance, described by one review (Wilson & Berne, 1999) as "a patchwork of opportunities—formal and informal, mandatory and voluntary, serendipitous and planned—stitched together into a fragmented and incoherent 'curriculum'" (p. 174). The second element focuses on creating the kind of teacher workplace in which teachers experience both structural supports for professional growth and an organizational culture or ethos conducive to professional learning. This element entails a mind-set among school leaders that is consistently attuned to the importance of teacher learning and to the various ways in which learning opportunities might be constructed in the fabric of everyday work.

CONCLUSION

This chapter builds selectively on the available research to suggest where schools might make important strides through investment in teacher learning. Its basic premise is that when a school systematically supports professional learning it is more likely to be effective with students. Schools that exhibit a high level of success with students, sometimes against considerable odds, tend to supply consistent portraits of work environments conducive to teacher learning. In these schools, teacher learning arises out of close involvement with students and their work; shared responsibility for student progress; access to new knowledge about learning and teaching; sensibly organized time; access to the expertise of colleagues inside and outside the school; focused and timely feedback on individual performance and on aspects of classroom or school practice; and an overall ethos in which teacher learning is valued and professional community cultivated. School leaders could go some distance toward creating such an environment by generating professional community, promoting and organizing activity that sustains a focus on teaching and learning and ensuring that other workplace conditions enhance rather than impede teachers' PD and commitment to teaching.

NOTES

This chapter is abridged and adapted from the 2006 paper of the same title (Little, 2006), published and reprinted by permission of the National Education Association © 2006. All rights reserved.

1. The evidence is consistent on this point. See findings from the nationally representative survey of elementary, middle and high school teachers reported by Garet, Porter, Desimone, Birman & Yoon (2001) and the

study of elementary teachers' participation in mathematics PD conducted by Cohen and Hill (2001).

2. For discussion of the broader range of workplace conditions that bear on professional learning opportunity and teacher retention, see Johnson et al. (2004) and Little (1999).
3. A thorough review of this literature is beyond the scope of this chapter. Taken more or less chronologically, some of the contributions include Little (1982, 1987, 1990); Rosenholtz (1989); Nias, Southworth and Yeomans (1989); Little and McLaughlin (1993); Siskin (1994); Louis and Kruse (1995); Newmann and Associates (1996); Westheimer (1998); Grossman, Wineburg and Woolworth (2001); McLaughlin and Talbert (2001); Achinstein (2002); Horn (2005).
4. In this case, the term *collective* refers to the aggregate of individual measures, but commonality of views (a high mean level and low variance on the reported items) suggests that a shared norm may be operating. That is, teachers in such a school would expect one another to take responsibility for student learning and would disapprove of those who do not.

REFERENCES

Achinstein, B. (2002). Conflict amid community: The micropolitics of teacher collaboration. *Teachers College Record, 104*(3), 421–455.

Ball, D. L., & Cohen, D. K. (1999). Developing practice, developing practitioners: Toward a practice-based theory of professional education. In L. Darling-Hammond & G. Sykes (Eds.), *Teaching as the learning profession: Handbook of policy and practice* (pp. 3–32). San Francisco: Jossey-Bass.

Banks, J., Cochran-Smith, M., Moll, L., Richert, A., Zeichner, K., LePage, P., Darling-Hammond, L., Duffy, H. & McDonald, M. (2005). Teaching diverse learners. In L. Darling-Hammond & G. Sykes (Eds.), *Teaching as the learning profession: Handbook of policy and practice* (pp. 232–274). San Francisco: Jossey-Bass.

Black, P., & Wiliam, D. (1998). Inside the black box: Raising standards through classroom assessment. *Phi Delta Kappan, 80*(2), 139–148.

Borko, H. (2004). Professional development and teacher learning: Mapping the terrain. *Educational Researcher, 33*(8), 3–15.

Bryk, A. S., Sebring, P. B., Allensworth, E., Luppescu, S., & Easton, J. Q. (2010). *Organizing schools for impro- vement. Lessons from Chicago*. Chicago / London: The University of Chicago Press.

Cohen, D. K., & Hill, H. C. (2001). *Learning policy: When state education reform works*. New Haven, CT: Yale University Press.

Cohen, D., Raudenbush, S., & Ball, D. (2003). Resources, instruction, and research. *Educational Evaluation and Policy Analysis, 25*(2), 1–24.

Desimone, L. M., Porter, A. C., Garet, M. S., Yoon, K. S. & Birman, B. F. (2002). Effects of professional development on teachers' instruction: Results from a three-year longitudinal study. *Educational Evaluation and Policy Analysis, 24*(2), 81–112.

Elmore, R. F. (2005). Building new knowledge: School improvement requires new knowledge, not just good will. *American Educator, 29*(1), 20–27.

Garet, M., Porter, A., Desimone, L., Birman, B. & Yoon, K. S. (2001). What makes a professional development effective? Results from a national sample of teachers. *American Education Research Journal, 38*(4), 915–945.

Grodsky, E., & Gamoran, A. (2003). The relationship between professional development and professional community in American schools. *School Effectiveness and School Improvement, 14*(1), 1–29.

Grossman, P., Wineburg, S. & Woolworth, S. (2001). Toward a theory of teacher community. *Teachers College Record, 103*(6), 942–1012.

Gutierrez, R. (1996). Practices, beliefs and cultures of high school mathematics departments: Understanding their influence on student advancement. *Journal of Curriculum Studies, 28*(5), 495–529.

Hargreaves, A. (1993). Individualism and individuality: Reinterpreting the teacher culture. In J. W. Little & M. W. McLaughlin (Eds.), *Teachers' work: Individuals, colleagues, and contexts* (pp. 51–76). New York: Teachers College Press.

Horn, I. S. (2005). Learning on the job: A situated account of teacher learning in high school mathematics departments. *Cognition and Instruction, 23*(2), 207–236.

Huberman, M. (1993). The model of the independent artisan in teachers' professional relations. In J. W. Little & M. W. McLaughlin (Eds.), *Teachers' work: Individuals, colleagues, and contexts* (pp. 11–50). New York: Teachers College Press.

Johnson, S. M., Birkeland, S. E., Donaldson, M. L., Kardos, S. M., Kauffman, D., Liu, E. & Peske, H. G. (2004). *Finders and keepers: Helping new teachers survive and thrive in our schools.* San Francisco: Jossey-Bass.

Kazemi, E., & Franke, M. L. (2004). Teacher learning in mathematics: Using student work to promote collective inquiry. *Journal of Mathematics Teacher Education, 7,* 203–235.

Knapp, M. S. (2003). Professional development as a policy pathway. *Review of Research in Education, 27,* 109–157.

Lampert, M. (2001). *Teaching problems and the problems of teaching.* New Haven, CT: Yale University Press.

Lee, V. E., & Smith, J. (1996). Collective responsibility for learning and its effects on gains in achievement and engagement for early secondary school students. *American Journal of Education, 104*(2), 103–147.

Little, J. W. (1982). Norms of collegiality and experimentation: Workplace conditions of school success. *American Educational Research Journal, 19*(3), 325–340.

Little, J. W. (1984). Seductive images and organizational realities in professional development. *Teachers College Record, 86*(1), 84–102.

Little, J. W. (1987). Teachers as colleagues. In V. Richardson-Koehler (Ed.), *Educators' handbook: A research perspective* (pp. 491–518). New York: Longman.

Little, J. W. (1990). The mentor phenomenon and the social organization of teaching. *Review of Research in Education, 16,* 297–351.

Little, J. W. (1999). Organizing schools for teacher learning. In L. Darling-Hammond & G. Sykes (Eds.), *Teaching as the learning profession: Handbook of teaching and policy* (pp. 233–622). San Francisco: Jossey-Bass.

Little, J. W. (2003). Professional community and the problem of high school reform. *International Journal of Educational Research, 37*(8), 693–714.

Little, J. W. (2006). *NEA Best practices working paper: Professional community and professional development in the learning-centered school.* Washington, DC: National Education Association.

Little, J. W., & Bartlett, L. (2002). Career and commitment in the context of comprehensive school reform. *Teachers and Teaching: Theory and Practice, 8*(3), 345–354.

Little, J. W., Gearhart, M., Curry, M. & Kafka, J. (2003). Looking at student work for teacher learning, teacher community, and school reform. *Phi Delta Kappan, 85*(3), 184–192.

Little, J. W., & Horn, I. S. (2007). 'Normalizing' problems of practice: Converting routine conversation into a resource for learning in professional communities. In L. Stoll & K. Seashore (Eds.), *Professional learning communities: Divergence, depth and dilemmas* (pp. 79–92). London: Open University Press.

Little, J. W., & McLaughlin, M. W. (1993). Perspectives on cultures and contexts of teaching. In J. W. Little & M. W. McLaughlin (Eds.), *Teachers' work: Individuals, colleagues, and contexts* (pp. 1–8). New York: Teachers College Press.

Louis, K. S., & Kruse, S. D. (1995). *Professionalism and community: Perspectives on reforming urban schools.* Thousand Oaks, CA: Corwin Press.

McLaughlin, M. W., and Talbert, J. E. (1994). Teacher professionalism in local school contexts. *American Journal of Education, 102*(2), 123–153.

McLaughlin, M. W., and Talbert, J. E. (2001). *Professional communities and the work of high school teaching.* Chicago: University of Chicago Press.

Meier, D. (1992). Reinventing teaching. *Teachers College Record, 93*(4), 594–609.

Newmann, F. M., and Associates. (1996). *Authentic achievement: Restructuring schools for intellectual quality.* San Francisco: Jossey-Bass.

Newmann, F., & Wehlage, G. (1995). *Successful school restructuring: A report to the public and educators by the center on organization and restructuring of schools.* Madison, WI: Center on Organization and Restructuring of Schools.

Nias, J., Southworth, G. & Yeomans, R. (1989). *Staff relationships in the primary school: A study of organizational cultures.* London: Cassell.

Rosenholtz, S. (1989). *Teachers' workplace.* New York: Longman.

Saxe, G. B., Gearhart, M. & Nasir, N. (2001). Enhancing students' understanding of mathematics: A study of three contrasting approaches to professional support. *Journal of Mathematics Teacher Education, 4,* 55–79.

Secada, W. G., & Adajian, L. B. (1997). Mathematics teachers' change in the context of their professional communities. In E. Fennema & B. S. Nelson (Eds.), *Mathematics Teachers in Transition* (pp. 193–219). Mahwah, New Jersey: Lawrence Erlbaum Associates.

Shepard, L., Hammerness, K., Darling-Hammond, L., Rust, F., Snowden, J. B., Gordon, E., Gutierrez, C. & Pacheco, A. (2005). Assessment. In L. Darling-Hammond & J. Bransford (Eds.), *Preparing teachers for a changing world* (pp. 275–326). San Francisco: Jossey-Bass.

Shulman, L. (1986). Those who understand: Knowledge growth in teaching. *Educational Researcher, 19*(2), 4–14.

Siskin, L. S. (1994). *Realms of knowledge: Academic departments in secondary schools.* London: Falmer.

Stein, M. K., Silver, E. A. & Smith, M. S. (1998). Mathematics reform and teacher development: A community of practice perspective. In J. Greeno & S. Goldman (Eds.), *Thinking practices in mathematics and science learning* (pp. 17–52). Hillsdale, NJ: Erlbaum.

Stokes, L. (2001). Lessons from an inquiring school: Forms of inquiry and conditions for teacher learning. In A. Lieberman & L. Miller (Eds.), *Teachers caught in the action: Professional development that matters* (pp. 141–158). New York: Teachers College Press.

Talbert, J. (1995). Boundaries of teachers' professional communities in U.S. high schools: Power and precariousness of the subject department. In L. S. Siskin & J. W. Little (Eds.), *The subjects in question: Departmental organization and the high school* (pp. 68–94). New York: Teachers College Press.

Wenger, E. (1998). *Communities of practice: Learning, meaning, and identity.* Cambridge: Cambridge University Press.

Westheimer, J. (1998). *Among schoolteachers: Community, autonomy and ideology in teachers' work.* New York: Teachers College Press.

Wilson, S. M., & Berne, J. (1999). Teacher learning and the acquisition of professional knowledge: An examination of research on contemporary professional development. *Review of Research in Education, 24,* 173–209.

Part II

Perspectives for Teacher Learning in Multiple Contexts

3 Professional Learning
Creating Conditions for Developing Knowledge of Teaching

John Loughran

INTRODUCTION

A considerable literature exists that describes a diversity of views on the nature of teachers' professional knowledge (their knowledge of teaching). As Munby, Russell and Martin (2001) explained, there has been considerable tension around how teachers' knowledge is conceptualized not least because of the stark differences surrounding what knowledge is and what counts as knowledge.

Fenstermacher (1994) described two types of knowledge: formal knowledge and practical knowledge. Formal knowledge he described as a type of knowledge developed using conventional scientific approaches that ultimately serve to be generalized and applied across contexts. On the other hand, practical knowledge is developed by teachers based on their experiences of classroom teaching. Formal knowledge is developed by researchers external to the classroom and stands in contrast to practical knowledge that is developed by teachers in idiosyncratic ways that are contextually bound. Formal knowledge may speak to teachers about general aspects of teaching and learning but, by its very nature, tends to falter under the pressure of the day-to-day realities of teaching. As teaching is problematic, it is commonly the case that the subtleties and idiosyncrasies of the practice setting call for pedagogic responses that are embedded in teachers' experiences of practice rather than on generalized rules, propositions or procedures.

When Wideen, Mayer-Smith and Moon (1998) considered these two forms of knowledge, they focused their attention on the notion of utilization. They concluded that knowledge is often described from a 'producer-user' perspective and explained how that influences understandings of knowledge and its perceived usefulness. From a producer-user perspective, researchers create the knowledge and teachers are assumed to apply it in their practice. Clearly then, arguments about that which comprises teachers' professional knowledge, what it looks like and how it might be interpreted and implemented through classroom actions is no simple task. Adding to these difficulties is an inherent contradiction about the nature of teaching that follows along similar lines to that of the producer-user arguments about knowledge. Cochran-Smith and Lytle (2009) capture this contradiction well:

> It is now broadly assumed by nearly everybody interested in improving schools—researchers, policymakers, school-based leaders, politicians, parents—that teachers and other practitioners are the key to educational change. . . . Recognizing that [they] . . . are critical to the success of all efforts to improve education is clearly an idea whose time has come . . . [However,] behind the current educational regime is a kind of back-to-the-future enterprise that, despite its rhetoric, makes certain assumptions: teachers are primarily technicians; the goal of teacher learning initiatives is to make teachers more faithful implementers of received knowledge and curriculum; subject matter is a more or less static object to be transmitted from teachers to students; the purpose of educational systems, which are the bellwether of the health of the economy, is to produce the nation's workers; and students' learning can be adequately assessed through standardized tests. (pp. 1–2)

If teaching is understood in the way described in the preceding, then it is not difficult to see why a view of knowledge as formal rather than practical holds sway in the perceived importance of that which might govern the practice of teaching. Challenging dichotomous and/or contradictory views of teaching (and views of teachers' knowledge that underpin practice) then matters if expertise in teaching is to be better understood and more highly valued. This is not to suggest that formal knowledge does not count, rather, that the expert pedagogue finds an appropriate balance between the advice available; that is, what might comprise formal knowledge and what they learned and know through their experience in the practice setting. Neither type of knowledge is more or less important, both serve to inform across the range of situations confronted by teachers in their planning, execution and review of teaching. However, an abiding issue is that formal knowledge is more easily stated and recognizable than practical knowledge because formal knowledge is often recognized as propositional in nature whereas practical knowledge is implicitly embedded in practice.

Teachers' knowledge of practice is largely tacit and so is easily misunderstood and/or misinterpreted by academics, educational policy makers, bureaucrats and even teachers themselves. Yet as Cochran-Smith and Lytle highlighted (2009), teachers' professional knowledge is fundamental to quality classroom teaching and learning and inextricably linked to the quality of teaching in the classroom. It therefore seems obvious that creating conditions for enhancing the development of knowledge of teaching is crucial to a strong and vibrant teaching profession; and doing so matters because:

- It is important to be able to recognize and articulate the expertise that is encompassed in quality practice—for oneself and for the wider community.
- There is a continual need to communicate and share knowledge of practice with others in ways that extend beyond the simple accumulation of tips and tricks as the sole measure (or expectation) of classroom expertise.
- The skills teachers develop and use to manage the dilemmas and tensions inherent in working with 25 or so different students each lesson is a basis for knowledge of practice.
- Teachers' professional knowledge encapsulates the very essence of what it means to be an accomplished practitioner in more meaningful ways than high-stakes testing and other imposed accountability measures.

Understanding teachers as producers of knowledge is important. Supporting that aspect of teachers' work occurs when opportunities for professional learning are made available that focus on helping them to capture, articulate and portray their professional knowledge of teaching (Loughran, 2009). This chapter explores the outcomes of two ongoing professional learning projects conducted over extended periods of time that have specifically sought to develop teachers' knowledge of practice through professional learning designed to help participants better value their knowledge, skills and abilities as pedagogues.

PROFESSIONAL LEARNING

No area in education has been more roundly criticized than professional development. Detractors see it as brief and rarely sustained, deficit oriented, radically under-resourced, lacking in intellectual rigor or coherence, treated as an add-on rather than as part of a natural process, politically imposed rather than professionally owned, and trapped in constraints of a bureaucratic system that poses barriers to even modest levels of success. In short, it is an ill-designed, pedagogically naïve, demeaning exercise that often leaves participants more cynical and no more knowledgeable, skilled or committed than before. The challenge that lies before us, therefore, is determining how we can take this vitally important endeavor and make it more effective, more relevant, and more meaningful. (Guskey, 2008, p. xiii)

It is not difficult to see why programs designed to offer professional development (PD) to teachers can be viewed in a less than favorable light. The consequence of program design based on commonly held views about the nature and application of knowledge (in accord with those described by

Wideen et al. [1998] and Cochran-Smith & Lytle [2009]) influence not only the structure of PD but also the way it is delivered. As a consequence, PD is often cynically viewed by teachers as a one-way process of transmission with the intention of the information being absorbed one day and put into practice the next; however, congruency between PD intentions/aspirations and outcomes does not appear to be the norm.

Guskey (2008) certainly offers a number of compelling reasons for the lack of change as a consequence of PD and many others support his view (Borko, 2004; Fullan, 2001, 2007; Mockler, 2005). In a recent study by Wei, Darling-Hammond, Andree, Richardson and Orphanos (2009) in which they examined the nature of PD programs and practices across the United States, their conclusion was that "the structures and supports that are needed to sustain teacher learning and change and to foster job-embedded professional development in collegial environments fall short [of that which is necessary for real change]" (p. 27). Further to this, Webster-Wright (2009), following an extensive review of the PD literature, found that:

> the majority of this PD literature . . . both research and practice based, has a focus on programs and content rather than on learning experiences. In fact, PD practices have been critiqued as "mired in update and competency approaches" (A. Wilson, 2000, p. 78). An update perspective stresses the obsolescence of present knowledge that accompanies rapid change. This perspective reinforces the view of learning as "filling up" a reservoir of knowledge in a professional's mind that will run dry if left too long. (p. 712)

What quickly emerges in any analysis of the PD literature is that a fundamental shift in the underpinning assumptions and purposes of teacher development is needed if PD is to be taken seriously by teachers and begin to influence the quality of teaching and learning in schools.

One way of catalyzing a shift away from the underpinning intentions of PD as an exercise in topping up or implementing mandated change is to begin to challenge the structure and purpose of PD by supporting approaches to knowledge growth based on notions of professional learning. By so doing, a greater emphasis might then be placed on practices that encourage genuine professional learning by being: sustained over time (Garet, Porter, Desimone, Birman & Yoon, 2001); responsive to the specifics of school and classroom contexts (Lieberman & Miller, 2001); underpinned by research and practice-based evidence (Borko, 2004); and supported by professional learning communities and collaboration (Hayes, Mills, Christie & Lingard, 2006; Hoban, 2002; Wegner, 1998). Hence, approaches to PD as "something done to teachers" (Guskey, 2008, p. xiv) might be replaced by professional learning practices whereby working with teachers to better support the development of their skills, knowledge and abilities in ways that are responsive to their particular pedagogical needs, issues and concerns might be facilitated (Berry, Clemans & Kostogriz, 2007). Two longitudinal professional learning programs based on such practices are Science Teaching and Learning (STaL; Berry, Loughran, Lindsay & Smith, 2009) and Leading Professional Learning (LPL; Clemans et al., 2009).

STaL and LPL are residential programs organized across the school year (program days 2–3 months apart) with ongoing (between program) school-based support for participants. STaL is specifically designed for science teachers and LPL is organized for those teachers with responsibility for leading the professional learning of their colleagues. Working from a teacher-as-learner perspective, the programs purposely adopt an approach similar to that described by Putnam and Borko (1997) in that they "ground teachers' learning experiences in their own practice by conducting activities at school sites, with a large component taking place in individual teachers' classrooms" (p. 6). Both programs focus on supporting teachers in articulating, developing and valuing of their professional knowledge of practice and culminate in a case writing day in which participants reflect on the work they did during their school-based project from which they write a case about a specific learning situation.

Case writing follows the approach described by Shulman (1992) in which a dilemma/issue/concern is central to the case. At the heart of case writing is the intention that teachers' professional knowledge of practice will begin to stand out in ways that are identifiable and articulable (Lundeberg, 1999) and, through publishing and disseminating the resultant cases, there is the hope that a greater sense of valuing teachers' knowledge might emerge; not just for participants but also for other teachers who read the cases. Therefore, it is participants' personal experiences of learning about their knowledge of practice that is fostered, captured and disseminated through these programs. Each program is therefore constructed and conducted in ways that explicitly demonstrate a shift away from a view of PD as the 'delivery of information' to that of an approach based on fostering genuine personal professional learning.

RESEARCHING PROFESSIONAL LEARNING

The STaL project has been funded by the Catholic Education Office (Melbourne), developed and conducted collaboratively with the Science Education Research team at Monash University. STaL has been an ongoing project that has gradually been developed and refined over time; it is currently in its sixth year. Lindsay (2006) described the purpose of the project in the following way:

> The Catholic Education Office Melbourne has developed the Science Teaching and Learning (STaL) Project in partnership with the Faculty of Education at Monash University in the belief that effective sharing

and collaboration between teachers provides them with valuable learning opportunities. The STaL project embraces the idea that teachers are producers of specialized knowledge about teaching and learning. Teachers hold a rich and precious knowledge about what they do, and this knowledge is continually developed and refined within the confines of their classrooms (Loughran, Berry, & Mulhall, 2006). This knowledge remains largely tacit, yet the education community would benefit significantly from encouraging this teacher knowledge to be much more explicit. The cases that comprise this book are an attempt to do just that; make the tacit explicit. (p. 3)

In a similar way, the LPL project was funded by the Department of Education and Early Childhood Development (DEECD), developed and conducted collaboratively with the Pedagogy and Professional Learning Research group at Monash University. LPL has also been an ongoing project that has gradually been developed and refined over time; it is currently in its third and final year. LPL was based on the view that:

the quality of teachers is a key determinant of variation in student achievement . . . in order to be effective, teachers need a deep understanding of their subject area, knowledge of how students learn specific subject matter and a range of strategies and practices that support student learning. The research also affirms that engaging teachers in high quality professional learning is the most successful way to improve teacher effectiveness . . . [and as] teaching is a dynamic profession and, as new knowledge about teaching and learning emerges, new types of expertise are required by educators. (DEECD, 2005, p. 3)

One way of capturing participants' professional knowledge has been through their case writing that stands out as an obvious research product (see Berry et al., 2008; Berry & Keast, 2009; Clemans et al., 2009; Loughran & Berry, 2006, 2007, 2008, for examples [n ≥ 250] of published cases). However, as both projects are based on a view that developing teachers' professional knowledge of practice is important, then a consideration of participants' understandings of the nature of their knowledge, how it is developed and valued matters. Both projects have attempted to do this (and continue to do so) by following up with participants through semi-structured interviews with volunteers a year after program conclusion in order to canvas their perceptions on these issues following their learning experiences.

In her reflection on involvement in the STaL program Colquhoun (2006) stated that:

[STaL] was an invaluable experience that gave us an opportunity to reconnect the importance of teaching with purpose. Too often we (teachers) are overwhelmed with course content which relentlessly drives the quality and depth of information delivered to students. This program gave us time out from the daily demands of school to personally reflect on our teaching from cognitive and practical perspectives. . . . As educators we regularly make assumptions about what students bring into the classroom. These assumptions primarily impact on our lesson planning, influencing the path of learning we perceive that needs to be created. But how well do we construct this path to really meet the students' learning needs? Do all students have the opportunity to integrate their prior views into their learning as the topic progresses? . . . The sessions we were involved in encouraged us to personally reflect on and, as a consequence, to affirm what in our practice was successful and to identify areas in our teaching which could be strengthened through trialling alternative teaching procedures and strategies. It also highlighted the importance of using the partnership with students to gain constructive feedback—they are often the best critics!—and to refine our practice. . . . Seldom do we sit down as a faculty and discuss how a concept is taught or what procedures are used. . . . We need to acknowledge and tap into the wealth of teaching knowledge and experience which is already in our faculties and rate this as an important and essential aspect of our meetings. . . . "Where is our teaching currently at and what are we doing about it? Is it working? How can I/we make it better?" On the one hand these appear simple questions, on the other, responding to them can lead to a powerful improvement in teaching. Participating in this program has clearly identified for me the lack of collegial opportunities we have in school to share our knowledge of practice but it has also prompted me to recognize and acknowledge the depth of experience available within schools. (pp. 11, 14)

Colquhoun raises a number of issues about teachers' professional knowledge that are important when thinking about professional learning. Understanding teachers' perspectives on these issues clearly matters when thinking about what a professional learning program might look like and how it might serve the needs and concerns of teachers as producers and users of knowledge of practice. (In the following sections, indicative quotes and pseudonyms have been employed.)

Professional Knowledge

It is interesting to consider from an academic perspective that which might be described as teachers' professional knowledge of practice. However, in many ways, it could be argued that academic interpretations and views have little bearing on the reality of that which matters to teachers in their day-to-day practice; the theory practice gap is certainly ever clear and present to many teachers. In the majority of interviews with participants, first responses to questions about their professional knowledge of practice were predicated on how they "managed a classroom full of children." Hence, their immediate touchstone of knowledge seemed to be that of knowledge of classroom management. There was a clear view that "if you can't manage the students, you can't teach them." It was not until discussions acknowledged and then moved beyond this point that other aspects of participants' professional knowledge emerged. However, as noted earlier, much of teachers' knowledge of practice is tacit, so not surprisingly, many struggled to state clearly what they thought their professional knowledge of teaching really comprised (beyond that of their knowledge and skills in classroom management).

> *Emma:*   Teachers' knowledge, there's heaps. In particular for our school, there's discipline. There's the individual students. There's the dealing with the individual needs of the students. There is dealing with the issues with parents and the students and the curriculum and what they're doing in the classroom. There's the issues of the policies in the school; dealing with discipline which is huge. In this school it's huge. And expanding that to the individual learner; how they're coping in the classroom and how are you adjusting your teaching to address the needs of the students. So that's a really—a big issue that I'm constantly dealing with every day. So I guess it's sort of one of those things. You actually know. Oh, not know but because of your years of experience, you're probably aware that you can pick up on a child; what's happening or what's not happening with them and go, "Well I need to go in that direction, I need to go that direction." And I think that comes with a lot of years of experience.

Interestingly, although they found it difficult to categorically define teachers' professional knowledge they had very little difficulty in offering ways in which it might be developed:

> *Anita:*   I've changed my thinking a lot having done these courses on that and I think that teachers can gain a lot more professional knowledge by talking to each other in more structured ways. So, being given like—we've got quite a big school here—and it's just really made me realize that we don't use each other's expertise enough and that's what I'm trying to build into our structure now. So that I think, you know, there's a lot of knowledge to be gained from people working together all the time, being given time to reflect and think about what they're doing and I think a lot of the strategies that I've learnt through that course and this course that I'm

	currently doing [LPL], can set those conversations up so that they, that people do get a lot more out of them.
Kay:	Um, well, quite a variety of different ways and one is to analyze their current practices. Also reading and observing quality learning in action or quality teaching, I suppose, in action. It's then trialling things in their own classroom and it's seeking and getting quality feedback. It's also being supported in terms of resourcing and time; it's in terms of structure that's placed around the learning as in: "Is there the provision for time for them to talk together, to reflect?"; "Are there perhaps some thinking tools that they might be using that would enhance their learning and their understanding?" And it comes down to a willingness and the professionalism of course of the person who's presenting the learning as well.
Brad:	Relationships, communication, teamwork, collaboration, professional reading. Professional learning through Action Research, Lesson Study, Coaching, Mentoring and attending professional development sessions that require you to do a "project" or "hands-on" task in your school/workplace, so you can learn from your mistakes and learn through doing. Taking risks and finding your way forward when there is no way forward that you know of. Tenacity, persistence, support from your colleagues, collaboration. Looking at the Big Picture and staying focused on the outcome, instead of getting bogged down in the little problems that could stop you from reaching your destination.
Jan:	By having a really strong collegial environment around and by having people to talk to. It's no good getting lectured; you don't improve. But actually sitting down and talking to people and sharing in a really non-threatening environment is for me how I develop professional knowledge. We share books, we share ideas but it's only when I get to sit around and talk to people and write stuff and feel professional.

It is not difficult to see then that the notion of "doing" and "learning through experience" are critical to these teachers' views about what it means to develop their knowledge of practice. As both the STaL and LPL programs used case writing as a vehicle for helping teachers to articulate their knowledge of practice, participants' views of their case writing experiences are also quite revealing.

Case Writing

Drawn from the fields of business and law, the idea of cases is as a way of capturing the essence of a situation and inviting the reader into the complexities of that situation. As they have been developed and used in teaching, cases illustrate the problematic nature of practice and the competing issues and concerns that are central to particular pedagogic situations. Cases are therefore constructed in ways that examine specific issues/dilemmas/concerns in ways that demonstrate the complexity of practice in action. From an academic perspective, cases offer many possibilities for "looking into teaching" and offer quite compelling data germane to teachers' professional knowledge. How they are viewed by teachers is therefore important in beginning to think about what cases might mean for the articulation and development of knowledge of practice. (Again, these are indicative responses from participants.)

> *Natalie:* I've certainly read them all [published cases] and I was very proud of the one I put in; very proud of the one I put in. . . . The process of writing is a very useful one. It's only when we actually talk over often, something that's happened, an experience or an issue or a problem or we write about it, but in the process of talking about it or the process of writing about it, it becomes clear, you clarify a lot of issues in your own mind. That actual process is a very good learning experience for yourself. I'm an English teacher, I guess, originally and I know how important it is to write things down and to talk things through, because it is a learning experience. There's a synergy that happens when you talk with people you can come to a better set of understandings. The shared understandings are often much more powerful than if you just thought about it yourself but the actual process of writing something down does something in the brain I think, it clarifies things, it helps you come to your own, well, I call it an epiphany often, you know it makes you think about things. You get a deep learning; deep meaningful. You make connections when you actually write things down. It's the self-discipline required, I suppose, the process you go through is a very worthwhile one. So I enjoy that very much, but I must admit, I like writing anyway . . . it was a very creative exercise and the result was fantastic; the book is great! I've got a couple of copies. I'm so proud of what I wrote. How often do you make yourself sit down and write something like that? You just don't get the time and I really appreciated making—having someone make me do that. So I really loved doing that and it's good to delve in and read some more short stories, cases.
>
> *Emma:* The book I found was really good. That was actually because I was able to communicate with other teachers who are on similar lines [to me] so that was good. Yeah. . . . It made me really think in depth of actually about: What are the issues?; What are the very fine details?; and things that I never actu-

ally, don't appear, you know, in the Big Picture but suddenly when you think about it and suddenly you start writing about it you go, that was an issue that I hadn't even looked at; hadn't thought about. Hadn't addressed and then [in being] able to write it down, it made it clearer. A lot clearer and then I was able to make it more concise . . . it made me more aware of who's going to read this . . . they read it and they can understand perhaps where I'm coming from. I think it's been excellent to do that. It took awhile. It was very hard. Oh, like drawing blood. But I got there and when you're not used to doing those sort of things, it's a great skill, you know, as a starting point. I figure it's a starting point but it's a great skill to actually learn and to actually write down and then to read each other's and then because you read each other's and . . . you can actually understand in their writing where they're actually coming from and I think that's really good. I found that really enlightening. In fact, I have it [the cases book] up there and every now and then when I've got 5 [minutes]; I read it. No I think it's important because each teacher has different perspectives on the way they work and on the way they deal with issues and I think . . . often you can pick up on ideas that they've done and they've dealt with and think "oh well, I'll try that" and that's another idea. That's another thing I found out of the book. So it's been a very good learning curve for me. Huge, yeah.

It is interesting to see how persistent the ideas of time and reflection appear to be and how through writing about their experiences, the status of these teachers' knowledge of practice is raised: "I'm very proud of the one [case] I put in"; "it made me aware of who is going to read this." However, at the center of all discussions about their professional knowledge is the issue of experience as a teacher and what that means in terms of being able to "do teaching."

For participants in the STaL and LPL programs, it appears as though expertise is framed not so much around what they know but what they are able to do. Knowing and doing may be inextricably linked, but for these participants, it is clear that knowing is derived of doing, rather than the other way around. Hence, and as is demonstrated over and over again through analyses of the content of the published cases, arguments about that which comprises teachers' knowledge is more an issue of interest to academics than teachers. What matters to (these) teachers is their expertise in being able to do teaching, not how they construct it in theoretical terms. They continually noted that they had limited time and opportunity to reflect in more formal ways on their practice and that the expectations for their work does not normally extend to writing about or sharing their knowledge in ways such as that demonstrated through their cases.

Despite the limited opportunities for documenting and sharing their knowledge of practice in more formal ways, there is little doubt that these teachers valued their case writing opportunity and had a certain amount of pride in the published product (cases book). The cases offered these participants a new way of articulating and sharing their knowledge of practice that they appreciated.

Trudy: To write the case, I didn't even know where to start and I remember a conversation we had about what I did in the classroom. What was important to me that made me consider working the way I did . . . I had to stop and step out . . . I am a bit of a control freak type, kind of, and it was that letting go. Even though you can still have control, but let the kids come up with an answer instead of me having to provide the answers. That was a huge learning thing for me. Actually number one, to take the time to step back and reflect on what I do. I know what my strengths are and what my weaknesses are, but at the same time to really give yourself the time to do it and think about what to do to perhaps try something different. I think writing the case made me reflect on it even more. . . . I think it was important for me to actually be put in a situation where, actually in a grown up way, a professional way, reflect on what it is that I do every day in your classroom. I think as educators maybe we don't [do that enough] because we are too busy to do it. You get to school, you've got a job, we are very good at "yes, yes, fine, I'll do it, bang let's go" but are we as good at [what we do] well, let's stop, let's take a step back and ask if it is working or not, what's the good in it, what's the area that maybe I should let go or improve on. I think, if nothing else, that was a really important thing from writing the case.

PROFESSIONAL LEARNING NEEDS

As the previous two sections demonstrate, these participants found it difficult to define their professional knowledge of practice. Just as Polanyi (1966) suggested so long ago, their knowledge is tacit. But, when given an opportunity to explore their tacit knowledge through case writing, they began to wrestle with their understanding of their knowledge of practice and began to value not just what they did as teachers, but also that which informed and directed their teaching actions.

Earlier in this chapter arguments were presented about the importance of a shift from a PD to a professional learning approach to enhancing teachers' knowledge of practice. Interestingly, when asked about their professional learning needs, participants found it difficult to categorically state what they required. However, it is obvious that the approach they sought was not one of mandated change and system-imposed up-skilling, rather they wanted to learn about how to direct and develop their own professional learning through a deeper consideration of their knowledge of practice.

> *Interviewer:* What do you feel you still need with regard to professional learning?
> *Kay:* Um, lots more personal knowledge I guess. I need to continue to practice my craft and to refine it. . . . I guess I need to fine-tune that. I need the time. The time is still the greatest factor I think, to be able to get into classrooms and see with a lot more detail what's happening and to be able to analyze the impact of the professional learning that might happen. So I guess I need tools to help me to know where the changes have occurred and the value of those changes, so I guess that's how to gather and analyze data, etc.
> *Sally:* I think developing professional knowledge is about sharing. It's about attending things that are important for the level that you're at. Not just attending professional learning for the sake of it; to say tick the box, I've done that. But to actually recognize what your needs are and then to attend something that's bridging the gap between where I was and where I want to be. . . . I would love to do more writing, some more of those cases and things like that because I suppose in the last 12 months from where I was then, I could actually—would love to have the opportunity to have that time to sit back and actually reflect on some of the things that have happened along the journey.

CONCLUSION

From a teacher's perspective, the need to know what to do and how to do it (practice) is much more important in the teaching and learning crucible of the classroom than the reasons for so doing (theory). That is not to suggest that reasons (theory) for actions do not matter, rather that they do not necessarily overtly direct the doing (practice). The reasons for doing tend to be tacit because, in the culture of teaching, there is little time for, or expectation to, make pedagogical reasoning more explicit. Jeff Northfield (see Loughran & Northfield, 1996), a teacher educator who returned to classroom teaching, recognized this very point explaining how he experienced it in the following manner:

The theories and the 'recommendations' seem to neglect the routine and contextual complexity of the classroom setting. Many of the 'theories' seem less useful from a teaching perspective. How do they apply to 7D on a Monday last period? Unpredictability is a factor—perhaps the theories come into play as I interpret the situation and respond to the way I see the situation unfolding. The best research in the world will have little impact until the conditions of teaching allow teachers time and opportunities to consider ideas in relation to the classroom contexts they experience. (pp. 21–22)

The views of these participants (STaL and LPL from which the data for this chapter is drawn), support Northfield's observations. As highlighted in the literature time and time again, the theory–practice gap (see, for example, Korthagen, Kessels, Koster, Langerwarf & Wubbels, 2001) influences understandings of teaching in many ways. The gap is viewed differently depending on the perspective of the observer (somewhat simplistically academics tend to see the gap from a theoretical perspective, teachers from a practical perspective), and so creating conditions under which the theory–practice gap might be viewed differently matters if possibilities for bridging the gap are to be seriously considered.

In an extensive study of learning to teach, Nilsson (2008) argued that "in order to learn from practical experience it is reasonable to suggest that experiences must be reflected and reasoned upon" (p. 34). In the busyness of teaching, teachers are not commonly afforded the time and conditions conducive to reflection and reasoning. Therefore, creating conditions for this to be the case is important. Nilsson's concern to do so for her students of teaching led her to create conditions for them to see their practice with new eyes that helped them to reconsider:

> their own teaching again through the video recordings . . . [they] were able to frame and reframe their practice . . . and therefore gain new insights into what they were doing and how. Reflecting in this way created new possibilities for them to make the tacit in their practice explicit and to begin to consider how the different knowledge bases on which their teaching was based influenced their developing orientation . . . [to] teaching. (p. 136)

Similarly, the STaL and LPL programs used a cases approach to encourage participants to frame and reframe their practice in order to bring to the surface new perspectives on their teaching. As experienced teachers, they did not so much need to see their teaching through videotapes (although that could clearly also be helpful), but they did need time to reflect on what they did in the classroom, how and why. In so doing, they found that aspects that were once tacit could be described and articulated in ways that made the knowledge underpinning their actions explicit for themselves and others. As a consequence, their professional learning was enhanced and they began to see into the theory–practice gap in new ways and take more control of their learning about their professional knowledge of teaching. Building on these new beginnings offers real possibilities for influencing the ways in which knowledge of teaching might be understood, developed and shared within the profession and lead to enhanced valuing of teaching itself. The challenge is for all of those involved in designing PD is to begin to make the shift to embrace professional learning—designers and teaches alike.

REFERENCES

Berry, A., Blaise, M., Clemans, A., Loughran, J. J., Mitchell, J., Parr, G., et al. (2008). *Leading professional learning: Cases of professional dilemmas*. Melbourne: Department of Education and Early Childhood Development.

Berry, A., Clemans, A. & Kostogriz, A. (Eds.). (2007). *Dimensions of professional learning: Identities, professionalism and practice*. Dordrecht: Sense Publishers.

Berry, A., & Keast, S. (Eds.). (2009). *Looking into practice: Cases of science teachers' professional growth*. Melbourne: Monash University and the Catholic Education Office Melbourne.

Berry, A., Loughran, J. J., Lindsay, S. & Smith, K. (2009). Supporting teacher research to develop knowledge of practice. *Research in Science Education, 39*(4), 575–594.

Borko, H. (2004). Professional development and teacher learning: Mapping the terrain. *Educational Researcher, 33*(3), 3–15.

Clemans, A., Berry, A., Blaise, M., Keast, S., Loughran, J., Parr, G., et al. (Eds.). (2009). *Willing to lead: Leading professional learning*. Melbourne: Department of Education and Early Childhood Development.

Cochran-Smith, M., & Lytle, S. L. (2009). *Inquiry as stance: Practitioner research for the next generation*. New York: Teachers College Press.

Colquhoun, Y. (2006). Cases: A teacher's perspective. In J. Loughran & A. Berry (Eds.), *Looking into practice: Cases of science teaching and learning* (2nd ed.) (pp. 11–14). Melbourne: Monash University and the Catholic Education Office Melbourne.

Department of Education and Early Childhood Development. (2005). *Professional learning in effective schools: The seven principles of highly effective professional learning*. Retrieved March 11, 2009, from http://www.eduweb.vic.gov.au/edulibrary/public/teachlearn/teacher/ProfLearningInEffectiveSchools.pdf

Fenstermacher, G. D. (1994). The knower and the known: The nature of knowledge in research on teaching. In L. Darling-Hammond (Ed.), *Review of research in education* (pp. 3–56). Washington, DC: American Educational Research Association.

Fullan, M. (2001). *The new meaning of educational change* (3rd ed.). New York: Teachers College Press.

Fullan, M. (2007). Change the terms for teacher learning. *Journal of Staff Development, 28*(3), 35–36.

Garet, M., Porter, A., Desimone, L., Birman, B. & Yoon, K. S. (2001). What makes professional development effective? Results from a national sample of teachers. *American Educational Research Journal, 38*(4), 915–945.

Guskey, T. R. (2008). Foreword. In R. Bourke, A. Lawrence, A. McGee, J. O'Neill & J. Curzon (Eds.), *Talk about learning: Working alongside teachers* (pp. xiii–xv). North Shore: Pearson Education New Zealand.

Hayes, D., Mills, M., Christie, P. & Lingard, B. (2006). *Teachers and schooling making a difference*. Sydney: Allen and Unwin.

Hoban, G. F. (2002). *Teacher learning for educational change: A systems thinking approach*. Buckingham: Open University Press.

Korthagen, F. A. J., Kessels, J., Koster, B., Langerwarf, B. & Wubbels, T. (2001). *Linking practice and theory: The pedagogy of realistic teacher education*. Mahwah, NJ: Lawrence Erlbaum Associates.

Lieberman, A., & Miller, L. (Eds.). (2001). *Teachers caught in the action: Professional development that matters*. New York: Teachers College Press.

Lindsay, S. (2006). Cases: Opening the classroom door. In J. Loughran & A. Berry (Eds.), *Looking into practice: Cases of science teaching and learning* (pp. 3–6). Melbourne: Catholic Education Office (Melbourne) and Monash University.

Loughran, J. J. (2009). *What expert teachers do: Teachers' professional knowledge of classroom practice*. Sydney: Allen and Unwin.

Loughran, J. J., & Berry, A. (Eds.). (2006). *Looking into practice: Cases of science teaching and learning* (2nd ed. Vol. 1). Melbourne: Monash Print Services.

Loughran, J. J., & Berry, A. (Eds.). (2007). *Looking into practice: Cases of science teaching and learning* (Vol. 2). Melbourne: Monash Print Services.

Loughran, J. J., & Berry, A. (Eds.). (2008). *Looking into practice: Cases of science teaching and learning* (Vol. 3). Melbourne: Monash Print Services.

Loughran, J. J., Berry, A. & Mulhall, P. (2006). *Understanding and developing science teachers' pedagogical content knowledge*. Dordrecht: Sense Publishers.

Loughran, J. J., & Northfield, J. R. (1996). *Opening the classroom door: Teacher, researcher, learner*. London: Falmer Press.

Lundeberg, M. (1999). Discovering teaching and learning through cases. In M. A. Lundeberg, B. B. Levin & H. Harrington (Eds.), *Who learns what from cases and how: The research base for teaching and learning with cases* (pp. 3–23). Mahwah, NJ: Lawrence Erlbaum Associates, Inc.

Mockler, N. (2005). Trans/forming teachers: New professional learning and transformative teacher professionalism. *Journal of In-Service Education, 31*(4), 733–746.

Munby, H., Russell, T. & Martin, A. K. (2001). Teachers' knowledge and how it develops. In V. Richardson (Ed.), *Handbook of research on teaching* (4th ed.) (pp. 877–904). Washington, DC: American Educational Research Association.

Nilsson, P. (2008). *Learning to teach and teaching to learn: Primary science student teachers' complex journey from learners to teachers. Linköping university, Norrköping, Department of Social and Welfare Studies*. Norrköping: The Swedish National Graduate School in Science and Technology Education, FontD.

Polanyi, M. (1966). *The tacit dimension*. Garden City, NY: Doubleday.

Putnam, R. T., & Borko, H. (1997). What do new views of knowledge and thinking have to say about research on teacher learning? *Educational Researcher, 29*(1), 4–15.

Shulman, J. H. (1992). *Case methods in teacher education*. New York: Teachers College Press.

Webster-Wright, A. (2009). Reframing professional development through understanding authentic professional learning. *Review of Educational Research, 79*(2), 702–739.

Wegner, E. (1998). *Communities of practice: Learning, meaning and identity*. Cambridge: Cambridge University Press.

Wei, R. C., Darling-Hammond, L., Andree, A., Richardson, N. & Orphanos, S. (2009). *Professional learning in the learning profession: A status report on teacher development in the U.S. and abroad*. Dallas, TX: National Staff Development Council.

Wideen, M., Mayer-Smith, J. & Moon, B. (1998). A critical analysis of the research on learning to teach: Making the case for an ecological perspective on inquiry. *Review of Educational Research, 68*(2), 130–178.

4 A Multi-Metaphorical Model for Teacher Knowledge and Teacher Learning

John Wallace and Judith Mulholland

INTRODUCTION

Teacher learning is based on the powerful idea that teachers are not just teachers, but also learners. In preparing to teach; in interacting with students, colleagues and other professionals; and in the act of teaching, teachers are engaged in learning to build their professional knowledge. While there is much agreement about the importance of teacher learning, there is considerable discussion and debate about the nature of this knowledge base (Fenstermacher, 1994; Kennedy, 2002; Munby, Russell & Martin, 2001) with different research communities employing their own metaphorical representations of, and ways of analyzing, teacher knowledge.

In this chapter we attempt to bridge these different research strands by adopting a multi-metaphorical approach to the analysis of teacher knowledge (and hence teacher learning). We begin with the conceptual by reviewing, elucidating and summarizing the different metaphorical representations of teacher knowledge to be found in the literature. In the second section of the chapter, we describe how these metaphors can be understood in terms of individual-cognitive and the collective-situative perspectives on learning. We conclude by arguing for a multi-metaphorical model of teacher learning, entailing the creation of a variety of formal and informal opportunities for learning to proceed in multiple contexts (settings, communities and learning foci).

FOUR METAPHORS OF TEACHER KNOWLEDGE

We summarize our reading of the teacher knowledge literature in terms of four sets or clusters of metaphors, each illuminating different but related aspects of teacher knowledge. Different views about teacher knowledge are elucidated by different metaphors, enabling us to view a nonphysical thing such as knowledge as an entity (such as a computer), an activity (such as crafting), a state (such as complexity) or an orientation (such as change). We have named the four metaphors: teacher knowledge as *computer*, whereby knowledge is viewed as an interactive database or sets of skills and under-standings; as *craft*, whereby teachers are seen as artisans whose skills exist in accomplished performance against a backdrop of the teaching context; as *complexity*, whereby knowledge is developed in complex interaction with the total environment and inseparable from this environment; and as *change*, whereby knowledge grows, evolves or develops over time.

We acknowledge that like most systems of classification, the categories we have chosen show a degree of overlap and that some types of teacher knowledge may fit more than one category. For example, while we argue here that the notion of change has sufficient metaphorical distinctions to warrant a separate category, we acknowledge that it could also be seen as a (sub)characteristic of the other three metaphors. In some cases, a knowl-edge concept is firmly attached to a particular metaphor (for example, Polanyi's, 1958/1998, notion of tacit knowledge is clearly associated with craft). In other cases, the original concept has been considerably expanded and co-opted so that it sits within more than one metaphorical cluster (Shul-man's, 1986, notion of pedagogical content knowledge [PCK] would be one example). Further, we are not suggesting that in every case, the original authors saw the metaphorical connections that we are proposing. In sum-mary, these four categories do not exhaust the possibilities for describing teachers' knowledge. However, we find the metaphor categories useful in assisting us to understand how various approaches to teacher learning can be associated with different representations of teacher knowledge.

Teacher Knowledge as Computer Database

The computer or knowledge database metaphor is derived from cogni-tive science whereby teachers' knowledge is likened "to the set of rules, definitions, and strategies needed by a computer to perform as an expert would in a given task environment" (Wilson, Shulman & Richert, 1987, pp. 105–106). Like Feldman (1997), we are not suggesting that the brain is a computer, but rather that the computer provides a metaphor for a way of representing teachers' knowledge. In the world of computers, for exam-ple, a knowledge base or database provides an expert system. Hence, the use of this metaphor in educational circles has developed into a discus-sion of expert teaching, often focusing on the differences between novice and expert teachers. The metaphor is frequently employed for purposes of teacher accreditation and in the professionalization debate (Darling-Ham-mond & Youngs, 2002; Gardner, 1989). Its most important contribution, however, is its representation of teaching as a profession conducted by those possessing a special knowledge base rather than an occupation carried out by any knowledgeable person (Turner-Bisset, 1999, 2001).

The database metaphor owes much to the original work of Lee Shulman (1986, 1987). In a lecture on the study of teaching in 1983, Shulman first identified "subject-matter knowledge and its interaction with pedagogy"

(Gess-Newsome & Lederman, 1999, p. ix) as a missing paradigm in research on teaching. This idea was brought to fruition in his now seminal papers where the term *pedagogical content knowledge* (PCK) was coined and defined as "pedagogical knowledge which goes beyond knowledge of subject matter . . . to the dimension of subject matter knowledge for teaching" (Shulman, 1986, p. 9). Since that time, PCK has come to be thought of as a special blending of subject matter knowledge and knowledge of pedagogy, long considered as separate, into a type of professional understanding unique to teachers (Shulman, 1987). PCK is often used to define what it is that teachers know and how this knowing differentiates them from other knowers of particular subjects. In many respects, the work of Dewey (1902) foreshadowed the concept of PCK. Dewey explained that teachers know their subjects differently from others, in that teachers were concerned not with subject matter for its own sake, as were other scholars, but with subject matter as but one part of the whole experience of education for a child. So important has the notion of PCK become that, in more recent times, researchers have called for subject matter knowledge to be taught to teachers as PCK so that teachers can more readily transform their own understandings for the classroom (Marks, 1990). Since Shulman's initial PCK work, researchers have debated the knowledge categories to be included and definitions of PCK have evolved over time (van Driel, Verloop & de Vos, 1998). However, in many ways, the notion of PCK has come to epitomize the computer or knowledge base metaphor of teachers' knowledge.

In the two decades since Shulman's early work, the knowledge base movement has developed into a major industry of research into the essential components of, and impacts upon, the knowledge base. Lists of such knowledge types, clustered in different ways and with different emphases, abound in the literature. They include content knowledge, general pedagogical knowledge, curriculum knowledge, PCK, knowledge of learners, knowledge of educational contexts, knowledge of educational aims, purposes and values and moral dispositions. However, it is difficult to isolate elements of teacher knowledge in research situations, as teachers have a holistic or integrated understanding of their work (Loughran, Milroy, Berry, Gunstone & Mulhall, 2001). The concept of PCK, for example, has fuzzy boundaries, challenging those who attempt to assign knowledge to its categories (Gess-Newsome, 1999), with aspects likely to fit more comfortably within other metaphors (craft, for example).

Given that the classification of knowledge into types does not represent a reality but is rather a system to assist thinking about teacher knowledge (Borko & Putnam, 1996), the computer database metaphor has both advantages and limitations. One advantage is that it provides a way of demonstrating what it is that teachers know, the complexity of the knowledge types and in being able to show in some sense that teachers "know that they know" (Fenstermacher, 1994, p. 51). The knowledge base also can be useful in analyzing teacher performance (Turner-Bisset, 2001), although in recent times it has been associated with accountability measures that are seen to restrict and undervalue the role of the teacher (Donmoyer, 1995; Sockett, 1987). Moreover, analyzing teaching performance by discussing individual knowledge types is not useful if the aim of analyzing teaching is to improve practice, in which all knowledge types are closely intertwined (Hiebert, Gallimore & Stigler, 2002). Hence the importance of other metaphors that allow for a more holistic view of teacher knowledge.

Teacher Knowledge as Craft

A major critique of the knowledge as computer metaphor is that it focuses primarily on scientifically derived or propositional knowledge rather than craft knowledge—or as Ryle (1949) put it, "knowledge that" rather than "knowledge how." According to Orton (1993), trying to capture knowledge of how teaching is done is problematic. He calls this the "tacit problem" (p. 6) or the difficulty in making an argument that connects "the causes of a complex skill, which is a psychological and descriptive matter, and the reasons why a complex skill is judged to be effective, which is an intellectual or logical matter" (p. 7). It is argued that the tacit (Polanyi, 1958/1998), craft-based nature of teaching challenges the very notion of a knowledge base for teaching. Van Manen (1995) similarly describes teaching as a type of "active understanding of how we find ourselves here as teachers with certain intentions, feelings, passions, inclinations, attitudes and preoccupations" (p. 47). He claims that it may be impossible to define this knowing conceptually and that practice, rather than being applied knowledge or theory, may be the reality that gives meaning to our theorizing.

Many researchers have, however, attempted to describe those forms of teachers' knowledge that can be grouped broadly under the metaphor of knowledge as craft. According to Grimmett and Mackinnon (1992), craft knowledge emphasizes a knowing how to teach learned from experience, central to which is the purpose of understanding and motivating learners. For some, understanding the nature of craft knowledge or the wisdom of practice (Christensen, 1996; Kennedy, 2002) "can only be attained in social practice or by personal experimentation" (Duncan, 1998, p. 1). Such approaches to studying teachers' knowledge may incorporate studies of PCK, reflective practice, narrative inquiry, teacher biography and action research. The craft knowledge central to such research is not the craft born of an unthinking apprenticeship; it is the craft of the accomplished artisan or artist. The idea of craft is well captured in the work of Roth and Tobin (2000), who develop the idea of praxeology or the amalgam of practice and reflection and discussion on practice that are central to learning to teach.

The research genres incorporating the knowledge as craft metaphor have in common an elucidation of teacher wisdom that takes account of the tensions and dilemmas inherent in diverse teaching contexts and emphasizes "judgment . . . intuition, care and empathy for pupils" (Grimmett & Mackinnon, 1992, p. 428). In other words, the lived experience of teaching and teachers is the subject matter of those whose work can be seen as contributing to the understanding of the craft knowledge of teachers. The craft metaphor can also lead to an alternative conception of PCK that, although having subject matter knowledge as its precursor, is formed largely in practice (van Driel et al., 1998) as teachers interact in classrooms and remake their own understandings of the concepts they teach in order to facilitate the learning of their students. The notion of teachers' practical knowledge (Connelly & Clandinin, 1985; Elbaz, 1983; Munby & Russell, 1994) also sits within the purview of craft knowledge, since it is "anchored in classroom situations and include[s] the practical dilemmas teachers encounter in carrying out purposeful action" (Munby et al., 2001, p. 880).

The complex nature of teaching, its situatedness and embodiedness are themes from this work. Research into craft knowledge has the potential to have greater impact on improvement of teaching than traditional social science research because of these features (Fenstermacher, 1994). However, some have argued that such features make the findings of studies of craft knowledge difficult to apply in teacher education and professional development (PD). Orton (1993) sees the problem as one of how to decide whether generality or meaning should have the upper hand in understanding the research findings. Another challenge to the validity of craft knowledge or personal knowledge is that all teachers, both effective and ineffective, have personal knowledge (Snow, 2001). Some commentators call for ways of systemizing personal knowledge and testing its claims against other research findings (Hiebert et al., 2002; Snow, 2001).

The need to envisage knowledge as existing beyond the boundaries of the individual knower is emphasized by some whose work could still be considered a study of craft, because of the emphasis on the person of the knower. Examples are work by Barnett and Hodson (2001) encompassing the importance of peers in knowledge development, and work by Clandinin and Connelly (1996) in which individual knower and the setting in which knowledge is developed are seen as mutually influential. Barnett and Hodson (2001) describe a form of teacher knowledge as "pedagogical context knowledge." They define it as "what good teachers know, do and feel" as they participate in "the minutiae of everyday classroom life" (p. 436). This knowledge is derived from multiple sources, experience as a teacher, emotional responses to teaching and interacting in the classroom, content knowledge and school and government policies. Teaching networks and teacher interaction with peers are the primary sources of this knowledge, which is obviously personal and involves feeling as well as propositional knowing.

Clandinin and Connelly (1996) describe teachers' knowledge in terms of a "professional knowledge landscape" that accounts for the ways in which personal knowledge is shaped by professional context. In other words, teacher knowledge sits within a context consisting of the teacher's own knowledge, the situation or landscape of the teacher's work and the way in which the work situation is oriented toward public policy and educational theory (Clandinin & Connelly, 1996). The landscape provides an interface between personal craft knowledge, personal history, the school and findings of educational research and educational policy, where "sacred stories" from theory and policy connect or contrast with "secret stories" from classroom life and "cover stories" for public explanation (Clandinin & Connelly, 1996, p. 25). In this way personal knowledge can be aligned with school context, research findings and current policy.

The craft metaphor is most valuable because of its acknowledgment of teaching as more than just propositional knowledge applied in a teaching context. This metaphor takes account of the lifeworld of teachers by emphasizing the importance of practice and context on what is known. Teacher's actions and emotions are seen as part of what is known. However, the importance of individual and context in the craft view of teacher knowledge have led to a lack of clarity about what can be generalized to other situations and problems in making embodied, tacit knowledge more explicit. Other metaphors allow for better integration of the multiple facets of and influences on what teachers know.

Teacher Knowledge as Complexity

While the preceding metaphors of computer and craft (particularly craft) incorporate aspects of the complexity and contextual nature of teachers' knowledge, a common thread in these metaphors is the centrality of the teacher—as decision maker, user of the knowledge base or actor influencing and being influenced by a context (Feldman, 1997, 2002). Our third teachers' knowledge metaphor of complexity problematizes the role of the teacher and brings the ideas of complexity and context to a new level. We argue that this metaphor offers some contrasting and emerging ideas about teachers' knowledge, each possible and helpful in liberating us from previous ways of seeing.

Ideas about complexity and context are central to the notion of situated learning, which has also been applied to teachers' learning (Greeno, 2003; Lave & Wegner, 1991; Peressini, Borko, Romagnano, Knuth & Willis, 2004; Putnam & Borko, 2000). Under this notion, knowledge and its expression in ways of thinking and of discussing ideas are seen as products of a social environment in which interpersonal interactions are critical (Putman & Borko, 2000). The learning community both shapes and is shaped by the individuals who comprise it (Putman & Borko, 2000). The question then is not about knowledge transfer across contexts, as with a craft or knowledge base metaphor, but what constitutes successful participation in a context. Learning then becomes "the process of recontextualizing resources and discourses in new situations" (Peressini et al., 2004).

Thus teaching involves recontextualization rather than application, and contexts are pivotal. It would be important to know, for example, what other participants in the same setting thought and knew in order to understand the teaching of any individual in a setting. Such ideas contrast with those described earlier, in that context or situation is the focus of explanation or interest and not the knowledge held by individuals or its enactment in different situations.

A related complexity-based image is one of teaching as a "way of being" (Feldman, 2002, p. 1038). This notion, borrowed from existentialism, emphasizes that teaching is a way of "being in the world in which action, understanding, and situation continuously interact with one another to result in who we are and what we do in the world" (p. 1040). Teacher understanding and knowledge from this perspective are not "explicit or tacit knowledge operated on by rule systems" (p. 1040) that could be learned in one situation and applied to another, but knowledge derived in "immersion in the situations" that arise in the classroom and the meaning that teachers make from these situations. The power of this most holistic of teaching images is that it allows for the inclusion in our understanding of teaching of such diverse areas as teacher identity, teaching self (Acker, 1999), emotion in teaching (Zembylas, 2004) and the moral nature of teaching (Sockett, 1987). Feldman's description of teaching situations as having "web like structures that extend not only through time and space but also across human relations" (p. 1040) brings to mind Clandinin and Connelly's (2000) dimensions of the narrative landscape: context; temporality (past, present, future); self and others; and location.

Davis and Sumara (2000) critique current metaphors of knowledge, which they suggest, are based on classical geometry, for example, the base or foundation, the building or a construction and linear terms like *path* or *spiral* (akin to the computer and change metaphors of teacher knowledge). As an alternative, these authors propose fractal geometry and fractal images as an alternative visual metaphor allowing current theories of knowledge and knowing to become compatible, relational and "nested in one another" (p. 821). Fractal images are "scale independent" (p. 825) meaning that closer inspection of such an image does not result in the discovery of a simpler structure constituting a part of the whole, so that ideas like "foundations, structures and hierarchies are challenged by notions of infinite regress, nestedness, and implicate orders" (p. 825). Closer inspection of a fractal image results in the revelation of smaller images each similar to and just as complex as the image of the whole. The term "self-similarity" (p. 825) describes this phenomenon.

The strength of the metaphor of the fractal image is the acknowledgment of complexity, complexity that resists simplification and leads to a view of the universe as "ever-unfolding, self-transcendental and relational" (Davis & Sumara, 2000, p. 827). The concept of nestedness is evoked to explain the relationship between part and whole. The part is not a fragment of the whole but "a fractal out of which the whole unfolds and in which the whole is enfolded" (p. 828); "The part is a pattern within a web of relationships" (p. 835). This idea of the fractal as nested allows the study of parts to be of value and frees us from the necessity of seeking always to comprehend the whole, for example, teacher knowledge in all its complexity. It also allows us to understand discourses of knowledge and knowing as "nested recursions rather than intersections of . . . discrete regions" (p. 830). Thus teacher knowledge might be seen as the knowing of individual teachers, the personal embodied craft that is part of personal history, nested in the discourse of particular settings, nested in turn in the shared discourse of the teaching profession, nested in wider community and culture, ever-extending layers of connectedness and complexity. We are free to value and study each level of nestedness, acknowledging its complexity and relatedness to other levels without undue emphasis on boundaries and delineations.

Each of the metaphors in this set shares something with ecological metaphors in that the parts are continuously interacting. Stability is a state of dynamic equilibrium between parts rather than a static state. An important feature of the study and understanding of complex systems is "embededness and . . . intertwinings, not . . . boundaries" (Davis, Sumara & Luce-Kapler, 2000, p. 174). Thus in teaching, the learning community, the way of being, the narrative landscape, the fractal image and the nested recursions and what a teacher knows are seen as dynamic, changing and enmeshed in social settings. The individual cannot be isolated, but must be seen in interaction with the context. Wideen, Mayer-Smith and Moon (1998) criticized the literature on learning to teach for its narrow focus and argue for a more ecological approach to teacher preparation. Teacher knowledge metaphors that show knowledge as a complex system extending beyond the boundaries of the individual provide an additional rich focus to the study of teaching.

Teacher Knowledge as Change

While the images of computer, craft and complexity bring to mind different aspects of the nature of teachers' knowledge, in each of these metaphors the notion that knowledge changes over time is largely assumed rather than directly explained. For example, the computer database metaphor assumes that the various components of teacher knowledge will change through teacher exposure to largely theoretical inputs (Marks, 1990). The craft metaphor places more emphasis on changing knowledge in context, particularly through biography and practical experience (Louden, 1991; Wallace & Louden, 1992). The complexity metaphor focuses on the quintessentially social character of teacher learning and the interrelationships between agent, activity and world (Lave & Wegner, 1991). All three metaphors assume (hold out the hope) that knowledge develops (improves) from day to day and throughout a teacher's career. While acknowledging the implicit change dimension in the previous metaphors, we have chosen to separately and explicitly address this phenomenon in our final metaphor of teacher knowledge as change.

For the most part, studies of teacher knowledge using the computer metaphor have been conducted *in situ*, examining and describing teachers' knowledge on the spot, as a static phenomenon. Studies comparing the knowledge bases of expert and novice teachers (Borko, Bellamy & Sanders, 1992; Reynolds, 1992) and longitudinal studies of individuals as they develop as teachers (Arzi & White, 2004; Mulholland & Wallace, 2005; Richardson & Placier, 2001) fit within this metaphor. Teacher knowledge as change often incorporates related metaphors, such as growth or stages of a journey. In our own work, for example, we used the metaphor of a tree to depict the change and growth of an elementary science teacher's knowledge over a decade of teaching (Mulholland & Wallace, 2005). The tree metaphor showed the continuity of the teachers' knowledge, with the richness and diversity of branches representing the different types of knowledge and connected to original experiences via the trunk. Types of knowledge that did not develop or flourish at particular times or contexts were represented as shoots and branches that were smaller and stunted in comparison with others. The power of this metaphor is that it can be used with each of the knowledge metaphors. The tree at any one time could be considered as the existing knowledge base composed of matter accumulated by growth over time. The tree could also represent craft knowledge because it is a living organism, dependant on the environment that influences it and is influenced by it. The unique shape and structure of the tree tells the life history of it as an individual organism. Trees, however, can be considered as fractal images (see Davis et al., 2000, p. 16), complex, ever changing, each branch an image of the whole, a living part inseparable from the ecosystem in which it is embedded.

We have also used the metaphor of a journey to describe teacher knowledge changes (Mulholland & Wallace, 2000, 2003). This metaphor allowed us to describe the challenges teachers face in developing expertise or better understanding of their lifeworlds. For example, we described a first-year teacher's experience of teaching as border crossing (Aikenhead, 1996) from the subculture of the university into the subculture of the school and learning to teach science in an elementary classroom as border crossing from teaching other subjects, better suited to an elementary context, to teaching science (Mulholland & Wallace, 2003). The border-crossing metaphor helped capture the beginning teacher's sense of not knowing, of being a stranger (Reynolds, 1992) and the difficulties faced by generalist elementary teachers when trying to teach a specialist subject such as science. The problems encountered and the solutions tried in both situations are respectively hazards on the border between the cultures and the teachers' attempts at border crossing. The cultural border crossing inherent in personal learning in new situations gives insight into the development of craft; the values, beliefs and ways of being in the world change as well as propositional knowledge. When an individual teacher is viewed as nested within overlapping layers of social meaning, self, family, classroom, school, profession, society, world and universe, the boundaries between each are borders where knowledge is formed and reformed in an interactive way.

Constructivist theories of knowledge and learning use the metaphor of a building or construction erected by the learner to represent knowledge (Tippins, Tobin & Nichols, 1995). Such metaphors allow what is known to be seen as incomplete, under development and able to be reconstructed. Construction requires effort on the part of the learner. Teachers' knowledge can be understood as developing over time with practice and reflection and always under construction (Louden & Wallace, 1994). Teaching itself has been regarded as an act of learning (Osborne, 1998).

While the change metaphor also applies to the computer, craft and complexity knowledge clusters, the notion of change brings with it particular and unique images of teaching. The metaphors of change have much to offer in understanding initial teacher education and the in-service PD of teachers. In a world where rapid change has come to be expected, lifelong learning is seen as important in the life of all citizens, both to improve the economic situation of individual and society and as a means of personal satisfaction and fulfillment for the learner (Delors, 1996). In such a context, learning is doubly important to those involved in education, as they are responsible for encouraging others to learn and in continuing their own ongoing development. Each metaphor in the change cluster clarifies different aspects of learning. The growing tree allows appreciation of continuity and dependence on context, the cultural border crossing emphasizes the difficulty of real change involving the individual as risk taker, and construction, the importance of learner and learner involvement in acts of coming to know.

A MULTI-METAPHORICAL APPROACH
TO TEACHING AND LEARNING

In this chapter we propose that teacher knowledge be understood from a variety of metaphorical standpoints, as computer (whereby knowledge is an interactive database), as craft (whereby knowledge is developed through experience), as complexity (whereby knowledge is developed in complex interaction with the environment) and as change (whereby knowledge evolves over time). In doing so, we argue that teachers learn about teaching in a variety of ways. Some ways—as illustrated by the computer and change metaphors—are more in keeping with an individual-cognitive perspective on knowing whereby knowledge and beliefs are the primary factors that determine action. Others—as exemplified by the craft and complexity metaphors—are aligned with a more collective-situative view, which holds that "knowledge and beliefs, the practices that they influence, and the influences themselves, are inseparable from the situations in which they are embedded" (Borko & Putnam, 1996, in Peressini et al., 2004, p. 73). Concomitant approaches to teacher learning include (from the individual-cognitive end of the range) PD workshops, conceptual change strategies and the teacher standards movement, and (from the collective-situative end of the range) problem-based learning, case methods, video study, teacher self-study, action research and collaborative learning communities.

As Wallace and Loughran (in press) argue, the advantage of individual-cognitive approaches is that generalized solutions to curriculum problems can be identified and widely disseminated. Further, teachers can pick and choose offerings depending on their perceived needs and motivations. The disadvantage is that these activities are typically not grounded in the teacher's practice, and are often conducted in isolation from the communities they are intended to serve. Further they can tend to fragment rather than consolidate teacher knowledge. While collective approaches are more locally effective, they are often complex and unwieldy and suffer from a lack of transferability. However, as Peressini and his colleagues (2004) point out, the individual-collective dichotomy is misleading, and the relationship between context and individual reasoning is reflexive: for example, "students contribute to the development of practices within the classroom; these practices, in turn, constitute the immediate context for [teachers'] learning" (p. 71).

Like many other scholars, we favor a pragmatic model of teacher learning that incorporates multiple metaphors and theoretical positions. As Cobb and Bowers (1999) argue, the "choice between any particular case being a pragmatic one that depends on the purposes at hand" (p. 6). Such a position highlights the interrelatedness of elements within systems and the notion of "individual-in-social-action" used by Hoban (2002) to represent the interaction of the cognitive and the situated.

In arguing for a multi-metaphorical approach to teacher learning, we agree with the position that teacher learning:

> takes place in multiple learning contexts, combining out-of-school, theory and practice-based learning experiences with ongoing support for teachers to learn from their students and integrate ideas into their classroom practice . . . These models have individual and collective components. They foster classroom-based, teacher research within a context of theory-driven ideas, and collegial and other support. They also attempt to build a discourse community around . . . education, across the school but also in the wider school community. (Wallace & Loughran, in press)

Supporting teacher learning entails the creation of formal and informal opportunities for learning to proceed in multiple contexts (settings, communities and learning foci). Ball and Cohen (1999, p. 25) refer to a "pedagogy of professional development" comprising of the tasks and materials of practice, the discourse to support learning with these tasks and materials and the roles and capabilities of leaders who provide guidance and support for this work. In this chapter we have provided examples of how teachers build their various knowledges—including knowledge of 'what' (computer metaphor), knowledge of 'how' (craft metaphor), knowledge as 'recontextualization' (complexity metaphor) and knowledge as 'growth' (change metaphor). A multi-metaphorical model recognizes that learning takes place in various discourse communities, inside and outside schools. Optimizing teacher learning requires that the various components of the education enterprise—students, teachers, school leaders, research-based inputs, academic and systemic supports, etc.—be brought together to build local relevance and ownership while developing both individual and collective learning.

CONCLUSION

Teacher learning is, we maintain, a central tenet for educational reform. In this chapter we argue for a multi-metaphorical model of teacher learning that encompasses both the individual-cognitive and the collective-situative stances on learning. Here we agree with Sfard (1998) who takes the position that:

> the sooner we accept the thought that our work is bound to produce a patchwork of metaphors rather than a unified, homogeneous theory of learning, the better for us and those whose lives are likely to be affected by our work. (p. 12)

This position recognizes that teachers operate as individuals, making choices about levels of engagement, processing information and reflecting and acting on that information. Teacher learning is also a social enterprise, contextually embedded, and inextricably linked to the learning of others—to students' learning, colleagues' learning and organizational learning.

Like Wallace and Loughran (in press), we argue for an approach to teachers' learning that focuses on research with and by teachers, on building teachers' knowledge about teaching and for practice, and recognizes the inextricable connection between teachers' learning and students' learning. We also understand that teacher learning often takes place in contexts removed from the classroom, such as universities, school boards and professional conferences. In this chapter we have described examples from the four metaphors of computer, craft, complexity and change of how teachers build their knowledge in different ways. We are not saying that anything goes, but rather we advocate a well-planned, considered and supported program of professional learning that enables teachers to learn in different ways and over time, in different contexts with a variety of settings, communities and learning foci. Contexts should be spread across the different metaphors rather than confined to a particular approach, with the metaphorical balance depending on the needs of the individual teacher and her or his community.

Simply stated, teacher learning is about teachers building and sustaining knowledge of classroom practice across various discourse communities. Teacher learning is complex because it is about the complicated interplay among different approaches, between the individual and the collective, and the cognitive and the situative. In this chapter we have argued for a multi-metaphorical model of teacher learning that acknowledges this complexity and that marshals the various components of the education enterprise to respect and support teachers' attempts to build knowledge of their own practice.

NOTES

1. This chapter uses some material from Mulholland and Wallace (2008).

REFERENCES

Acker, S. (1999). *The realities of teachers' work: Never a dull moment.* London: Cassell.
Aikenhead, G. S. (1996). Science education: Border crossings into the subculture of science. *Studies in Science Education, 27,* 1–52.
Arzi, H. J., & White, R. T. (2004, April). *Seeking change in teachers' knowledge of science: A 17-year long study.* Paper presented at the annual meeting of the American Educational Research Association, San Diego, CA.
Ball, D. L., & Cohen, D. K. (1999). Developing practice, developing practitioners: Towards a practice-based theory of professional education. In L. Darling-Hammond & G. Sykes (Eds.), *Teaching as the learning profession: Handbook of policy and practice* (pp. 3–32). San Francisco: Jossey-Bass.
Barnett, J., & Hodson, D. (2001). Pedagogical context knowledge: Toward a fuller understanding of good science teachers. *Science Education, 85*(4), 426–453.
Borko, H., & Putnam, R. (1996). Learning to teach. In D. Berliner & R. Calfee (Eds.), *Handbook of educational psychology* (pp. 673–708). New York: MacMillan.
Borko, H., Bellamy, M. L. & Sanders, L. (1992). A cognitive analysis of patterns in science instruction by expert and novice teachers. In T. Russell & H. Munby (Eds.), *Teachers and teaching: From classroom to reflection* (pp. 49–70). London: Falmer Press.
Christensen, D. (1996). The professional knowledge-research base for teacher education. In J. Sikula, T. J. Buttery & E. Guyton (Eds.), *Handbook of research on teacher education* (2nd ed.) (pp. 38–52). New York: Simon and Schuster Macmillan.
Clandinin, D. J., & Connelly, F. M. (1996). Teachers' professional knowledge landscapes: Teacher stories—stories of teachers—school stories—stories of schools. *Educational Researcher, 25*(3), 24–30.

Clandinin, D. J., & Connelly, F. M. (2000). *Narrative inquiry.* San Francisco: Jossey-Bass.

Cobb, P., & Bowers, J. S. (1999). Cognitive and situated learning perspectives in theory and practice. *Educational Researcher, 28*(2), 4–15.

Connelly, F. M., & Clandinin, D. J. (1985). Personal practical knowledge and the modes of knowing: Relevance for teaching and learning. In E. Eisner (Ed.), *Learning and teaching the ways of knowing* (pp. 174–198). Chicago: University of Chicago Press.

Darling-Hammond, L., & Youngs, P. (2002). Defining "highly qualified teachers": What does "scientifically-based research" actually tell us? *Educational Researcher, 31*(9), 13–25.

Davis, B., & Sumara, D. J. (2000). Curriculum forms: On the assumed shapes of knowing and knowledge. *Journal of Curriculum Studies, 32*(6), 821–845.

Davis, B., Sumara, D. J. & Luce-Kapler, R. (2000). *Engaging minds: Learning and teaching in a complex world.* Mahwah, NJ: Lawrence Erlbaum Associates.

Delors, J. C. (1996). *Learning: The treasure within* (Report to UNESCO of the International Commission on Education for the Twenty-First Century). Paris: UNESCO.

Dewey, J. (1902). *The child and the curriculum.* Chicago: University of Chicago Press.

Donmoyer, R. (1995, April). *The very idea of a knowledge base.* Paper presented at the annual meeting of the American Educational Research Association, San Francisco, CA.

Duncan, B. J. (1998). *On teacher knowledge: A return to Shulman.* Retrieved August 19, 2004, from http://www.ed.uiuc.edu/EPS/PES-yearbook/1998/duncan.html

Elbaz, F. (1983). *Teacher thinking: A study of practical knowledge.* New York: Nichols.

Feldman, A. (1997). Varieties of wisdom in the practice of teachers. *Teaching and Teacher Education, 13*(7), 757–773.

Feldman, A. (2002). Multiple perspectives for the study of teaching: Knowledge, reason, understanding, and being. *Journal of Research in Science Teaching, 39*(10), 1032–1055.

Fenstermacher, G. D. (1994). The knower and the known: The nature of knowledge in research on teaching. *Review of Research in Education, 20,* 3–56.

Gardner, W. (1989). Preface. In M. Reynolds (Ed.), *Knowledge base for the beginning teacher* (pp. ix–xii). Oxford: Pergamon Press.

Gess-Newsome, J. (1999). Pedagogical content knowledge: An introduction and orientation. In J. Gess-Newsome & N. G. Lederman (Eds.), *Examining pedagogical content knowledge: The construct and its implications for science education* (pp. 3–17). Dordrecht: Kluwer.

Gess-Newsome, J., & Lederman, N. G. (Eds.). (1999). *Examining pedagogical content knowledge: The construct and its implications for science education.* Dordrecht: Kluwer.

Greeno, J. G. (2003). Situated research relevant to standards for school mathematics. In J. Kilpatrick, W. G. Martin & D. Schifter (Eds.), *A research companion to principles and standards for school mathematics* (pp. 304–332). Reston, VA: National Council of Teachers of Mathematics.

Grimmett, P. P., & Mackinnon, A. M. (1992). Craft knowledge and the education of teachers. In G. Grant (Ed.), *Review of research in education* (pp. 385–456). Washington, DC: American Educational Research Association.

Hiebert, J., Gallimore, R. & Stigler, J. W. (2002). A knowledge base for the teaching profession: What would it look like and how can we get one? *Educational Researcher, 31*(5), 3–16.

Hoban, G. F. (2002). *Teacher learning for educational change: A systems thinking approach.* Buckingham: Open University Press.

Kennedy, M. M. (2002). Knowledge and teaching. *Teachers and Teaching: Theory and Practice, 8*(3/4), 355–370.

Lave, J., & Wegner, E. (1991). *Situated learning: Legitimate peripheral participation.* Cambridge: Cambridge University Press.

Louden, W. (1991). *Understanding teaching: Continuity and change in teachers' work.* London: Cassell.

Louden, W., & Wallace, J. (1994). Knowing and teaching science: The constructivist paradox. *International Journal of Science Education, 16*(6), 649–657.

Loughran, J., Milroy, P., Berry, A., Gunstone, R. & Mulhall, P. (2001). Documenting science teachers' pedagogical content knowledge through PaP-eRs. *Research in Science Education, 31*(2), 289–307.

Marks, R. (1990). Pedagogical content knowledge: From a mathematical case to a modified conception. *Journal of Teacher Education, 41,* 3–11.

Mulholland, J., & Wallace, J. (2000). Beginning elementary science teaching: Entryways to different worlds. *Research in Science Education, 30*(2), 151–171.

Mulholland, J., & Wallace, J. (2003). Crossing borders: Learning and teaching primary science in the pre-service to in-service transition. *International Journal of Science Education, 25*(7), 879–898.

Mulholland, J., & Wallace, J. (2005). Growing the tree of teacher knowledge: Ten years of learning to teach elementary science. *Journal of Research in Science Teaching, 42*(7), 1–16.

Mulholland, J., & Wallace, J. (2008). Computer, craft, complexity and change: Explorations into science teacher knowledge. *Studies in Science Education, 44*(1), 41–62.

Munby, H., & Russell, T. (1994). The authority of experience in learning to teach: Messages from a physics methods class. *Journal of Teacher Education, 45,* 86–95.

Munby, H., Russell, T. & Martin, A. K. (2001). Teachers' knowledge and how it develops. In V. Richardson (Ed.), *Handbook of research on teaching* (4th ed.) (pp. 877–904). Washington, DC: American Educational Research Association.

Orton, R. E. (1993). *Two problems with teacher knowledge.* Retrieved August 19, 2004, from http://www.ed.uiuc.edu/EPS/PES-yearbook/93_dics/ORTON.HTM

Osborne, M. D. (1998). Teacher as knower and learner: Reflections on situated knowledge in science teaching. *Journal of Research in Science Teaching, 35*(4), 427–439.

Peressini, D., Borko, H., Romagnano, L., Knuth, E. & Willis, C. (2004). A conceptual framework for learning to teach secondary mathematics: A situative perspective. *Educational Studies in Mathematics, 56*(1), 67–96.

Polanyi, M. (1958/1998). *Personal knowledge: Towards a post critical philosophy.* London: Routledge.

Putnam, R., & Borko, H. (2000). What do new views of knowledge and thinking have to say about research on teacher learning? *Educational Researcher, 29*(1), 4–15.

Reynolds, A. (1992). What is competent beginning teaching? A review of the literature. *Review of Educational Research, 62*(1), 1–35.

Richardson, V., & Placier, P. (2001). Teacher change. In V. Richardson (Ed.), *Handbook of research on teaching* (pp. 905–947). Washington, DC: American Educational Research Association.

Roth, M., & Tobin, K. (2000, January). *Learning to teach science as praxis.* Paper presented at the annual meeting of the Association for the Education of Teachers of Science, Akron, OH.

Ryle, G. (1949). *The concept of mind.* New York: Barnes and Noble.

Sfard, A. (1998). On two metaphors for learning and the dangers of choosing just one. *Educational Researcher, 27*(2), 4–13.

Shulman, L. S. (1986). Those who understand: Knowledge growth in teaching. *Educational Researcher, 15*(2), 4–14.

Shulman, L. S. (1987). Knowledge and teaching: Foundations of the new reform. *Harvard Educational Review, 57*(1), 1–22.

Snow, C. E. (2001). Knowing what we know: Children, teachers, researchers. *Educational Researcher, 30*(7), 3–9.

Sockett, H. T. (1987). Has Shulman got the strategy right? *Harvard Educational Review, 57*(2), 209–219.

Tippins, D., Tobin, K. & Nichols, S. (1995). A constructivist approach to change in elementary science teaching and learning. *Research in Science Education, 25*(2), 135–149.

Turner-Bisset, R. (1999). The knowledge bases of the expert teacher. *British Educational Research Journal, 25*(1), 39–55.

Turner-Bisset, R. (2001). *Expert teaching: Knowledge and teaching to lead the profession*. London: David Fulton Publishers.

van Driel, J. H., Verloop, N. & de Vos, W. (1998). Developing science teachers' pedagogical content knowledge. *Journal of Research in Science Teaching, 35*(6), 673–695.

van Manen, M. (1995). On the epistemology of reflective practice. *Teachers and Teaching: Theory and Practice, 1*(1), 33–50.

Wallace, J., & Louden, W. (1992). Science teaching and teachers' knowledge: Prospects for reform of elementary classrooms. *Science Education, 76*(5), 507–521.

Wallace, J., & Loughran, J. (in press). Science teacher learning. In B. Fraser, K. Tobin & C. McRobbie (Eds.), *International handbook of research in science education* (2nd ed.). Dordrecht: Springer.

Wideen, M., Mayer-Smith, J. & B., Moon. (1998). A critical analysis of the research on learning to teach: Making a case for an ecological perspective on enquiry. *Review of Educational Research, 68*(2), 130–178.

Wilson, S. M., Shulman, L. S. & Richert, A. E. (1987). "150 different ways" of knowing: Representation of knowledge in teaching. In J. Calderhead (Ed.), *Exploring teachers' thinking* (pp. 104–124). London: Cassell.

Zembylas, M. (2004). Emotion metaphors and emotional labor in science teaching. *Science Education, 88*(3), 301–324.

5 The Transformative Potential of Teacher and Student Voices
Reframing Relationships for Learning

Mary Kooy and Dana Colarusso

INTRODUCTION

Research and interest in teacher learning have increased exponentially in the last 20 years. Educational reforms characterized by higher student expectations, achievement and performance have drawn attention to the key role of teachers in actualizing the new curriculum, policies and practices for their classrooms. In tandem with growing awareness of the incommensurability between policy mandates and teacher change, a body of research has accrued on teacher development with particular emphasis on social learning contexts.

Traditionally, teacher learning has been variously defined and distributed in a complex network of formal and informal opportunities, and woven into fragmented, disparate patches of "curriculum" (Ball & Cohen, 1999). Formal learning consisting primarily of top-down forms of professional development (PD) continues to dominate (Borko, 2004; Clark, 2001; Kooy, 2006a).

Even while teacher learning is researched, discussed, socialized and theorized, traditional approaches remain the mainstay (e.g., the "one-shot" workshop). This suggests that both the practical experience of teachers and their understandings of student perspectives and learning processes are disregarded.

The critical role of teachers in realizing educational change, however, suggests that their perspectives are vital to the planning and implementation of both professional learning and learning improvement plans for students. This requires reimagining and repositioning teachers as agents of change, empowered by ongoing opportunities to actively shape their learning in line with their knowledge from practice (Cook-Sather, 2007). For their new knowledge to translate into effective teaching practice, moreover, teacher voices need to be included in the ongoing pursuit of improved student learning and achievement (Guskey, 2008).

A considerable body of research supports professional learning shaped in social contexts (Dufour & Eaker, 1998; Kooy, 2009; McLaughlin, 1995). In dialogue with others (Bakhtin, 1986), teachers develop their knowledge and understanding. In this respect, research on teacher learning mirrors research describing all learning as negotiated, social in nature and therefore developed through dialogic interaction. This critical relationship between teacher learning and student learning goes underresearched, yet is central to the capacity for teacher knowledge to translate into classroom practice. Teachers with access to professional learning experiences that allow them to communicate their tacit knowledge of teaching and student learning are empowered through dialogue in a social context (Kooy, 2009; Polanyi, 1966; Tharpe & Gallimore, 1988). Learning is effective as it invokes "changes in practice itself—in other words, what happens when teachers enact their new knowledge or skill in their daily work with students or each other" (Knapp, 2003, p. 114).

Even with rigorous and ongoing teacher learning, a gap remains. Those most affected by teaching—the students—have historically been left out of the dialogue on learning. Levin (2000) observed:

> The history of education reform is a history of doing things to other people supposedly for their own good . . . Even though all the participants in education will say that schools exist *for* students, students are still treated almost entirely as objects of reform. (p. 155)

Curriculum guidelines ask teachers to 'assess data' (student work) and to 'monitor' and 'observe' student achievement. *Listening* and *responding* to student self-representations of their learning experiences remains a rarity in school practice. Yet, teachers are not only best situated to listen and respond, but also to act on and create the dialogic learning experiences that unlock the potential of student voice to influence reform at multiple levels. Greater inclusion of student perspectives in classroom as in professional dialogue informs and improves ('professionalizes') teacher pedagogy, helps students become better learners, and ultimately, shifts the emphasis from object to subject for both teacher and students. The value-added benefit of including student voice and perspective in school learning depends for translation and transformation on classroom teachers who, ultimately, "not only translate what they gather, but are translated by it" (Cook-Sather, 2007, p. 829).

We suggest that research on teacher learning (e.g., Kooy, 2006a; Little, this volume; Lodge, 2008; Wineburg & Grossman, 1998) intersects with research on student voice (e.g., Cook-Sather, 2009; Mitra, 2008; Rudduck & McIntyre, 2007) and develops an interdependency that reflexively builds and transforms. In that way, core competencies of collaboration, critical thinking and problem solving develop for both teachers and their students.

CONTEXT AND BACKGROUND

Teacher Learning that Matters

Growing indications that teachers are critical players in educational change who need direct involvement in their learning (Kooy, 2006a, 2009; Shechtman, Roschelle, Haertel & Knudsen, 2010), and that highly skilled teachers contribute to improvement and higher achievement in student learning, led to the push to raise teacher competence and skill. While evidence for government-funded programs and new opportunities for PD emerged, most teacher learning continues to be directed and prescribed by those in authority.

Teacher learning has historically been a patchwork of opportunities ranging from informal conversations with colleagues to the district-mandated "one-shot" workshop. The short-term content knowledge gained is both short-lived and fails to materialize in classroom instruction (Clark, 2001; Kooy, 2006a; Shechtman et al., 2010). Wilson and Berne (1999) found that "the collective and negative reports of generations of teachers about traditional in-service programs" exposes a gap around:

> what exactly it is that teachers learn and by what mechanisms that learning takes place. What knowledge do teachers acquire across these experiences? How does that knowledge improve their practice? These questions are left unanswered. (p. 174)

Nieto observed more than a decade ago that "trying to solve the problems of public schools through more vituperative, technical decrees is absurd" and "(re)forming school structures alone will not lead to differences in student achievement . . . if such changes are not accompanied by profound changes in how we as educators think about our students" (1994, pp. 395–396). Franke, Carpenter, Levi and Fennema (1998) found that: "Engaging teachers in current reforms requires more than showing them how to implement effective practices" (p. 1). Despite the lack of empirical evidence about what and how much teachers learn in traditional PD, the more sinister implication reflects that teacher knowledge and professional learning is undervalued, even ignored, and leaves teachers underprepared for creating change or improving learning in their classrooms (Franke et al., 1998; Shechtman et al., 2010; Wilson & Berne, 1999). Consequently, the quick-fix workshop reinforces conceptions of knowledge transmission as uncomplicated and linear and leaves teachers ill equipped to move forward, to make meaningful change. This becomes even more complicated when added to excluding teachers in dialogue on reforms, policies, programs and curriculum.

More recent conceptions and research on teacher learning is most clearly represented in professional learning communities: teachers learning with colleagues in social contexts (Little, this volume; Lodge, 2008; Werder & Otis, 2010; Willms, Friesen & Milton, 2009). Bringing together aspects of learning that include the social, teacher knowledge, collaboration and co-construction of new knowledge (Kooy, 2006a) is altering the PD landscape. Ongoing professional learning in supportive, social contexts accepts teachers as critical stakeholders in education (Bauch & Goldring, 1998; Franke et al., 1998). It follows, as research suggests, that teachers need to be empowered themselves to empower others (Bauch & Goldring, 1998; Muncey & McQuillan, 1991).

The popularization of professional learning communities has resulted in widespread adoption in Ontario, Canada and elsewhere (Ontario Ministry of Education [OME], 2007). The concept, however, widely and idiosyncratically interpreted, takes on different configurations when observed in local settings and since programmatic research has not accompanied the swell of professional learning communities, too little information guides policy and practice.

Some research is beginning to disrupt the discourse (e.g., see Little, this volume) and identify marks of effective professional learning. Shared key words and concepts include such qualities as: community, collaboration and teachers as active learners; choice; ongoing and developmental; arising from teacher issues, knowledge and questions; dialogue on students, learning and teaching (see especially Kooy, 2006a, 2006b; See also Attema-Noordewier et al., Little and van Veen et al., this volume).

Student Voice and Perspective for Teaching and Learning

Most schools are not structured to encourage student voice; instead, the structures often conflict with adolescent needs. Established hierarchies and power relations counter any force to negotiate and alter existing patterns. Fielding (2004) observed that:

> Students, under pressure to soak up more and more information in increasingly shorter periods of time, put huge pressure on teachers to 'deliver' thicker and thicker sets of notes and often feel let down if some folders are thinner than others and irritated if pedagogy strays from the dull and dutiful. (p. 308)

In such contexts, both teachers and students risk becoming merely functionaries for received knowledge. But this presents a complex conundrum. Even when teachers prepare to resist the narrowed perceptions of learning as transmission and initiate including student voice and establish social groupings for dialogue and learning, many students are not immediately prepared to abandon the familiar. Over 30 years ago, Rudduck's (1977) research found students exerted a powerful push back to established routines and practices in classrooms. She found change untenable unless teachers proceed from powerful knowledge, understanding and commitment. This indicates that students, like their teachers, need awareness and understanding of the purpose and means for change. Rudduck and Flutter (2003) observed:

> [Students'] images of self as learner were largely shaped by the messages that the school transmitted, often unwittingly. And at the same time, teachers had constructed pictures of pupils and their reputations and it was often the fixed nature of these images that made it difficult for pupils to think that change was possible. (p. 54)

This challenges the dominant pedagogy of the school and the existing curriculum models; that is, against curriculum as delivery and for curriculum as a shared making of meaning.

Pressures from educational ministries to improve and achieve (mostly defined as test scores) feeds the compulsion to sweep controversies under the rug and breeds unwillingness to tolerate and support the difference of opinion including student voice requires (Mitra, 2008).

A growing number of studies disrupt these commonplaces of education (Schwab, 1973) to reveal that more dialogic, participatory and democratic practices go further to support successful learning in school (Kooy, 2009). In Dartmouth, Nova Scotia, for example, a middle school includes students "as equal partners in school decision-making processes. Students and teachers are building their own professional learning community to co-design learning environments that make students more interested learners" (Dunleavy and Cooke, 2010, p. 2).

The Canadian research landscape, particularly through the national CEA, has taken the issue of student voice seriously. Their task is complex given that in Canada (geographically, the second largest country in the world) each province (10) and territory (3) regulates and funds its own K–12 education system. Nevertheless, the CEA makes a significant contribution by considering and accounting for the larger, national view and making its research nationally accessible and available. Research such as *What Did You Do in School Today? Exploring the Concept of Student Engagement and Its Implications for Teaching and Learning in Canada* (Dunleavy and Milton, 2009, pp. 18–19) describes research conducted across Canada (e.g., through surveys such as "Tell them from me" and "What did you do in school today?") as well reporting on work done in specific educational jurisdictions such as Alberta and British Columbia.

The OME has begun to attend to student voice and learning in schools. Student perspectives, however, are gathered outside classrooms (in panels, through surveys, for instance). In a document entitled *Student Voice*, for instance, the Ministry website calls on students to apply for "Speak Up" projects for their schools, offering assurances they will "get more engaged in their learning and their school community" and "have a voice." The call continues:

> we want to hear what you have to say about your education. We want to help you make your school a place where everyone feels welcome and where you are empowered to speak your mind, get involved, and become active citizens and leaders. (OME, 2010, p. 1)

Rudduck and McIntyre's (2007) warning not to deflect attention on student voices away from classrooms into the more general, contextual schooling issues reverberates here. Moreover, what is done with the data that is collected remains ambiguous and too general to inform and provoke teacher action in classrooms.

The apparent lack of transparency, transition and follow-through has not gone unnoticed by those most directly affected. The CEA reports that:

> Increasingly, young people are demanding to know what the surveys they participate in will be used for. In the summer of 2010, for example, five Social Planning Councils in Ontario conducted youth focus groups to "test-drive" a draft survey designed to measure students' confidence in learning and in their futures. When asked to identify effective ways of involving them as partners in school and community planning and change, the young people—many of whom are marginalized—said they were tired of being asked about things that don't matter to them, and given empty promises of change. (Dunleavy and Cooke, 2010, p. 1)

Similarly, students who participated in follow-up focus groups after being surveyed in the "What did you do in school today?" initiative remind us that they are often frustrated by being the objects of research without knowing its purpose or effect: "I would like to see some results from this survey. I don't want you to just have this survey sitting in the basement ten years from now. I want to learn from it and not make me waste my time" (The Learning Bar, 2010, p. 1). Students want to know the nature of the gathered data, see the results and evidence of impact. In other words, students want to see a transition from collecting data on student voice to active student involvement in their own learning.

In 2009, the CEA reported a challenge to the transitions required:

> We invite students to share their opinions, but how often do we invite them to become an integral part of classroom practice and co-design their everyday experiences of learning? And yet we know that students are both willing to and highly capable of shaping decisions about the content, process, and outcomes of their learning. (Dunleavy and Cooke, 2010, p. 1)

Educational researchers have begun examining how an increase in student voice in schools offers students the opportunity to participate in decisions that shape their lives and the lives of their peers (Fielding, 2001; Levin, 2000). Stronger forms of student voice initiatives can be considered "youth–adult partnerships" (Camino, 2000), relationships in which both teachers and students contribute to decision-making processes, learn from one another and promote change (Jones & Perkins, 2004; Jones, 2004; Mitra, 2008). The literature on student voice contributes significantly as prefigurative practice for more challenging and transformative educational experiences in schools (Rudduck & Flutter, 2003; Fielding, 2004; Cook-Sather, 2009). Fielding (2004) argues that given the rich and abundant research literature on student voice, it is "surprising that only a very small proportion of the literature has taken us back to theoretical foundations that underpin both the advocacy and the emerging realities of student voice in school and community renewal" (p. 295).

To continue the conversation, I use a longitudinal research study (Kooy, 2006–2010) that included students in school-based learning communities as a vehicle for thinking about the link between teacher and student voices, the indications and implications of transitions and transformations and dialogical and relational learning.

THE LONGITUDINAL STUDY

Context and Background of the Study

Since 2006, I have maintained a research project that included secondary teachers (since 2000) and students with the aim of foregrounding students' words and interpretive frames and their value for teacher learning. I speak from inside the reflective practice of eliciting student perspectives and learning.

In 2000, I initiated a 4-year research project on PD with a group of nine teachers who began teaching the same month. Although novices, we negotiated establishing a social context for reading and developing professional relationships. The teachers enthusiastically elected to continue the collaborative learning experience of the book club modeled in my preservice English Methods course in a teacher education program the year before. The teachers mutually selected books (annually) and discussed them in seven annual book club meetings. Narratives from the texts were always surrounded by stories of teaching and learning. The teachers attested to the book club's power for developing relationships, professional knowledge, dialogical learning and the support needed to stay in the profession (all nine remain secondary teachers). This research was documented in a book entitled *Telling Stories in Book Clubs: Women Teachers and Professional Development* (Kooy, 2006a).

The Study Enters Phase Two

The selected section of the longitudinal study offers a location to examine student negotiations of knowledge in site-based, out-of-class, social contexts. From 2006 to 2010, continuing research funding allowed us to develop the research program further. Six of the original teachers agreed to continue (three moved out of the area). The teachers agreed to carry forward their professional learning into each of their schools.

As this critical point in the research, we proceeded inductively observing how the teachers interpreted and acted on their knowledge to establish learning communities in their schools. They created a format and put out a call for participant members. While this meant ceding control, it allowed for teacher learning to emerge and evolve without boundaries or explicit expectations. Simultaneously, we listened to and observed how teacher knowledge transitioned into their schools and thus, as researchers, positioned ourselves as learners.

All six teachers organized book clubs outside regular classes. This unexpected development disrupted my assumptions that teacher knowledge would move linearly into classrooms and their teacher practice. I learned that the complex process of transforming or, in Cook-Sather's term, *translating* (2009, pp. 222–227) professional knowledge is anything but linear. The teachers translated their experiences with learning communities, making choices within the context and lived realities of their schools, adjusting and adapting the construct they created.

A 4-Year Book Club Study

This report focuses on one of the three school-based groups (4 years in progress) involving students. Evelyn, the research teacher and a novice teacher colleague (Becky), created a mother–daughter group with 14 black girls (just entering Grade 9) and three of their mothers. The membership of this group, unlike the others, remained intact throughout their secondary schooling and is, therefore, ideally located to explore the development of student voice. The group developed a process for text selection (collaborative, annually); format; meeting time (6 p.m.) and frequency; and discussion (informal, dialogic).

Research funding provided the books for each participant; the school provided food. For each meeting, two research team members observed, videotaped and, occasionally, participated in the discussions. Semi-structured group interviews were conducted biannually (at the beginning and end of each of the 4 academic years, 2006–2010). Data included annual surveys and videotapes of all book club meetings, interviews, planning sessions and field notes.

Uncovering the Dialogues on Learning and Teaching

At their urban high school, the group of 14 black students, three of their mothers and two teachers read books together for 4 years (Grades 9 to 12, 2006–2010). They met every 6 weeks at 6 p.m., allowing some mothers to join after work. Students took a bus home after school and returned—some with younger siblings in tow—to gather for a hot meal and discussion.

The Catholic secondary school these girls attended had undergone significant change in its demographics over the 15 years before the research. The suburb emerged in the 1950s with a largely English and Scottish population. In the 1990s, a wide mixture of affordable housing emerged, attracting a large influx of low-income immigrant workers (a 2006 Census noted immigrants constituted 53% of the population). As high-rise apartment blocks began filling the surrounding low socioeconomic landscape, the white population began their exit. By 2002, the school's population was primarily black and poor, with many single-parent family units.

Evelyn, the research teacher, spent her high school years at the school (when it was primarily white students) and returned to teach after completing her BEd in 2000. The demographic shift in the school, she observed, had a pronounced effect on the programs, curriculum and student expectations. Few students who joined the group when they entered Grade 9 (2006) were expected to successfully complete secondary school, let alone remain in the book club. Over the 4 years, the unexpected shifts in student performance, in commitment to the book club and each other, surprised the teachers and administration. At the first meeting, two girls snickered at the other girls as they discussed why they joined the book club; they confessed they had never read an entire book. And yet they stayed; and they began reading and became readers and leaders in the group. From the first year, the girls (eight of whom had never personally owned a book) would make daily trips to Evelyn's class with an oft-repeated question: "Is the book here yet, Miss?"

At the onset of this research in 2006, the school was in disrepair, dark and outdated. The group met in the library with 20 people seated around a long table, reading, talking and learning. By the end of the second year, however, a new larger school building opened and our meeting space moved to a brightly lit and spacious staff room. At each meeting, members filled their plates in the kitchen and seated themselves on sofas and comfortable chairs around a large coffee table.

The girls, three of their mothers, the teacher researchers and the two teachers who attended consistently and most often completed the readings, ready to discuss. When, routinely, someone would appear at the door and ask to join, the girls would assemble and again decide "no new members."

In the 4 years, the students matured, developed, became avid readers, engaged in increasingly complex dialogues, questioned, challenged, disagreed and debated. Their dialogue, discourse, text selection, relationships, interdependency and learning in a social context developed intricately and substantially. Evelyn and Becky, as facilitators, spoke noticeably less and listened more, increasingly deferring to the students engaging in dialogue. Students delved into burning issues on their own terms. Mothers, on the other hand, began to contribute more, suggesting titles, relating personal stories. Together, the members shifted from a diverse group to a committed community.

The students' self-led discussions usually extended significantly beyond the planned hour and ranged across multiple points of interest in the novels, often leading to deep debate: on how much sympathy the main character deserves (Winter, the errant daughter of a drug dealer in *Coldest Winter Ever*), on the trustworthiness of strangers (*Lovely Bones*); on whether and when it's right to engage in a physical fight (*The Color Purple*), on what can be done about the signs of suicide (*13 Reasons*), on the moral fortitude of the main character (*PUSH*).

Sometimes a book club meeting produced a bursting forth, a cacophony of disparate opinions with particular voices vying for dominance at various points. At other times, the book (although mutually selected) failed to capture most readers. At one point (fall 2009) when most students admitted disliking the selected book, they used the opportunity to engage in a dialogue about reading itself. Their critical perceptions, developed through 4 years of experiences, prepared them to conduct a comparative assessment on books they read for school: *Flowers for Algernon*, *A Clockwork Orange* and Shakespearean plays. They questioned why some fictional works appealed (or not) in the classroom. Their questioning focused on their recent school English reading: Was *Flowers for Algernon* boring, or was it the way it was taught? How can *A Clockwork Orange* be made more accessible when even the movie is hard to understand? And why, Latrice wondered aloud, is Shakespeare so predominant in the curriculum?

When a fellow student lamented the boring responsibility of reading Shakespeare in the early modern verse, Latrice pushed to the heart of her question: "But that's not exactly what I mean—it's not just that I'm bored . . . why is Shakespeare such a *must*?" Perceiving the conversation turned on critiquing the value of learning Shakespeare, she insisted, "No, no, no, I'm not saying I don't like Shakespeare—Shakespeare is good, but why do teachers push it so much? Three, four, five books on Shakespeare— some people want variety." Clearly, Latrice was not contesting the merit of Shakespeare but rather, invoking the *rationale* for Shakespeare's centrality in her schooling. Much like the students in the CEA "Student Voice" project (Dunleavy & Milton, 2009), she voiced the learner's need to understand not only the 'what' but the 'wherefore' of engagement. This calls attention to the learner's position as blind subject of inherited choices. Latrice's words test the freedom and authenticity of this dialogic space against the classroom experience, to penetrate the wizard's fortress: Why this book and not others? Why your choice and not mine? We translate: "Why leave me out of the conversation when it so directly impacts my life and learning?"

The budding critics also considered teaching approaches as critical for students' motivation or lack of it to engage in reading. Shantel reflected: "I think if a book is boring, what could make it more interesting? Not everything has to relate to our lives—but give us a visual . . . activities we can understand." She added a specific example: "Mrs. J made us take a play and rearrange it—we got bonus points for the best lines, did games with the book." Jacquie noted the drop in engagement when motivation is weak: "Miss B said she opened our bank accounts to put ten cents in each time we read (aloud), but I still said no."

Kadisha related the outcome of an independent study unit the previous year as she continues to weave the themes of choice and engagement. Students could choose two of three books: *Catcher in the Rye*, *To Kill a Mockingbird* and *The Scarlet Letter*. Kadisha did not find this level of choice helpful. *The Scarlett Letter* mystified her:

I tried my hardest. I went through the first page, and it was dense—like three-pages-in-one condensed. And it was so boring. I didn't understand what was going on—nothing. And lots of people felt that way . . . We all talked about it, came to school: "Oh did you read this part?"— "Yeah, yeah, yeah."

Kadisha's anecdote suggests the teacher's ongoing responsibility to review curriculum in light of student input and feedback; she creates dialogic possibilities for effective learning. Without this, even choice, creative teacher efforts and the student's best intentions can end in frustration.

Uncovering Teacher Dialogue on Learning and Teaching

The development and power of student voice in the book club was a revelation for the teachers. A final interview with book club founder Evelyn and novice teacher Becky revealed their changing perceptions of the interactive relationship between teacher and student learning. Evelyn reflected on her rationale for the mother–daughter book club, which she introduced with an invitation to all Grade 9 girls and their mothers:

I knew I wanted it to have students participate—as opposed to being a teacher book club. . . . Literacy is an issue—especially in our community—and I don't know how much students are exposed to these "grown-up experiences" and mature ways of dealing with books. . . . I thought . . . if we started them young, then it would be something they could carry through their entire lives—skills (they could) enjoy in their personal lives. And, I wanted to invite parents—my own research indicated that parent involvement was one of the problems in inner-city schools. What was I hoping? I don't know. To be quite honest, I did not know it would last 4 years. I was hoping it would last the 1 year. If they came from September to June, then I would have considered that a success.

Evelyn's vision for the book club clearly derives from an intimate knowledge of her school community; her role as teacher researcher thus provides a model of the value of teacher voice in professional learning.

Becky's overall impression confirms the success of Evelyn's vision:

I was really amazed—I couldn't believe how critical the girls got with the book, without being led by any teacher. It was great to hear the moms—the first meeting was at the (school site) and . . . moms at that meeting . . . were very eager to give their views of the books and how they differed from their daughters—I liked the relaxed feel of it, how we had a meal together.

Becky further reflects on the importance, in this social learning experience, of resisting the temptation to direct student talk in the routine manner of a homework check:

> I think it was worth it for us not to be like, "Okay, now Julie what do you think?" because that's how they would feel in the classroom. . . . Now if she didn't read the book, she's automatically feeling put down—she didn't do the job that she was supposed to do—and already it's a negative feel when it's supposed to be a positive and safe space. So, I think calling people out would make it not safe and not enjoyable.

Becky raises the changes she observed when Evelyn left for a maternity leave and another colleague replaced her. Members seemed uncomfortable, uncertain with the change:

> She was doing her best, but she didn't know the culture of the book club. Because you're coming from a teacher in the classroom and you think this is like a classroom but it's not a classroom anymore—we're in a totally different setting [in this book club].

Evelyn and Becky had to confront their ingrained reservations against certain kinds of literature. This was a focal point in the decision of the girls and their mothers to read *The Coldest Winter Ever*, a novel set in a black ghetto featuring graphic sexuality and violence. Evelyn reflects: "I still don't know if I agree if that was a good book to read—but maybe the learning was that it wasn't my decision to make in that context." Asked whether the results of the meeting affirmed the decision to include the book, Evelyn replies:

> Absolutely. The discussion was around the fruitless end of this girl's doings—the thing they loved about it (the same thing they loved about *PUSH*) ... was how real these stories were—the fact that they know people who live like this. "This is real, we see it—Why are you trying to hide this from us when we live it or at least know people who live it?" It was their way of saying, "Do you not know where we come from—the communities we live in? This is nothing new to us. But we like it because it is finally reflecting our reality." And I think they love this real talk.

The teachers recognized that "the books that engaged the girls reflected black, urban experience. These were extreme stories, heavy, hard stories, but they loved the language of it, the voice in these novels; that made it very real for them" (Evelyn). By the same token, over time, their literary tastes broadened, as Becky recalled: "I think the girls are (now) happiest when it is more of a mix . . . Last year we did three books about gangs. By the third book, the girls were sick of it—"This is too much—we need something different"—they came to a point of being able to voice their need for something different."

It is notable how often Evelyn and Becky's reflections include imagined paraphrases of the girls' voices, as if they absorbed the habit of translating and internalizing the voiced and tacit meanings of the girls' participation. Observing changes in the girls changed the teachers' perspectives. For example, reflecting on blind spots of the research with respect to transfer to classrooms, Evelyn relates:

> I wasn't seeing how they were doing in their English classes, and I wasn't their English teacher, so I couldn't see the direct link between book club and their improved writing. I was surprised, to be honest, when at the end of year 1 we did that recap and some of them were saying they felt that they were stronger readers.

Becky relates another proof of success—the development of a new culture of book talk as the excitement for reading of book club participants spilled over to other students:

> How quickly they finish the books when they love the books is amazing to me ("When are we getting the next book? I finished the book in 2 days") because they're not that quick in doing their homework. . . . there are 10 or 12 committed (student) members but so many more students have gotten those books, are talking about those books, want to join our club. So through their participation they spread literacy in our school by showing and lending the books that they got from Mary to their friends—(who) read the books we discussed (and) once they finished spoke so highly of them.

Asked whether such a development—of students reading voluntarily—was unusual, she replied, "Yes, at our school, I would say, yeah." Evelyn added, "[The book club] gets them talking amongst each other, spans grades, creates a culture in the school—so new girls coming in see this and it's cool."

Further impact on the "success" of the girls' schooling emerged in their unfolding commitment, maturity and active role in shaping the course of the book club. Evelyn related how the nervous, giggling Grade 9 girls of the first book club meeting transformed over 4 years:

> [I]n the early years, the first two, it was still teacher driven in the sense we had to remind them, "here are the books; this is when we meet"— and some meetings, only some showed up . . . I really feel that over the last 2 years, they have taken ownership.

To demonstrate, the research teachers recount a recent meeting where they did not explain the presence of two new assistant researchers.

Latrice interrupted to say, "I don't want to be rude but no one introduced the new people to us." The researcher hosts immediately apologized. Becky explains:

> I think the first part is the protective part—Who are these people coming into our very private and personal space, and, we weren't told of this in advance . . . And the second part is Latrice is a responsible and polite woman. . . . It goes back to them having a voice of their own and not relying on the teacher.

A pronounced growth in openness to intersubjective and intercultural learning occurred. In contrast to the less than satisfactory experiences of prescribed reading in school, the teachers relate the students' response to *The Book of Negroes*.

Evelyn: The whole discussion around the history of slavery and how we understand it and why we need to understand it. It was electrifying. It was a real shared dialogue.

Becky: And no one was afraid to say her true opinions . . . Kadisha accepted Jacquie's ideas but felt her own way about it: "No, this is not how I feel"—her conviction . . . which I think is a sign of growth as well, because before they might have (said), "You know what? Yeah, I see your point" but now they're very driven in their own ideas.

Transformative Student Voices

A common portrait revealed the girls and their moms (occasionally with baby siblings, aunts or cousins) squished closely together on couches around coffee tables. One would stroke another's hair or play with another's scarf. Babies would be shared from one set of arms to another. Books would be clasped and rifled by speakers and nonspeakers alike. Some whispered their opinions on comments made to each other rather than claiming the floor. Others would half leave their seats and wave their arms wildly in anticipation of winning the floor. Mothers and daughters sometimes openly negotiated their difference of opinion.

During 4 years of the book club, their personal identities emerged: one had a father in prison, another had direct experience of rape, several knew individuals who attempted or committed suicide, some had been directly involved in gang fights, one became pregnant but continued to attend, graduated and is attending college. As each year passed, their relationships developed and opened the way for transformative, relational learning.

While 'evidence of success' does not include test results or grades in their classes, they succeeded. Without exception, this cohort of students graduated from high school and currently attends college and university in the area. In their final year, Janine had a baby, graduated and currently attends college. Latrice blossomed as a leader in her own right, becoming president of the school student council in her final year. Evelyn successfully applied for and received the school districts' Exemplary Practice Award (photos, a formal reception, honor and respect in the school followed). Confidence in their ability to learn and teach resulted in a presentation to the school teaching staff about what the book club meant to them and what they learned about reading and talking about books in school.

As the graduates faced leaving, they pondered how to continue the book club experience in their lives. Hence, they had become readers, spending valuable time after school hours reading (at home, on the bus, with their friends and mothers). Their dedication to reading books without the 'reward' of marks or credits, their largely self-directed discussion and debate of literature and current issues, their ongoing engagement with the potent ideas and alternative perspectives of authors and peers, constitute powerful alternative evidence of student success.

DISCUSSION

We discuss three significant areas of teaching and learning that matter: (a) what we are learning from the research about student voice; (b) teacher learning; (c) students, voice and perspective: implications of speaking up.

The Study: the "So What" of Student Voice

While we make no attempt to draw conclusions, we nevertheless have confidence in the data developed over 4 years with the same group, to inform and drive our observations and further inquiry. The group of 14 black girls who constituted the membership of the book club (2006–2010) developed into an interdependent community of learning who disrupted expectations (low, at school, poverty, e.g.) and rose above their marginalized social and economic positions. Over time, the book club space, experiences, texts, relational learning and interdependency, among other things, made them confident enough to stay in school and not only survive, but thrive. All worked to create a new vision of themselves as strong(er) women who, together and individually, began to redraw the boundaries and limitations of their histories (Shor, 1996).

The literacy practices in the deregulated spaces of the book clubs produced forms of textual engagement that schooled spaces often do not. School and literacy boundaries dissolved as students selected the literature and socially and collaboratively negotiated meaning. They became active producers of their own meanings and uses of texts.

The students recognized and named the effects of their dialectical practices in the book club and realized the distinctions between in and out of school literacy practices. Repeatedly in interviews, they explored their developing stances as critical readers (noting, for instance, the effects on reading for in-school courses) Nevertheless, their knowledge of and insights into classroom texts, practices and learning, for the most part, remained outside classroom doors. Too much school improvement research neglects student voice and a focus on learning (Lodge, 2008). The students in the study reveal the powerful potential and possibilities of their voices to transform classroom learning.

Teachers and Learning

While the teachers in the study attested to accruing pedagogical and content knowledge for teaching, our research did not include observations in their classes and, thus, we limited our discussion to the outside-of-class experiences and teacher self-report. We recognize the link to practice is weak in this study (see also Wineburg & Grossman, 1998) and deserves further, in-depth study (Kooy, 2010).

Much research has been conducted on teachers in professional learning communities. For teachers to create dialogic spaces in the texture of their teaching requires them to practice and equip themselves. Lodge (2008) observed: "The skills required for dialogue have to be learned by both adults and young people and are best learned by engaging in the process. The focus of the dialogue needs to be on learning if learning is to improve and learners get better at it" (p. 8).

Watkins's (2001) model for learning may be helpful for explaining how teacher learning develops in four ways that include to: (a) notice, (b) talk about, (c) reflect on and (d) learn *about* learning. Teacher learning sets out to help teachers find the moments to encourage these four activities and apply them to their planning, review and evaluation. Learning innovative practices (writing to learn, jigsaw, e.g.) to enhance capacity for student learning positions teachers to become "committed learners" (Carnell & Lodge, 2002, p. 67). Moreover, awareness that students bring experiential knowledge to discussions on curriculum and knowledge development in classrooms has the potential to shift and even alter teacher perceptions of pedagogy and content.

Speaking Up: Students, Teachers, Voice and Perspective

A remarkable synchronicity between teacher and student learning exists in this study. Understanding the ways students collaboratively construct meaning of their in-class learning in light of their out-of-class learning is a critical contribution to the literature on, and critical need for, student voice and perspective for teacher learning to matter. The reflexive relationship between teaching and learning indicates that "involving students in dialogue about their own learning" not only "helps young people become better learners," but also helps "teachers improve their pedagogy" (Kordalewski, 1999), creating a reflexive reciprocity.

The multiple external resources that inform teacher knowledge for action require active and meaningful participation. This reconstitutes the boundaries and widens the circle of inclusion. Similarly, learning that matters to students (that is, makes a positive contribution and difference) requires active participation in the learning experiences (Puneet Bhatti, Chauhan, Grewal & Sachdeva, 2010). This reflexive and interdependent relationship requires both students and teachers to assume teaching and learning roles. Palmer (1998) observed:

> The real threat to community in the classroom is not power and status difference between teachers and students but the lack of dependence that those differences encourage. Students are dependent on teachers for grades—but what are teachers dependent on students for? If we cannot answer that question with something as real to us as grades are to students, community will not happen. When we are not dependent on each other, resource allocation in educational environments where quality, improvement, and achievement have become common watchwords, community cannot exist. (p. 139)

When students interrogate and help construct educational experiences, they teach their teachers how to reevaluate curriculum and pedagogy, and simultaneously to learn how to expand knowledge of their students' learning processes and lives and to strengthen habits of inquiry, reflection and dialogue as key to the improvement of practice. By including themselves in the dialogic learning experiences they devise for their students, teachers can gain valuable cultural knowledge (ethnic as well as other individual and collective life experiences) and develop a "listening pedagogy" (Paciotti & Boluck, 2009) that nourishes professional efficacy while also supporting the self-efficacy and motivation of their students. "When students have a voice in classroom processes, they share in decision-making and the construction of knowledge. The teacher, consequently, becomes a co-learner and facilitator as well as a source of knowledge" (Kordalewski, 1999, p. 1). It is, after all, a nonnegotiable need to improve learning that takes into account the reality that students themselves (not teachers) decide what they will learn (Olson, 2003).

The shared principles arising from the students in the longitudinal study include: *Community, dialogue, choice, collaborative problem posing and solving, questioning, multiple perspectives, negotiation of meaning, motivation, beginning with personal knowledge and questions, connections to content, learning.* These key concepts and their expressions grew from a vital social learning environment and influenced the wider school culture. Simply providing the conditions (enhanced by food and literature) for teacher and student voices to be heard created potential for transforming teaching and learning, teacher selves and learner selves (Shechtman et al., 2010).

The study demonstrates how teacher learning that matters values teacher voices as singularly informed with learning with, and about, students. To understand how to engage dialogically with student voices, professional learning communities must complete the ecology by nurturing this professional vision of teachers and by promoting the social constructivist approaches that support teachers' ability to cultivate and learn from student voice.

NOTES

The research described in this study was funded by the Social Science and Humanities Research Council of Canada.

REFERENCES

Bakhtin, M. (1986). *Speech genres and other late essays.* (V. McGee, Trans.). Austin: University of Texas Press.

Ball, D., & Cohen, D. (1999). Developing practice, developing practitioners: Toward a practice-based theory of professional education. In G. Sykes & L. Darling-Hammond (Eds.), *Teaching as the learning profession: Handbook of policy and practice* (pp. 3–32). San Francisco: Jossey-Bass.

Bauch, P., & Goldring, E. (1998). Parent–teacher participation in the context of school governance. *Peabody Journal of Education, 73*(1), 15–35.

Borko, H. (2004). Professional Development and Teacher Learning: Mapping the Terrain. *Educational Researcher, 33*(8), 3–15.

Camino, L. (2000). Youth–adult partnership: Engendering new territory in community work and research. *Applied Developmental Science, 4*(1), 11–20.

Carnell, E., & Lodge, C. (2002). *Supporting effective learning.* London: Paul Chapman.

Clark, C. (2001). *Talking shop: Authentic conversation and teacher learning.* New York: Teachers College Press.

Cook-Sather, A. (2007). Translating researchers: Re-imagining the work of investigating students' experiences in school. In D. Thiessen & Cook-Sather, A. (Eds.), *International Handbook of Student Experience in Elementary and Secondary School.* Dordrecht: the Netherlands, 829–872.

Cook-Sather, A. (2009). *Learning from the student's perspective: A sourcebook for effective teaching.* Boulder, CO: Paradigm Publishers.

DuFour, R., & Eaker, R. E. (1998). *Professional learning communities at work: Best practices for enhancing student achievement.* Washington, DC: ASCD/ National Education Services.

Dunleavy, J., & Milton, P. (2009). *What did you do in school today? Exploring the concept of student engagement and its implications for teaching and learning in Canada* (Research Report. Canadian Education Association). Retrieved May 28, 2009, from www.cea-ace.ca/publication/what-did-you-do-school-today-exploring-concept-student-engagement-and-its-implications-t

Dunleavy, J. & Cooke, M. (2010). *Illuminating the Blind spots. Climbing from student voice to student involvement.* Toronto: Canadian Education Association.

Fielding, M. (2001). Students as radical agents of change. *Journal of Educational Change, 2*(3), 123–141.

Fielding, M. (2004). Transformative approaches to student voice: Theoretical underpinnings, recalcitrant realities. *British Educational Research Journal, 30*(2), 295–311.

Franke, M., Carpenter, T., Levi, L. & Fennema, E. (1998, April). *Teachers as learners: Developing understanding through children's thinking.* Paper presented at the annual meeting of the American Educational Research Association, San Diego, CA.

Guskey, T. R. (2008). Foreword. In R. Bourke, A. Lawrence, A. McGee, J. O'Neill & J. Curzon (Eds.), *Talk about learning: Working alongside teachers* (pp. xiii–xv). North Shore: Pearson Education New Zealand.

Jones, K. (2004). *An assessment of community-based youth–adult relationships.* Unpublished dissertation, Pennsylvania State University, University Park.

Jones, K., & Perkins, D. (2004). Youth–adult partnerships. In C.B. Fisher & R. Lerner (Eds.), *Applied developmental science: An encyclopaedia of research, policies, and programs* (pp. 1159–1163). Thousand Oaks, CA: Sage.

Knapp, M. (2003). Professional development as a policy pathway. In R. Floden (Ed.), *Review of research in education* (pp. 109–158). Washington, DC: American Educational Research Association.

Kooy, M. (2006a). *Telling stories in book clubs: Women teachers and professional development.* New York: Springer.

Kooy, M. (2006b). The telling stories of novice teachers: Constructing teacher knowledge in book clubs. *Teaching and Teacher Education, 22*(6), 661–674.

Kooy, M. (2006–2010). *Teacher development in learning communities in and out of school: A follow-up longitudinal study.* Grant: Social Science and Humanities Research Council of Canada.

Kooy, M. (2009). Conversations and collaborations in communities of learning: Professional development that matters. In L. F. Deretchin & C. J. Craig (Eds.), *Teacher learning in small-group settings* (pp. 5–22). Lanham, MD: Rowman and Littlefield Education.

Kooy, M. (2010). *Teacher learning that matters: Expanding a longitudinal study into a technology-mediated professional community* (Grant Proposal). Social Science and Humanities Research Council of Canada.

Kordalewski, J. (1999). *Incorporating student voice into teaching practice [electronic resource].* Washington, DC: ERIC Clearinghouse on Teaching and Teacher Education. Retrieved December 8, 2010, from http://www.ericdigests.org/2000-4/voice.htm

Levin, B. (2000). Putting students at the centre in education reform. *Journal of Educational Change, 1*(2), 155–172.

Lodge, C. (2008). Engaging student voice to improve pedagogy and learning: An exploration of examples of innovative pedagogical approaches for school improvement. *International Journal of Pedagogies and Learning, 4*(55), 4–19.

McLaughlin, M. (1995). *Creating professional learning communities.* Keynote address at the National Association of Staff Development Council Annual Meeting.

Mitra, D. (2008). *Student voice in school reform: Building youth-adult partnerships that strengthen schools and empower youth.* New York: State University of New York Press.

Muncey, D., & McQuillan, P. (1991). *Empowering nonentities: Student perspectives.* Paper presented at the Biennial Meeting of the Society for Research in Child Development, New Orleans, LA.

Nieto, S. (1994). Lessons from students on creating a chance to dream. *Harvard Educational Review, 64*(4), 394–427.

Olson, L. (2003). The great divide. *Education Week, Quality Counts, 22*(17), 9–16.

Ontario Ministry of Education. (2007). *The literacy and numeracy secretariat. Professional learning communities: A model for Ontario Schools.* Toronto: OME.

Ontario Ministry of Education. (2010). *Student voice.* Retrieved December 31, 2010, from http://www.edu.gov.on.ca/eng/students/speakup/forums.html

Paciotti, K. & Bolick, M. (2009). A listening pedagogy: Insights of pre-service elementary teachers in multi-cultural classrooms. *Academic Leadership Live: The Online Journal,* 4(7).

Palmer, P. (1998). *The courage to teach: Exploring the inner landscape of a teacher's life.* San Francisco: Jossey-Bass.

Polanyi, M. (1966). *The tacit dimension.* Garden City, NY: Doubleday.

Puneet Bhatti, J., Chauhan, J., Grewal, G. & Sachdeva, S. (2010). Exceeding all expectations: Student-led initiatives in a North Delta school. *Education Canada, 50*(1), 28–31.

Rudduck, J. (1977). *Learning to teach through discussion.* East Anglia, UK: University of East Anglia Press.

Rudduck, J., & Flutter, J. (2003). *How to improve your school.* London: Continuum.

Rudduck, J., & McIntyre, D. (2007). *Improving learning through consulting pupils.* London: Routledge.

Schwab, J. (1973). The practical 3: Translation into curriculum. *School Review, 81,* 501–522.

Shechtman, N., Roschelle, J., Haertel, G. & Knudsen, J. (2010). Investigating links from teacher knowledge, to classroom practice, to student learning in the instructional system of the middle-school mathematics classroom. *Cognition and Instruction, 28*(3), 317–359.

Shor, I. (1996). *When students have power: Negotiating authority in a critical pedagogy.* Chicago: University of Chicago Press.

Tharpe, R., & Gallimore, R. (1988). *Rousing minds to life: Teaching, learning, and schooling in social context.* New York: Cambridge University Press.

The Learning Bar: School Survey Evaluation System for School Assessment and Evidence-Based Decision-Making (2010). Retrieved May 28, 2009 from http://www.thelearningbar.com/what-people-say.php.

Watkins, C. (2001). *Learning about learning enhances performance* (Research Matters Series No. 13). London: Institute of Education, National School Improvement Network.

Werder, C., & Otis, M. (Eds.). (2010). *Engaging student voices in the study of teaching and learning.* Sterling, VA: Stylus.

Willms, D., Friesen, S. & Milton, P. (2009). *What did you do in school today? Transforming classrooms through social, academic and intellectual engagement* (First National Report). Toronto: Canadian Education Association.

Wilson, S., & Berne, J. (1999). Teacher learning and the acquisition of professional knowledge: An examination of research on contemporary professional development. *Review of research in education, 24,* 73–209.

Wineburg, S., & Grossman, P. (1998). Creating a community of learners among high school teachers. *Phi Delta Kappa, 79,* 350–353.

6 Professional Development through a Teacher-as-Curriculum-Maker Lens

Cheryl Craig

INTRODUCTION

How teacher professional development (PD) is conceived, approached and studied communicates the view held of teachers. It also conveys the conception of knowledge underpinning teacher learning and how experience figures into the chosen perspective. Most often, others' prescriptions of what teachers should know and do takes precedence over teachers' personal professional understandings of their growth. In this chapter, a different image of teachers—teachers as curriculum makers—will be presented, along with a different notion of teacher knowledge, a personal practical view emerging from the narrative continuities of teachers' lives. The consequences of not focusing relentless attention on teachers as learners along the career/life span and all that "the paradigm of the practical" (Greene, 1994) has to offer will also be considered, together with the long-term impact on the teaching profession.

TEACHER IMAGES, TEACHER KNOWLEDGE

The dominant image of teachers as curriculum implementers upholds the position that teachers are merely agents of the state, paid to do its bidding. In this prevailing view, shifts in teachers' practices occur because policy makers at various levels of the system mandate changes that teachers must dutifully— due to legal requirements/subordinated line positions/lack of power—follow. Within this scenario, the teacher is a "technician, consumer, receiver, transmitter, and implementer of other people's knowledge" (Cochran-Smith & Lytle, 1999, p. 16). This image of teachers as being positioned in an educational conduit (Clandinin & Connelly, 1996; Craig, 2002), delivering curriculum products to students, has spread like wildfire in the teaching enterprise, particularly in the policy arena, but also significantly within the theoretical terrain due to theory's long-standing estrangement from practice (Schwab, 1969b). Clandinin and Connelly (1995) liken this top-down approach to change by injection, with each new injection resulting in new knowledge prescriptions for teachers. Sadly, externally imposed measures tend to be disconnected from what teachers have experientially come to know and do in their practices. This is highly problematic because teachers' practices reflect their personal practical knowledge in action (Connelly & Clandinin, 1985; Clandinin, 1986), not simply what others expect of them, although others' expectations enter the mix (Clandinin & Connelly, 1992).

But this prevailing paradigm ignores the existence of an alternate image of teaching, one that is more sensitive to teachers as active agents (Schwab, 1954/1978) and the mindedness Dewey (1908) afforded them. In this view, teachers are curriculum makers—"the fountainhead of the curriculum decision" as Schwab (1983, p. 241; also see Fox, 1985, p. 77) put it—who "*must* be involved in debate, deliberation, and decision about what and how to teach" (Schwab, 1983, p. 245; italics in original). The image of the teacher as curriculum maker focuses attention on the primacy of the teacher in organizing, planning and orchestrating classroom interactions because only the teacher is situated at the interstices of the curricular exchange and meets students face-to-face. Thus, curriculum is what happens—what becomes instantiated—in the moments when teaching and learning fuse. In that fusion (see Figure 6.1), teachers use student knowledge (learner commonplace), their teaching situations (milieu commonplace) and themselves (teacher commonplace) to make curriculum (typically organized around the subject matter commonplace) in a way that captures the continuity of experience (Dewey, 1938) that facilitates and develops learning and knowledge.

In a nutshell, knowledge culled from experience cannot be "tested, packaged, imparted and sent like bricks across countries to build knowledge structures that are said to accumulate" (Eisner, 1997, p. 7) because the teacher, like the student, is indispensable to the body of knowledge that exists (i.e., Dewey & Bentley, 1949; Fenstermacher, 1994) and essential to

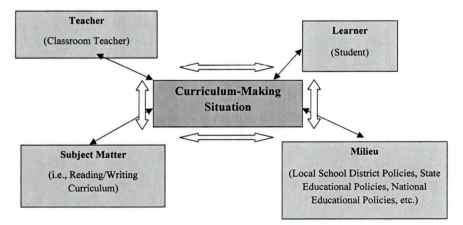

Figure 6.1   Schwab's commonplaces of curriculum.

the curriculum-making act (Schwab, 1983). In essence, the teacher is "the most responsive creator of curriculum" because he/she "negotiates the formal planned curriculum of governments and publishers within his/her practice, alongside the lives of learners" (Murphy & Pushor, 2010, p. 658). Consequently, in the teacher-as-curriculum-maker image, attention turns from written plans, authorized textbooks and government mandates (Clandinin & Connelly, 1992; Connelly & Clandinin, 1988), which typically privilege the subject matter commonplace and confine the teacher to a dispenser of knowledge role, to curriculum as it is lived within the context of people's lives (Downey & Clandinin, 2010), a mingling of Schwab's four curriculum commonplaces (teacher, learner, subject matter, milieu) mediated by the teacher. And, in stark contrast to lists of codified knowledge, stripped from context, disembodied from persons and devoid of relationship, what emerges are the most important aspects of teacher knowledge, which are "ephemeral, passionate, shadowy and significant . . . for the most part . . . reflect[ive of] teachers' lives" (Connelly & Clandinin, 2004, p. 42).

TEACHER KNOWLEDGE, TEACHER PROFESSIONAL DEVELOPMENT, PUBLIC POLICY

When the image teachers are expected to live subjects them to policy makers who dictate and manipulate knowledge as if it could/should be possessed, measured and reified as an indicator of teacher effectiveness, the idea of teacher PD falls victim to the shifting whims of decision makers and takes the form of one-shot training sessions. Such one-size-fits-all sessions typically do not build on what individual teachers already know and do. Instead, teacher PD is approached generically—as if all teachers exhibit the same malady and are in need of the same antidote. Even more troubling is the underlying belief that teachers' knowledge is deficit and not simply in need of further cultivation, but requiring total replacement. This mind-set recently surfaced in my longitudinal work with Daryl Wilson, a middle-school literacy teacher in the United States, whose PD experiences I have studied since 1998 (Craig, 2010). Despite Daryl's stellar teaching record and ongoing teacher leadership role in his school, he was expected to abandon units of study that held great personal meaning for him and had been well received by his literacy students and their parents to teach what a consultant—unfamiliar with the students, school and district—declared more appropriate.

This type of external manipulation of the teaching/learning act is troubling from a teacher knowledge point of view and problematic from a policy perspective. As Cohen and Garet (1975), among others (Cremin, 1990; Olson & Craig, 2009, Tyack & Cuban, 1995), have maintained, educational policy tends to be a "grand story" of loosely connected ideas that are often based on "faulty logic" that "lack explanatory power" (Cohen & Garet, 1975, p. 17). Such policy stories have to do with "a large and loose set of ideas about how [things] work, [what] goes wrong, and how it can be set right" (p. 21). These grand stories take a system view; they see things from a distance and "small" because a "big" view (Greene, 2000) of how things play out, in particular teachers' classroom situations, has neither been fully recognized nor appreciated as the critically important linchpin in successful policy enactment. Greene (2000) further elaborated what she meant by "small" and "big" this way:

> To see things or people small, one chooses to see from a detached point of view . . . to be concerned with trends and tendencies . . . To see things or people big, one must resist viewing other human beings as mere objects . . . and view them in their integrity and particularity instead. (p. 10)

When big and small perspectives are linked with policy makers' approaches and behaviors, we find that what policy makers create is not a flexible framework that supports teachers as they interface with live students and inert curriculum documents (all the while drawing on their personal narrative histories and individual propensities), but frequently something more akin to "a bad eclectic" (Schwab, 1983). Put differently, various pieces of the policy puzzle do not fit snugly together despite teachers' valiant attempts to make them cohere in their face-to-face work with youth. Ultimately, different aspects of educational policy trace to different philosophical and pedagogical traditions that have accumulated over time, some of which conflict with one another.

In my research program, teachers in PD sessions have focused on arts integration (Craig, 2010) and readers' and writers' workshop (Craig, 2009b)—approaches seriously impeded by the U.S. No Child Left Behind Act (2002), despite arts integration and the workshop approach also receiving support from policy makers. The article, "The Contested Classroom Space: A Decade of Lived Educational Policy in Texas" (Craig, 2009a), captures several such theory-practice-policy collisions. The work suggests that the less-than-productive mixing of educational imperatives at the policy level, each justified by different theories, creates intractable tensions in teachers' practices and student learning due to the incommensurable nature of the eclectic that has been amassed, largely devoid of teachers' participation. For Schwab, potentially good practices (i.e., arts integration? readers' and writers' workshop?) built on less-than-good policies (i.e., No Child Left Behind?) suffer from "poisoning at the source" (Schwab, 1959/1978, p. 167). This further complicates the impossible roles of teachers (Schwab, 1959/1978) and teacher educators (Ben-Peretz, 2001). Not only are the forces of continuity and change with which teachers contend never ending, the management of the tensions arising from them has become increasingly unwieldy and politically charged, given the penalties associated with not complying with accountability mandates.

EXPERT KNOWLEDGE, TEACHER PROFESSIONAL DEVELOPMENT

So far, conflicting images of teachers and problems arising from less-than-ideal educational policies and the consequences both have on teacher knowledge and teacher PD have been discussed. Now, attention turns to a third major problem: expert knowledge and its relation to, and impact on, teacher PD. Returning to Schwab's 'practical,' particularly his common-places of curriculum, one finds that in PD pursuits (see Figure 6.2) teachers are positioned in the learner role (as opposed to their students) whereas staff developers and various other consultants, some of whom may be university professors, occupy the teacher commonplace typically reserved for class-room teachers. Milieu remains relatively the same as in other curriculum situations, but subject matter changes. It includes not only content knowl-edge from the disciplines, but also pedagogy and teaching dispositions as summarized, for example, in the National Council for Accreditation of Teacher Education (NCATE) standards in the United States (2001).

The reconfiguration of the curriculum commonplaces places the teacher in this particular curricular situation in the vulnerable role of (adult) learner and once again shines the spotlight on the teacher–learner relationship. How-ever, just as uneven power distribution exists in student–teacher relationships, power differentials are also present in teacher–staff developer relationships, particularly when PD takes the form of training sessions with teachers expected to uncritically accept the knowledge of the expert as 'best practice' rather than 'trying on' changes within the context of the teacher's classroom teaching and publically reconstructing a personal story of what it means to teach. In short, 'training' reduces the teacher to passive recipient (rather than active professional). Fueled by the technical rationalist philosophy, this approach assumes a homogeneity among teacher and student populations and reflects a deficit view—that is, teachers lacking skills (Darling-Hammond, 1993). Furthermore, training revolves around predetermined skills and com-petencies (Bullough & Gitlin, 1994) understood behaviorally and operating from a worldview that narrowly defines teaching and learning (Goodlad, 1994). Finally, "performance training sects" may emerge where trainers "trap

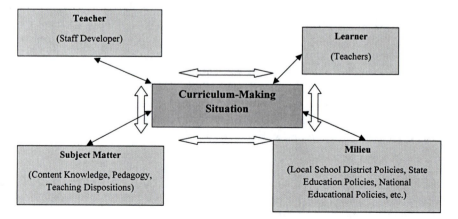

Figure 6.2   Changes in the commonplaces of curriculum configuration.

'underdeveloped' schools and their teachers within cycles of minimum competence" (Hargreaves, 2003, p. 191).

The issues and implications of teacher learners working with expert trainers who represent the teacher commonplace are significant. The core issues reflect the teacher-as-implementer image of teaching and echo Schwab's warning about the roots of particular policies undermining well-meaning practices. But two associated questions critical to this chapter's focus also need to be raised:

1. What is the difference between a teacher trainer and a consultant engaged in promoting teacher growth?
2. How does expert knowledge figure into the different roles and relationships?

To address these queries, I return to my longitudinal work with Daryl Wilson. Earlier, I spoke of Daryl's expert knowledge of himself as a teacher, his students as individual learners, his state's reading and writing curriculum and the particularities of his school context as it changed over time during his tenure at the campus. However, the expert trainer's knowledge discounted and undermined Daryl's professional knowledge of and approach to reading and writing. Daryl's colleague found herself defenseless, "like a butterfly under a pin" (Craig, in press). This raised the question of dominance and hierarchies and challenged the ways "experts" undermine the teacher as curriculum maker and fail to acknowledge teachers as professional knowledge holders from their own lived experiences as classroom teachers.

Daryl Wilson's stories of experience (Connelly & Clandinin, 1990), lived and told, relived and retold, reemerged and created new stories. Two years after the professional "training experience," Daryl attended a PD session led by literacy workshop expert whose approach significantly differed from the earlier trainer. This second literacy expert challenged the gathered teachers to develop tension and beauty in their writing through reflectively drawing on their personal experiences and telling and retelling their stories in a writers' workshop. Daryl returned to his school with drafts of his story as a teenage runaway. His active involvement (actually creating and "workshopping") a personal narrative, enabled him to engage his students using examples from his writing. His students created quality writing involving tension and beauty, emerging from their teen experiences. Daryl subsequently combined his and his students' writing and presented the work to his colleagues in a literacy department meeting. In response, Daryl's peers:

> made it clear to him that his teaching example resonated with them—and that it, along with his student work samples, were products to which they—and their students—would aspire. One colleague distinctly noted that his lesson was not a "zinger lesson"—a fail-proof lesson that would work anywhere, anytime—like the ones the initial staff developer used to teach their students or the lessons the teachers routinely carried back with them from their summer training sessions in [other states]. (Craig, 2010, pp. 432–433)

In this narrative exemplar (Lyons & LaBoskey, 2002), we see the consequences of different experts working together. The teacher as a learner is more than a receptacle to be filled with knowledge by an expert trainer (regardless of duration)—a "flavor of the month" training (an expression used by a high school teacher in an Olson and Craig inquiry [2001]). Schwab argued that teacher learning occurs when acknowledged experts (the consultant/Daryl) work with learners (Daryl/his students/his peers) in ways that attend to, and are mindful of, their wholeness as persons. For Schwab, learners must be approached "not only [as] minds or knowers but [as] bundles of affects, individual personalities, earners of livings . . . They are not only group interactors but possessors of private lives" (1969b, p. 9). In short, teachers' knowledge, emotions and identities unavoidably come into play in change initiatives (i.e., Craig, 2004; van Veen & Sleegers, 2009).

Connelly and Clandinin (2004) suggest that more realistic and individually satisfying goals be sought in teacher PD. They explain their reasoning as follows:

> We do not mean to imply that . . . formal teacher education be downplayed. [It is], of course, important. But we do think that, on the whole, there is more for most teachers to learn by coming, self-consciously, to grips with their own teacher knowledge than with what may be learned from a knowledge or skills for teaching workshop provided by others . . . Formal professional developers, must, of course, continue their work. This work should, we believe, be done in the context of an understanding of the significance of informal teacher education and, therefore, with a humble spirit and with modest expectations. (p. 42)

Having addressed the role of experts and potential clashes between teacher expertise and expert knowledge of different kinds held by consultants authorized to instruct teachers, I address an equally complex issue: teacher learning in small group settings and its relationship to teacher knowledge.

TEACHER KNOWLEDGE, TEACHER KNOWLEDGE COMMUNITIES, PROFESSIONAL LEARNING COMMUNITIES

Ineffective one-shot workshops with little or no impact on teachers' daily work, persistent calls for increasing student performance through standardized testing/accountability measures/punitive sanctions/negative press coverage and the issues swirling around expert knowledge have resulted in recasting teacher PD in terms of learning in community. Hence, leadership is ideally equitably distributed among participants (teachers/faculty/consultants) such as the fruitful way Kooy (2006) interacted in the various iterations of her book club project. Schwab historically favored teachers at all levels collaboratively sharing their knowledge. For him, teachers deliberating in community represent "a pooling of diversities of experience and insights" (Schwab, 1969a, p. 30). This opposes others of his time who declared teachers' communal learning a "pooling of ignorance" (Schwab, 1950/1978, pp. 107–108). Even today, modern critics—even some who theoretically align with the teacher-as-curriculum-maker image of teaching, view it as a ruse for giving teachers permission to 'do their own thing.' This misrepresents what the teacher-as-curriculum-maker approach intends (Grimmett & Chinnery, 2009, p. 134).

The futility of professional learning communities forced to fit personal, administrative and system-level agendas emerged in Daryl Wilson's inquiry into constructing teacher knowledge in communities (Craig, 1995a, 1995b) in the context of organized school reform (Craig, 2001). Early in the research, readers' and writers' workshop initiatives were couched in language of teacher learning within a professional learning community. However, I uncovered significant differences between teachers' knowledge communities developed around the teacher as curriculum maker and professional learning communities limited to externally imposed expectations and strategies (by school administrators/school district personnel and academic researchers; see Craig, 2009b).

My understanding of teachers' knowledge communities include:

> safe, storytelling places where educators narrate the rawness of their experiences, negotiate meaning, and authorize their own and others' interpretations of situations. They take shape around commonplaces of experience (Lane, 1988) as opposed to around bureaucratic and hierarchical relations that declare who knows, what should be known, and what constitutes 'good teaching' and 'good schools' (Clandinin & Connelly, 1996). Such knowledge communities can be both found and created. (Craig & Olson, 2002, p. 116)

Meanwhile, other educational researchers (e.g., DuFour, 2001, 2004; DuFour & Eaker, 1998; Fullan, 2002, 2004; Hargreaves, 2000) define professional learning communities. I adopt DuFour's conceptualization my study participants (administrators and teachers), had attended several of his workshops and thus, familiar to them. To DuFour (2001), professional learning communities "focus on learning rather than teaching, work collaboratively, and [are] accountable for results." DuFour (2004) observed that:

> people use the term to describe every imaginable combination of individuals with an interest in education—a grade-level teaching team, a school committee, a high school department, an entire school district, a state department of education, a national professional organization, and so on. (p. 6)

Table 6.1 compares my perspective with that of DuFour.

Table 6.1   Comparing Knowledge Communities (Craig) and Professional Learning Communities (DuFour)

Knowledge Communities	Professional Learning Communities
Organically lived	Administratively introduced
Can be found or made	Expected to be present
Commonplaces of experience	Focus on learning rather than teaching
Relational among individuals and across groups; collaborations emerge	Collaboration anticipated at the outset
May exist within member of various groups; also occur between teachers who interact for their own purposes	Any visible group within a school/ organization
Accounts of practice	Accountable for results
▼ Practical View of Knowledge	▼ Formal View of Knowledge

LINGERING ISSUES, LATENT POSSIBILITIES

In this chapter, I argue that the teacher as curriculum maker is foundational to high-quality teacher PD and a productive lens for approaching teacher learning. I surveyed the work of Schwab (United States) and Connelly and Clandinin (Canada) and supported those findings with what has more recently emerged in my own research program as a Canadian researching teacher learning in American school contexts for more than a decade. I wove other views of researchers who helped set the context for why the teacher-as-curriculum-maker image is so vitally important. In conclusion, I connect some major consequences regarding: (a) the boundaries between the two images of teaching, (b) the critics of the teacher-as-curriculum-maker image and (c) the teacher-as-curriculum-maker image and its relationship to teacher education along the continuum.

The prevailing image of the teacher as curriculum implementer dominating the reform, administration and some teaching research literature, significantly counters the image of the teacher as curriculum maker, diminishing its possibilities as a viable lived alternative. At the same time, the binary images are not helpful. While boundaries do exist between the teacher as curriculum implementer and the teacher as curriculum maker, they are not discrete. Ideally, they are porous, with ideas and practices flowing reflexively.

Furthermore, teachers in the curriculum-making role work diligently to account for the policies, programs and mandates of their educational contexts. This calls for research inquiries that focus on the ways prescribed formal knowledge and developing informal (practical) knowledge intersects. Here, I would include such perceived anomalies as the direct teaching of reflective practice and the indirect knowledge encountered in teacher development experiences. This requires further investigations.

Second, at the 2009 American Educational Research Association Meeting, a colleague shared his impression that work involving the teacher-as-curriculum-maker image/Schwab's 'practical' is currently considered "old-fashioned." This direct argument against practical teaching inquiries suggests the binary theory and practice split that continues to plague the research. Schwab (1969a) termed this a "flight from the field" to theory—or to what currently is the move to abstract empiricism. Such an approach ignores the complexities of learning itself, including the need to develop awareness of and move forward using the knowledge of learners and teachers alike.

Already in 1953, Cremin's article entitled "The Curriculum Maker and His Critics" argued against the domination of those who contest the knowledge and practice of teachers. Those conducting teaching and teacher education research need to consciously cultivate ways to collaboratively inquire so that research involving multiple stakeholders (teacher and academics, for instance) make their way into the creation of policies and programs that affect the lived learning lives of teachers and students.

Pedagogies that cultivate the teacher-as-curriculum-maker image can contribute to effective practice (see Connelly and Clandinin, e.g.). Other examples include: *Narrative Inquiries in Curriculum-Making in Teacher Education* (Canadians Kitchen, Ciuffetelli Parker & Pushor, 2011); Li (United States), Conle (Canada) and Elbaz-Luwisch (Israel) (2009). Many leading international researchers (i.e., Ben-Peretz, 2009; Cochran-Smith & Zeichner, 2005; Cochran-Smith & Lytle, 2009; Grimmett & Chinnery, 2009; Kwo, 2010) point to the teacher-as-curriculum-maker image as the illuminative path and call for its elaboration in fine-grained detail. Marking that territory continues to be a professional imperative and make a significant impact on the field.

REFERENCES

Ben-Peretz, M. (2001). The impossible role of teacher educators in a changing world. *Journal of Teacher Education, 52*(1), 48–56.

Ben-Peretz, M. (2009). *Policy-making in education: A holistic approach in response to global changes.* Lanham, MD: Rowman and Littlefield Education.

Bullough, R., & Gitlin, A. (1994). Challenging teacher education as training: Four propositions. *Journal of Education for Teaching, 20*(1), 67–81.

Clandinin, D. J. (1986). *Classroom practice: Teacher images in action.* Philadelphia: Falmer Press.

Clandinin, D. J., & Connelly, F. M. (1992). Teacher as curriculum maker. In P. Jackson (Ed.), *Handbook of curriculum* (pp. 363–461). New York: Macmillan.

Clandinin D. J., & Connelly, F. M. (1996). Teachers' professional knowledge landscapes: Teacher stories-stories of teachers-school stories-stories of school. *Educational Researcher, 25*(5), 2–14.

Cochran-Smith, M., & Lytle, S. (1999). The teacher research movement: A decade later. *Educational Researcher, 28*(7), 15–25.

Cochran-Smith, M., & Lytle, S. (2009). *Inquiry as stance: Practitioner research in the next generation.* New York: Teachers College Press.

Cochran-Smith, M., & Zeichner, K. (Eds.). (2005). *Studying teacher education: The report of the AERA panel on research and teacher education.* Washington, DC: American Educational Research Association (with Lawrence Erlbaum Associates).

Cohen, D., & Garet, M. (1975). Reforming educational policy with applied social research. *Harvard Educational Review, 45*(1), 17–43.

Connelly, F. M., & Clandinin, D. J. (1985). Personal practical knowledge and the modes of knowing: Relevance for teaching and learning. In .E. Eisner (Ed.), *Learning and teaching ways of knowing: The eighty-fourth yearbook of the National Society for the Study of Education* (pp. 174–198). Chicago: University of Chicago Press.

Connelly, F. M., & Clandinin, D. J. (1988). *Teachers as curriculum planners: Narratives of experience.* New York: Teachers College Press.

Connelly, F. M., & Clandinin, D. J. (1990). Stories of experience and narrative inquiry. *Educational Researcher, 19*(5), 2–14.

Connelly, F., M., & Clandinin, D. J. (2004). Canadian teacher education in transition. In Y. C. Cheng, K. W. Chow & M. C. Magdalena Mok (Eds.), *Reform of teacher education in the Asia-Pacific in the New Millennium: Trends and challenges* (pp. 35–43). Dordrecht: Kluwer Academic Publishers.

Craig, C. (1995a). Knowledge communities: A way of making sense of how beginning teachers come to know. *Curriculum Inquiry, 25*(2), 151–175.

Craig, C. (1995b). Safe places in the professional knowledge landscapes. In D. J. Clandinin & F. M. Connelly (Eds.), *Teachers' professional knowledge landscapes* (pp. 137–141). New York: Teachers College Press.

Craig, C. (2001). The monkey's paw: The relationships between and among teacher knowledge, communities of knowing, and top down school reform. *Curriculum Inquiry, 31*(3), 303–331.

Craig, C. (2004). The dragon in school backyards: The influence of mandated testing on school contexts and educators' narrative knowing. *Teachers College Record, 106*(6), 1229–1257.

Craig, C. (2009a). The contested classroom space: A decade of lived educational policy in Texas schools. *American Educational Research Journal, 46*(4), 1034–1059.

Craig, C. (2009b). Research in the midst of organized school reform: Versions of teacher community in tension. *American Educational Research Journal, 46*(2), 598–619.

Craig, C. (2010). Coming full circle: From teacher reflection to classroom action and places in-between. *Teachers and Teaching: Theory and Practice, 16*(4), 423–435.

Craig, C. (in press). 'Butterfly under a pin': An emergent teacher image amid mandated curriculum reform. *Journal of Educational Research.*

Craig, C., & Olson, M. (2002). The development of teachers' narrative authority in knowledge communities: A narrative approach to teacher learning. In N. Lyons & V. LaBoskey (Eds.), *Narrative inquiry in practice: Advancing the knowledge of teaching* (pp. 115–129). New York: Teachers College Press.

Cremin, L. (1953). The curriculum maker and his critics. *Teachers College Record, 54*(5), 234–245.

Cremin, L. (1990). *Popular education and its discontents.* New York: Harper and Row.

Darling-Hammond, L. (1993). Reframing the school reform agenda: Developing capacity for school transformation. *Phi Delta Kappan, 74*(10), 753–761.

Dewey, J. (1908). The practical character of reality. In J. McDermot (Ed.), *The philosophy of John Dewey* (pp. 207–222). Chicago: University of Chicago Press.

Dewey, J. (1938). *Education and experience.* New York: Collier Books.

Dewey, J., & Bentley, A. (1949). *The knower and the known.* Boston: Beacon Press.

Downey, C. A., & Clandinin, D. J. (2010). Narrative inquiry as reflective practice: Tensions and possibilities. In N. Lyons (Ed.), *Handbook of reflection and reflective practice: Mapping a way of knowing for professional reflective inquiry* (chap. 19). New York: Springer.

DuFour, R. (2001, Winter). In the right context. *Journal of Staff Development, 22*(1), 14–17.

DuFour, R. (2004). Schools as learning communities. *Educational Leadership, 61*(8), 6–11.

DuFour, R., & Eaker, R. E. (1998). *Professional learning communities at work: Best practices for enhancing student achievement.* Washington, DC: ASCD/ National Education Services.

Eisner, E. (1997). The promises and perils of alternate forms of data representation. *Educational Researcher, 26*(6), 4–10.

Fenstermacher, G. (1994). The knower and the known: The nature of knowledge in research on teaching. *Review of Research on Teaching, 20,* 3–56.

Fox, S. (1985). The vitality of theory in Schwab's conception of the practical. *Curriculum Inquiry, 15*(1), 63–87.

Fullan, M. (2002). The change leader. *Educational Leadership, 59*(8), 16–21.

Fullan, M. (2004). Leading in tough times. *Educational Leadership, 61*(7), 42–46.

Goodlad, J. (1994). *School renewal: Better teachers, better schools.* San Francisco: Jossey-Bass.

Greene, M. (1994). Epistemology and educational research: The influence of recent approaches
to knowledge. *Review of Research in Education, 20,* 423–464.

Greene, M. (2000). *Releasing the imagination: Essays on education, the arts, and social change.* New York: Teachers College Press.

Grimmett, P., & Chinnery, A. (2009). Bridging policy and professional pedagogy in teaching and teacher education: Buffering learning by educating teachers as curriculum makers: A review. *Curriculum Inquiry, 39*(1), 125–143.

Hargreaves, A. (2000). Four ages of professionalism and professional learning. *Teachers and Teaching: Theory and Practice, 6*(2), 151–182.

Hargreaves, A. (2003). *Teaching in a knowledge society: Education in an age of uncertainty.* New York: Teachers College Press.

Kitchen, J., Ciuffetelli Parker, D. & Pushor, D. (2011). *Narrative inquiries in curriculum-making in teacher education.* Bingley, UK: Emerald Group Publishing Limited.

Kooy, M. (2006). The telling stories of novice teachers: Constructing teacher knowledge in book clubs. *Teaching and Teacher Education, 22*(6), 661–674.

Kwo, O. (Ed.). (2010). *Teachers as learners: Critical discourse on challenges and opportunities.* Hong Kong: Comparative Education Research Centre, the University of Hong Kong and Springer.

Lane, B. (1988). *Landscapes of the sacred. Geography and narrative in American spirituality.* New York: Paulist Press.

Li, X., Conle, C. & Elbaz-Luwisch, F. (2009). *Shifting polarized positions: A narrative approach to teacher education.* New York: Peter Lang Publishing.

Lyons, N., & LaBoskey, V. (2002). *Narrative inquiry in practice: Advancing the knowledge of teaching.* New York: Teachers College Press.

Murphy, M. S., & Pushor, D. (2010). Teachers as curriculum planners. In C. Kridel (Ed.), *Encyclopedia of curriculum studies, Vol. 2* (pp. 657–658). Thousand Oaks, CA: Sage Publications.

National Council for Accreditation of Teacher Education. (2001). *Professional standards for the accreditation of schools, colleges, and Departments of Education.*

In National Council for accreditation of teacher education: The standard of excellence. Charlottesville, VA: NCATE.

Olson, M., & Craig (2001). Opportunities and challenges in the development of teachers' knowledge: The development of narrative authority in knowledge communities. *Teaching and Teacher Education, 17*(6), 667–684.

Olson, M., & Craig, C. (2009). Small stories and mega-stories: Accountability in balance. *Teachers College Record, 111*(2), 547–572.

Schwab, J. J. (1950/1978). Proceedings of the Educational Testing Services Annual Conference. In I. Westbury & N. Wilkof (Eds.), *Science, curriculum and liberal education: Selected essays* (pp. 107–108). Chicago: University of Chicago Press.

Schwab, J. J. (1954/1978). Eros and education: A discussion of one aspect of discussion. In I. Westbury & N. Wilkof (Eds.), *Science, curriculum and liberal education: Selected essays* (pp. 105–132). Chicago: University of Chicago Press.

Schwab, J. J. (1959/1978). The "impossible" role of the teacher in progressive education. In I. Westbury & N. Wilkof (Eds.), *Science, curriculum, and liberal education: Selected essays* (pp. 167–183). Chicago: University of Chicago Press.

Schwab, J. J. (1969a). *College curriculum and student protest.* Chicago: University of Chicago Press.

Schwab, J. J. (1969b). The practical: A language for curriculum. *School Review, 78*(1), 1–23.

Schwab, J. J. (1983). The practical 4: Something for curriculum professors to do. *Curriculum Inquiry, 13*(3), 239–265.

Tyack, D., & Cuban, L. (1995). *Tinkering toward utopia: A century of public school reform.* Cambridge, MA: Harvard University Press.

van Veen, K., & Sleegers, P. (2009). Teachers' emotions in a context of reforms: To a deeper understanding of teachers and reforms. In P. Schultz & M. Zembylas (Eds.), *Advances in teacher emotion research: Impact on teacher lives* (pp. 233–252). Dordrecht: Springer.

Part III

Foundations for Developing the Self in Teacher Learning

7 Promoting Quality from Within
A New Perspective on Professional Development in Schools

Saskia Attema-Noordewier,
Fred Korthagen and Rosanne Zwart

INTRODUCTION

For the past several years, the Dutch Institute of Multi-Level Learning (IML) has been organizing innovation projects designed to begin with the qualities, commitments and concerns of teachers or students themselves. The intervention focuses on promoting professional development (PD) of teachers and improving schools through 'quality from within.' Thus, it attempts to build teachers' awareness of their personal qualities, potential and inspiration that supports growth in their pedagogical views and abilities to coach others.

Despite a small number of staff workshop days, participants find the intervention highly successful (Korthagen & Vasalos, 2008). One primary school teacher observed:

> I have never felt more at home in my team than I do now. We are really talking to each other. That to me is the biggest outcome. And add to this the wonderful fact that it has already been channeled to the children. Life in the school is vibrant again.

A primary school principal added:

> Teachers' progress can be observed in the classroom. Even an 'old hand' tells me with a broad grin that he is doing things differently! I have also been able to observe. They are really involved in it. I also notice that relations between teachers and students are improving. Mutual understanding is genuinely growing. There is more openness between colleagues.

This research explores the impact of the *quality from within* approach on the PD of participating teachers from six primary schools, and on school culture as a whole. It further considers whether specific aspects of the approach encourage or hinder teacher growth. Other schools designing innovations for professional learning may benefit from the findings of this study. We formulated the following research questions:

1. What do the participants in the 'quality from within' projects perceive as the outcomes of the project and how do participants interpret these outcomes for daily practice?

We examine this question from two perspectives: (a) the primary process in the classroom, i.e., the outcomes both for the teachers and their students, and (b) the school as whole.

2. Do the participants perceive themselves as better facilitators of student and colleague learning as a result of the 'quality from within' projects?
3. What aspects of the project or of school or of themselves do the participants perceive as:

   a. developing the learning process and the outcomes?
   b. hindering or limiting the learning process and the outcomes?

The combined research questions include both what participants perceive as relevant (questions 1 and 3) and the predetermined criteria (question 2). Research methods include: an *evidence-based approach* to identify evidence for the effectiveness of a certain approach and a *value-based approach* that starts from the participants' values.

THEORETICAL FRAMEWORK

Educational Innovation Is Problematic

A 1998 review of a large number of studies found that most innovations for educational change fail (Holmes, 1998). Elliot (1991, p. 47) notes that teachers often do not feel taken seriously in their own professionalism and knowledge. Educational goals are often predetermined, without consultation with teachers (Korthagen, 2007). Innovators may know what needs to be changed in the classroom, but without consultations, teachers may or may not agree or act upon the innovation in ways innovators expect (Day, 1999). The top-down approach creates external pressure on the teachers, especially if the innovation is in tension with their needs and views. Often, teachers respond by showing fight, flight or freeze patterns. They actively resist (fight), try to escape from the pressure to change (flight) or become tense (freeze). For example, a common fight-or-flight response of teachers is to disparage or dismiss innovations as useless or impractical (Elliot, 1991).

Nevertheless, this top-down thinking and its ineffectual results still dominate the educational culture (Korthagen & Vasalos, 2008). It mirrors Schön's (1987) "technical-rationality model"; namely, if research indicates what is needed for good teaching, then teachers must learn and apply their new knowledge of the research outcomes in their teaching. Although this sounds logical, it appears not to work in practice. Many studies show that teachers rarely apply the theories presented to them (see, e.g., Cochran-Smith & Zeichner, 2005). This is a critical problem in educational innovation. A deadlock seems to follow as teachers reject innovations, regardless of their potential benefits for practice. Education seems urgently to need a solution to this widespread phenomenon.

Often educational innovators attempt to minimize the external pressures on teachers. By promoting 'ownership,' they make teachers 'owners' of the innovation. However, teachers *must* still *do* the something prescribed, which implies a top-down approach. When teachers resist, educational innovators express disrespect (see Hargreaves, Lieberman, Fullan & Hopkins, 1998). In sum, the overall picture is problematic: Educational experts and teachers do not really interact or seem to take each other seriously, and the conventional, top-down approach to educational innovation rarely succeeds. The *quality from within* approach essentially inverts the model into bottom-up instead of top-down.

Positive Psychology

Recently, the emergence of *positive psychology* helps us understand the psychological processes involved in teacher resistance to innovations that focus on deficits in teaching practices. Traditional psychology has focused on traumas, and on what is wrong with people consequently, on what has to be 'repaired.' Seligman and Csikszentmihalyi (2000) point out that this approach fails to contribute to personal well-being. Instead, they argue for emphasizing inner potential, or *character strengths*, such as enthusiasm, care, courage, determination and creativity. Ofman (2000) calls these *core qualities*, potentially present in people, already part of them. On the other hand, competencies such as 'giving a clear and unambiguous explanation' can be learned, even at a later age.

Personal qualities color a teacher's professional behavior and shapes a teacher's professional growth. Hamachek (1999, p. 209) observed: "Consciously, we teach what we know; unconsciously, we teach who we are." Almaas (1986, p. 148) refers to core qualities as 'essential aspects,' irreducible to more basic constituents. Whereas competencies can be divided into subskills, core qualities can be broadly applied—that is, they have high 'transfer value' (Korthagen, 2004). Tickle (1999) claims that the core qualities are neglected in education because of a dominantly technical and analytical perspective of teachers.

The 'quality from within approach' views the teacher (or student) as a whole person; therefore, it attends to core qualities as critical factors in teaching and learning. Thereby it validates the individual's irreplaceable contribution to their own and colleagues' professional growth and also progressively develops a more holistic approach to students and teachers while creating room for alternative ways of approaching problems in work and life.

Self-Determination Theory

Insights from positive psychology link to the Self-Determination Theory (SDT; see Deci & Ryan, 2000; Ryan & Deci, 2002; Evelein, 2005), that identifies three basic human psychological needs: autonomy, competence, and relatedness. Evelein (2005, pp. 45–46) found that if teachers are encouraged to identify and act on their personal strengths, they will enrich and fulfill their basic needs.

Autonomy refers to the need to express the authentic self, and experience the self as the source of behavior (Ryan, 1995; Ryan & Deci, 2002). Central in experiencing autonomy are the personal will, clear decision-making based on awareness of personal values and a feeling of responsibility for personal decisions (Hodgins, Koestner & Duncan, 1996). *Competence* refers to feeling effective in personal, ongoing interactions in the social environment. It implies that humans are born with the need to use their capabilities to influence their surroundings (Ryan & Deci, 2002). The need for *relatedness* refers to a longing for positive relations and engagement with others, that is, to care and be cared for by others, by belonging to a group or community (Baumeister & Leary, 1995; Ryan, 1995; Ryan & Deci, 2002). These basic psychological needs are essential to psychological health and growth, intrinsic motivation, well-being, optimal functioning, and self-actualization (Deci & Ryan, 2000; Ryan & Deci, 2002). Increased satisfaction of the basic psychological needs of teachers correlates with more effective teaching behavior (Evelein, 2005). In sum, active use of personal strengths may positively influence teaching and learning.

Quality from Within and Multilevel Learning

The principles of positive psychology and SDT inform the new 'quality from within' approach to PD developed by Korthagen and Vasalos (2008). This approach uses the qualities, commitment and inspiration that teachers (and students) already possess to promote further development. Fredrickson (2002) calls this the *broaden-and-build model*, which implies an extension of what already exists.

The principles of multilevel learning (MLL) used for PD (described by Korthagen & Vasalos, 2005; Meijer, Korthagen & Vasalos, 2009) accounts for the existing knowledge, qualities and motivations of teachers. It assumes that professional behavior becomes more effective and fulfilling (fulfilling the three basic psychological needs) when it connects to the deeper gradations within a person, particularly if they are in harmony.

In the onion model (Korthagen, 2004; see Figure 7.1) we distinguish six such layers: (a) environment, (b) behavior, (c) competencies, (d) beliefs, (e) identity and (f) personal mission (or spirituality). This sixth level represents personal ideals. Figure 7.1 questions are formulated to clarify each stratum. The center of the model represents 'core' qualities assumed to be located with each layer and influencing the inner layers.

We illustrate how the layers of the onion model play a role in teaching: Teacher Jennifer teaches fourth grade (*environment*). She sees herself (*identity*) as a 'guiding' teacher who supports children to develop themselves and teaches them how to learn. She feels she contributes to the world by developing children for becoming self-reliant adults (*mission*). She believes it important to help children find and assess their own answers to questions (*belief*). Therefore, she develops her skills to guide her students through the learning process (*competencies*), applying her qualities of patience and trust (*core qualities*). This example demonstrates the harmony among the levels, an *alignment* of the strata.

MLL promotes a harmonious connection between the outer and the inner layers of the onion model, namely, between the layers within the person and the external environment. Ryan and Deci (2002; Deci &

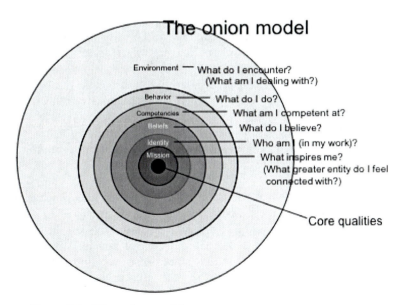

Figure 7.1   The onion model.

Ryan, 2000) call this interaction between a person and the environment a *positive organic-dialogical process* resulting in a high degree of fulfillment of the three psychological needs. The person's effective response to the demands of the situation (environment) is, simultaneously, personally fulfilling (person).

Making people aware of the inner layers of identity and mission promotes cognizance of their ideals and core qualities. If the outer layers conflict with the inner layers, disharmony (or no alignment) results. In our example, Jennifer quickly telling a student the right answer to a question (*behavior*) would contradict her mission to assist students to become self-reliant adults.

Recent empirical studies suggest that awareness of the different layers and especially alignment between those layers is important for education. Meijer et al. (2009) followed one novice teacher during seven lessons using the principles of MLL. The study describes both teacher growth and the supervisor's interventions, quoting from interactive dialogues, logbooks and interviews. We found the teacher became and felt more effective and more fully present as a teacher. The teacher's learning process as an integration of the personal and the professional were identified.

Hoekstra and Korthagen (in press) describe a study addressing if and how MLL-based supervision affects teacher learning. In a longitudinal mixed-method study, they documented the learning of one teacher over 2 years. In the first year she had no systemic support, but nevertheless was required to implement an educational innovation. During the second year, she received individual supervision based on MLL. She became aware of beliefs and patterns that previously inhibited her ability to change. The new knowledge precipitated significant changes in her learning, beliefs and classroom behavior. The findings suggest that MLL-based support can help teachers deal more effectively and personally in the learning process.

The 'quality from within' approach also involves methods called *core reflection*, based on the following key principles (Meijer et al., 2009):

1. promoting awareness of ideals and core qualities related to the situation reflected on, to strengthen awareness of identity and mission
2. identifying internal obstacles to acting out the ideals and core qualities
3. promoting awareness of the cognitive, emotional and motivational aspects embedded in ideals, core qualities and obstacles
4. promoting awareness (cognitively and emotionally) of the friction between 1 and 2, and the self-created nature of internal obstacles
5. developing trust in the process that comes from within the person
6. supporting inner potential within the situation under reflection
7. developing autonomy in using core reflection

In sum, essentially, core reflection develops awareness of core qualities, supports acting on these qualities and overcomes obstacles hindering the process.

Finally, the 'quality from within' as an innovative approach for PD begins with teachers' qualities, potential and inspiration. Teacher support provides models for transition to support their students. The 'quality from within' approach does not aim at a specific teaching outcome. If teachers connect with their inner strengths and inspiration and strive to apply that to their students, they construct personal approaches to effective and meaningful education.

CONTEXT OF THE STUDY

A variety of Dutch schools, departments of teacher education and other educational organizations have adopted the 'quality from within' approach. In this study, we examine implementation in six primary schools between June 2008 and June 2009. The project aimed to improve the quality already present in the schools in teachers, students and school principals. Hence, we aimed to begin by developing teachers' awareness of the qualities, potential and motivation. They learned to engage their core qualities in (self) reflection and coaching and reflected on their pedagogical view of the new methodology. We hypothesized that teachers would become better facilitators of student and peer learning. To achieve these goals, we applied an intervention in each school:

1. Building on the Needs and Concerns of the Participants

Three group meetings (1 day each) involved pedagogical approaches based on 'realistic teacher education' (Korthagen, Kessels, Koster, Lagerwerf & Wubbels, 2001). Problems encountered by the teachers in their work became the starting point for learning (as in MLL).

2. Practicing in Authentic Situations

Teachers practiced MLL methods in their classrooms with students. To increase their learning, classroom practice included coaching by trainers. Sometimes students attended group meetings or coaches joined the teachers in the classroom.

3. Promoting Individual Reflection

To achieve deep learning, we encouraged participants to write personal reflections, e.g., on problems arising in their work with students or colleagues, ideals and beliefs, core qualities and/or obstacles they faced.

4. Enhancing Transfer

To enhance transfer of new knowledge, teacher participants were encouraged to apply the new insights and practiced inter-collegial coaching in pairs and kept reflective logs. They emailed the reflections to trainers and the group. They also read several Dutch articles on MLL methods practiced in the group meetings. In addition, a developmental group was installed, which consists of two up to five teachers. Its aim was to monitor, guide and support the development within the school.

5. Promoting Reflection on the Team and School Level

Learning in school occurs both individually and socially. School principals, remedial teachers and student teachers joined the other teachers so that all school members participated in a whole-school learning process.

All participants in the school reflected on their educational identity and mission. Through connecting individual to group qualities, teachers discovered important elements of the deeper layers of school identity and mission. Essentially, this process provided a common language to support team discussions on the relationship between theory, vision and practice, as well as deepen individual teacher reflection on practice.

Moreover, making the innovation public—for example, by organizing an informative meeting for parents, other schools or educational institutions, the educational inspectorate and/or the local press—enabled a more complex, layered definition of the school's educational identity.

In sum, the project consists of school-based coaching, teaching and learning in classrooms and with colleagues. To fully understand the intervention, trainers must be experienced teacher trainers specifically equipped to guide the learning process on core reflection and MLL (see Korthagen & Vasalos, 2008).

METHOD

Design

This study followed six primary schools implementing the 'quality from within' approach over a period of 17 months. A mixed-method design allowed for triangulation and complementarity (Johnson & Onwuegbuzie, 2004). Figure 7.2 illustrates the timing of the meetings and data collection. Our particular focus is on the results of questionnaires at the moments Q1 and Q2 (N = 61), the first set of interviews (I1: N = 24) and the second (I2: N = 20). In addition, to capture the more longitudinal effects of the intervention, we report on the data of a third interview

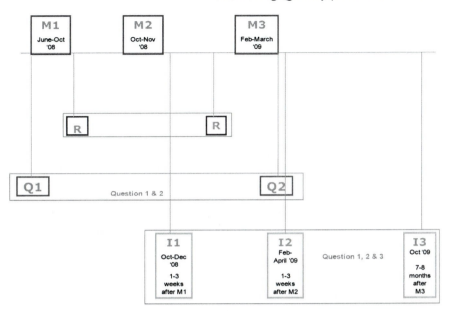

Figure 7.2   Timeline of the intervention and data collection period.

round (I3: N = 14). Unfortunately, given the ending of the training and the summer holiday, not all of the original participants could be interviewed for the third round.

Participants

Participants consisted of 61 primary school teachers from six schools located in six different, small to middle-size cities (three in the East and three in central Netherlands). The schools ranged from small (one school with five teachers) to large schools (30 teachers and two locations). Teachers taught from kindergarten through Grade 6. Teaching experience ranged from novices to teachers with 25 or more years of experience. We also interviewed 24 of the teachers in round 1, 20 in round 2 and 14 in round 3. They came from four schools (two in the East and two in central Netherlands). The first interview included 5 male and 19 female teachers.

The second interviews (within 3 weeks after the workshop period ended) also included school principals. We asked their views on (a) the development of the school during the project and (b) the essential characteristics of the intervention that made this development possible.

Data Collection

Four instruments are described in the following.

Questionnaire on Perception of Work

To measure what participants perceived as outcomes and whether they perceived themselves improved their facilitation of student and colleague learning, they responded to a questionnaire to indicate how they perceived (themselves within) their work, before and immediately after the project. The questionnaire measured the fulfillment of basic psychological needs. Based on a pilot study carried out in 2007, the questionnaire consisted of four subscales: (a) fulfillment of the basic psychological need for *competence*, (b) fulfillment of the basic psychological need for *relatedness*, (c) fulfillment of the basic psychological need for *autonomy* and (d) self-efficacy regarding the principles of coaching central to the 'quality from within' approach.

The first three scales derive from a study by Evelein (2005), who presented evidence of the validity and reliability of these scales. The fourth scale measures the teachers' self-perception of their own coaching competencies illustrating the 'quality from within' approach. Representative examples are:

Participants scored items on a 7-point Likert scale ranging from (1) *not true at all* to (7) *very true*. We present Cronbach's alphas of the scales for the first measurement moment (Q1) in Table 7.2.

All participating teachers (93) of the six schools filled out the questionnaire. Some teachers were unable to fill out both questionnaires because of

Table 7.1   Scales and Representative Items of the Questionnaire on Perception of Work

Variable	Example item
Need for autonomy	• I feel free at work to come up with my ideas and opinions • I feel I can decide for myself how I do my work • In my work I have to do what I am told (negative item)
Need for competence	• The people at work tell me I am good at what I do • I feel I am able to cope with my work • I feel little competence in my work (negative item)
Need for relatedness	• My colleagues are friendly towards me • I feel I have a bond with my colleagues • There are few colleagues who are close to me (negative item)
Self-efficacy in coaching students and colleagues by means of core reflection and MLL	• I feel competent in in-depth coaching • I can help people to express their personal qualities • When I coach other people I can deal with personal aspects

Table 7.2   Cronbach's Alphas of the Scales of the Questionnaire on Perception of Work

Scale	Number of items	Cronbach's alpha
Autonomy	8	.75
Competence	6	.67
Relatedness	8	.70
Self-efficacy in coaching	10	.88

illness, for example, or they had left the school. We excluded these teacher questionnaires from the data, resulting in a final sample size of 61 teachers representing six schools.

Reflective Reports

Reflective reports provided insight into what the participants perceived as the outcomes of the projects. They wrote reflective reports twice: Between the first two workshop days and between the second and last workshop day, focusing on what inspired them in the workshop, how the experience would affect their daily practice and on what supported and hindered their learning. The teachers sent their reports to the trainers and to their colleagues.

Semi-Structured Interviews

We conducted semi-structured interviews to study the teachers' experiences in depth. These interviews also focused on the (learning) outcomes of the project for the participants and what stimulated or hindered these outcomes. The interviews followed a detailed guideline probing the research questions through such subquestions as:

- What personal outcomes resulted from your participation?
- Do you notice any changes in the students?
- What aspects of the project influenced and determined the outcomes?
- What aspects hindered the outcomes?

We interviewed a subsample of six teachers at four schools: (a) halfway through the workshop period, (b) within 3 weeks after it ended and (c) approximately 7 to 8 months after it had ended. Based on their reflective reports, we found varied categories of teachers: The teachers represented several categories:

A. very enthusiastic about the project and seemed to learn a lot
B. slightly positive about the project and seemed to learn a few things

C. not enthusiastic about the project and seemed to learn little

D. Did not write a reflective report (hence we did not know to which of the first three groups they belong)

Two teachers from category A, C and D were selected randomly. In one school no teachers fell in category D, so we chose them from categories A and C. The teachers not interviewed belonged primarily to categories A and B.

Intervention Report

We asked the trainers in each school to identify (a) the characteristics of the specific intervention, (b) their opinion about the development and (c) their opinion about what was essential in the intervention to make this development possible. These data provided background information to help us interpret the results.

Data Analysis

Analysis of the Questionnaire

For the quantitative analysis we selected a pre-posttest design. Respondents included 61 teachers at six schools (i.e., observations [N = 122], nested within teachers [N = 61], nested within six schools [N = 6]). We included teachers for whom we had both a pretest and a posttest score. To assess whether the participants of the 'quality from within' projects showed an increase in the fulfillment of the three basic psychological needs and/or an increase in their perceived capacity to facilitate colleague and student learning a multifactor analysis of variance was computed (Bickel, 2007). We were interested in a fixed effect (of time) but had to take other effects into account too (e.g., it was possible that some teachers or schools performed better than others right from the beginning or that teachers within one school were more alike than teachers in other schools). Therefore, we tested multiple models and the best fit proved to be the model in which the random intercept was chosen at the teacher level. We discovered a school-effect for the autonomy scale only, although not significant. Therefore the results can be interpreted as effects of the group of teachers.

Analysis of the Interviews

The analysis of the interviews followed a grounded theory approach (Strauss & Corbin, 1998). First, four interviews were transcribed (two from category A and two from category C). From these transcripts, we discussed and developed categories for scoring the answers. The part of the interviews focused on the outcomes of the 'quality from within' approach (research questions 1 and 2) followed the quality from within onion model. To reduce the data into meaningful categories and with sufficiently high numbers per

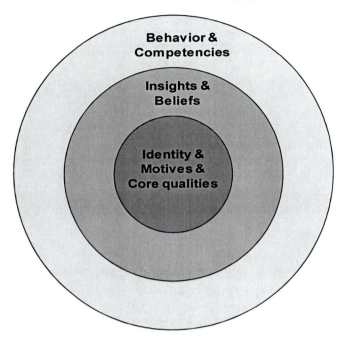

Figure 7.3 The simplified onion model.

category, we condensed the six layers of the model into three layers, by combining adjacent levels into one scoring category (Figure 7.3).

With the aid of the final scoring model, the lead researcher and two research assistants independently analyzed two interviews. Upon comparison, they agreed in most of the cases. Where interpretations differed, discussions led to an agreement that the findings of the primary researcher were valid.

FINDINGS

In the following sections we first report on the results as measured before and immediately after the intervention. In last section of the findings, we describe the longitudinal effects of the 'quality from within' approach.

Quantitative data: Outcomes of the 'Quality from Qithin' Project on the Fulfillment of the Basic Psychological Needs and on Self-efficacy in Coaching

For the whole group of teachers, the scores on the scales Autonomy and Self-Efficacy in coaching increased between the pretest and posttest ($p < 0.01$), a small but statistically significant effect (R^2 is .06 and .04, respectively). On the other scales the increase was not significant (see Table 7.3 and Figure 7.4).

Table 7.3   Means on the Pretest and Posttest for the Scales of the Questionnaire

Subscale	Pretest		Posttest		Time		
	Mean	SD	Mean	SD	b	se	P
Autonomy	5.11	.87	5.39	.71	.275	.08	.001**
Competence	5.64	.74	5.75	.71	.116	.08	.159
Relatedness	5.51	.71	5.63	.58	.117	.07	.114
Self-efficacy in coaching	4.74	.89	4.96	.78	.231	.08	.006**

(** p < 0.01)

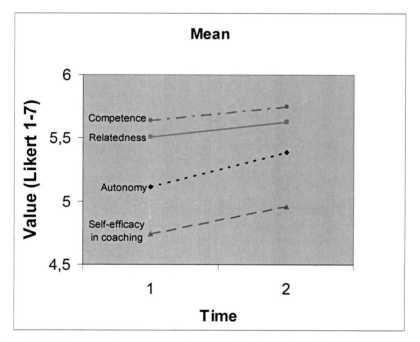

Figure 7.4   Means on the pretest and posttest for the scales of the questionnaire.

Qualitative data: Outcomes of the Quality from Within Project, as Reported in the Interviews

In the following sections, we report the qualitative results of the study. First, we describe the outcomes that the teachers perceive as important for themselves as teachers and/or as persons. Second, we report on the onion layers related to the learning outcomes and discuss individual differences. Finally, we present outcomes the teachers perceived as important for others.

Outcomes at the Individual Level

Table 7.4 summarizes teachers' perceptions of personal outcomes of the project. Percentages show the total of teachers who mentioned these outcomes. The table displays only outcomes mentioned by more than 50% of the participants in at least one interview round. This ensured the data was representative for all participants.

Table 7.4 Teachers' Perceptions of Personal Outcomes of the Project

Perceived outcomes	Illustrative example	I1(N = 24)	I2(N = 20)
Behavior and competencies			
Increased coaching skills (regarding coaching of students and colleagues); stronger focus on the emotional and motivational side of learning; let the other person find the solution, more structured coaching.	"I ask the children more about how they feel, and what they think. I have noticed that the children are then able to come up with their own solutions." "In coaching colleagues I pay more attention to the limiting beliefs teachers have about the students."	75%	85%
Feedback on core qualities (to students, colleagues, parents).	"I give more and more conscious feedback on core qualities."	63%	55%
Increased awareness of certain coaching skills.	"I became aware of the difference between giving a compliment and giving feedback on core qualities."	58%	45%
Insights and beliefs			
New and/or renewed insights and ideas about learning.	"One learns from positive feedback." "It is more useful to help someone find his own solution than presenting him with the solution."	75%	80%
Identity, motives and core qualities			
Increased awareness of one's own motives.	"I want to contribute to the well-being of the children." "I want the children to learn how to solve their own problems, so that they become self-reliant and autonomous."	71%	30%

(continued)

Table 7.4   (continued)

Perceived outcomes	Illustrative example	I1(N = 24)	I2(N = 20)
Identity, motives and core qualities (continued)			
Increased awareness of one's own professional identity.	"I feel there is more appreciation for me, that my experience really matters."	54%	55%
Increased awareness of one's own core qualities, like commitment, care, calmness, enthusiasm, honesty.	"I now have tools for looking completely differently at myself and a situation . . . more positively. That can give a complete shift. Instead of thinking 'ah, I am so busy' and feeling irritated, I now decide consciously to get in touch with my quality of care, and I decide to look at the positive side of the situation . . . In this way I see much more, and I feel a much lighter kind of energy."	63%	70%

Table 7.4 reveals that the reported outcomes of the 'quality from within' approach are rather similar for the first and second measurements. An exception is the category 'increased awareness of one's own motives.' In addition, Table 7.4 demonstrates that interviewees most frequently mentioned a perceived increase in coaching skills as an important outcome of the project.

Multilevel Learning

As described in the method section, we condensed the onion model into three levels by combining adjacent layers (see Figure 7.3). The three resulting levels are: (a) behavior and competencies, (b) insights and beliefs and (c) identity, motives and core qualities.

Table 7.5 shows the percentage of participants that mentioned outcomes at one, two or three of these levels for each interview round.

Table 7.5   Number of Levels on which Outcomes Were Reported

Levels of the reported outcomes	I1 (N = 24)	I2 (N = 20)
Three levels	75%	70%
Two levels	12.5%	25%
One level	12.5%	5%

Table 7.5 demonstrates that the teachers reported more two- and three-level learning at the second measurement. We noticed that all but one of the 14 participants interviewed three times (93%) mentioned individual outcomes at three levels in at least one interview round. This suggests that participating in the project resulted in MLL for the teachers.

Individual Differences in the Outcomes

When we analyzed the data, we found striking differences between the enthusiastic and less enthusiastic teachers. These differences seem to relate to their attitude towards learning in general. If they had an open, learning-oriented attitude, they were more enthusiastic about the project and seemed to learn more. Those with a less open attitude seemed to 'close up' from the beginning, although the positive experiences and enthusiasm of colleagues eventually and almost always influenced these less enthusiastic teachers. Sometimes, however, the profile was mixed, as with the example of a teacher who became more positive but maintained the conviction that, due to her many years of experience, the content of the project had little to offer her.

Outcomes Regarding Others: The Students, The Team and The School Principals

Table 7.6 shows that more than half of the teachers in at least one interview cited the most important perceived outcomes of the project for students, the team and the school principals:

Table 7.6   Outcomes of the Project Regarding the Students, the Team and the School Principals

Perceived outcomes	Illustrative example	I1 (N = 24)	I2 (N = 20)
Increased working and communicating skills and attitude of the students: better attitude towards working and learning, better group work, more independent in solving problems, more understanding of each other's feelings, giving more positive feedback to each other.	"At days that I use it [core reflection], I notice that the children are working quite well and that their attitude is much better, and their concentration as well." "They [the students] are learning more with and from each other." "The children are more motivated when it comes out of themselves, if it was their own idea or discovery . . . Then things are bubbling, and there is enthusiasm. (. . .) Autonomy is very important for students, if they see: this is my learning process." "If you mention such a core quality, then you see the children grow, they look proud, and their eyes start to shine, so they find it really cool. (. . .) Then you see that they feel good for the rest of the morning or afternoon."	67%	60%

(continued)

Table 7.6   (continued)

Perceived outcomes	Illustrative example	I1 (N = 24)	I2 (N = 20)
	"I believe that this positive approach will lead to better learning outcomes, because if they get this trust they will also use it."	67%	60%
Teachers experience more openness, safety and a deeper connected-ness in school.	"The barrier to be open to each other really diminished. We are also taking more time for each other. I find that very positive. (. . . .) Suppose you have a problem with something, then it will not be seen as your fault; you keep your own value." "We listen more to each other, and more often people say what they think of something."	75%	65%
Better management and coaching skills of the school principals.	"The principal asks and shares a lot about core reflection and about her ideals. That helps. (. . . .) And when I had a problem and talked to her about it during a break, she immediately worked it out with me through core reflection. (. . .) After 5 minutes I was ready and knew how to solve it. That was nice!" "The principal is much more decisive."	50%	45%

Table 7.6 demonstrates that similar to the personal outcomes, reported outcomes with respect to 'others' vary little between the first and second measurements.

Qualitative Data: Aspects of Stimulus and Obstruction

Aspects that Motivated the Outcomes

In Table 7.7 we summarize those aspects of the project, with regard to content, context and the individual teachers, mentioned by more than half of the teachers in at least one interview round as stimulating the learning process and the outcomes.

Table 7.7 demonstrates some aspects that support the process and outcomes of the project, such as the project aligning with the school development and culture. The development group can play an important role by focusing attention on the project during school weeks. An open attitude is important to keep the agenda alive for teachers, especially at the start of the project.

Table 7.7 Aspects that Stimulated the Process and Outcomes

Stimulating aspects	Illustrative example	I1 (N = 24)	I2 (N = 20)
Fitting in with the school (its development, culture, methods).	"We are together as a team for two years now, and are ready for reformulating our educational identity and mission. This project can help with this."	96%	25%
Paying attention to the project during the school weeks: during staff meetings, active developmental group, peer coaching, sharing of successes, inspiring conversations with the school principal.	"The installation of a developmental group, that is active and feels responsible, helps (. . .) [a developmental group] that brings it in at staff meetings, and does exercises that you can also do in your classroom. That is the way to keep it alive!"	71%	55%
Inspiring experiences during and after the workshop.	"When we practiced [with the core reflection model], I solved my biggest problem."	71%	60%
	"Two teachers that always have problems communicating with each other started to understand each other."		
Open and active attitude towards the project and your own learning.	"I think about the project and what I want with it. And I plan conversations [with the students] in order to practice and become competent at it."	63%	25%
	"At the end of each day I try to evaluate how I used core reflection and what the effects were."		
Quality of the trainer.	"The trainer is good at clarifying things."	33%	50%
	"The trainer is very positive."		

Aspects that Hindered the Process and Outcomes

In Table 7.8 we summarize aspects of the project such as content, context and individual teachers that obstruct an optimal process and positive outcomes. Selecting a relatively high percentage of less enthusiastic teachers for the interviews gave insight into the reasons why a smaller number of teachers were less positive. Table 7.8 shows the encumbering aspects most often mentioned.

Table 7.8   Aspects that Hindered the Process and Outcomes

Hindering aspects	Illustrative example	I1 (N = 24)	I2 (N = 20)
Lack of time and busyness during work	"We are so busy with many things that I have no time to practice this."	58%	45%
Workshop was not practical enough	"The workshop was different from how it is in the class room."	42%	30%
Resistance (to the focus on personal aspects of learning and to the focus on emotions)	"I felt a lot of resistance at the start (. . . .) I found it very fuzzy, and I am a direct person. (. . .) this question of 'what do you feel about that?'—it just does not fit me. I felt very irritated."	21%	30%

Table 7.8 demonstrates some aspects that hindered the process and outcomes of the project. Lack of time and being busy were most commonly cited.

Results of the Long-Term Outcomes of the Project

Analysis of the outcomes of research in teacher development often ends when the project ends. Researchers often fail to account for the more long-term effects of a PD intervention (Desimone, 2009; Borko, 2004). In this study, we also collected more longitudinal data by interviewing the teachers 7 to 8 months after the 'quality from within' project ended (I3). Since not all teachers could participate at that time (see method section), the longitudinal outcomes of the project reflect data from 14 teachers (see Table 7.9).

Table 7.9 demonstrates that the important individual outcomes still ring true for the teachers 7 to 8 months after the project. Groups that remained active might also affect the outcomes. One outcome, remarkably, emerges more strongly (I3): 'increased awareness of certain coaching skills.' One explanation could be that after participating in the project, teachers are not only aware of the coaching skills, but also continue to use the skills and, therefore, feel more competent. For example, at I1 they reported things like "I know now that I can give feedback on core qualities, but I find it hard to practice it in the classroom." At I2 and I3 they reported actually doing this more in the classroom and therefore felt no need to report awareness.

Our earlier findings that the outcomes were mostly situated at the three (reduced) onion levels remained stable. The third measurement (I3) revealed 57% (three levels), 36% (two levels) and 7% (one level). While these results do not prove an increase in outcomes reported at three levels in general, they do show that 7 to 8 months after the project ended most outcomes reported by teachers still connect to all three levels of the onion model. As

Table 7.9   Teachers' Perceptions of Longitudinal Personal Outcomes of the Project

Perceived outcomes	I1 (N = 24)	I2 (N = 20)	I3 (N = 14)
Behavior and competencies			
Increased coaching skills (regarding coaching of students and colleagues): stronger focus on the emotional and motivational side of learning; let the other person find the solution; more structured coaching.	75%	85%	79%
Feedback on core qualities (to students, colleagues, parents).	63%	55%	71%
Increased awareness of certain coaching skills.	58%	45%	29%
Insights and beliefs			
New and/or renewed insights and ideas about learning.	75%	80%	64%
Identity, motives and core qualities			
Increased awareness of one's own motives.	71%	30%	64%
Increased awareness of one's own professional identity.	54%	55%	57%
Increased awareness of one's own core qualities, like commitment, care, calmness, enthusiasm, honesty.	63%	70%	50%

this concurs with the idea of MLL, this seems a promising result for long-term effects of the 'quality from within' approach.

In Table 7.10 we present the longitudinal outcomes of the project regarding students, the team and school principals that were mentioned by more than half of the teachers in at least one interview.

Table 7.10   Longitudinal Outcomes of the Project Regarding the Students, the Team and the School Principals

Perceived outcomes	I1(N = 24)	I2(N = 20)	I3(N = 14)
Increased working and communicating skills and attitude of the students: better attitude to working and learning; better group work; more independent problem solving; more understanding of each other's feelings; giving more positive feedback to each other.	67%	60%	71%
Teachers experience more openness, safety and a deeper contact in school.	75%	65%	64%
Better management and coaching skills of the school principals.	50%	45%	57%

Table 7.11   Examples of Longitudinal Aspects that Stimulated the Process and Outcomes that Changed over Time

Stimulating aspects	I1(N = 24)	I2(N = 20)	I3(N = 14)
Open and active attitude	63%	25%	14%
Quality of the trainer	33%	50%	14%
Fitting in with the school (its development, culture, methods)	96%	25%	36%

Table 7.10 reveals that the important outcomes for the students, the team and the school principals remain 7 to 8 months after the project ended.

The data reveals another aspect, however: 'Paying attention to the project during the school weeks' and 'inspiring experiences during and after the workshop' appear to the same degree in the three instances. At the same time, Table 7.11 shows that other aspects were mentioned considerably less at I3. This indicates these aspects were especially important at the start of the project.

Two obstructing aspects emerged to the same degree in all three instances: "Lack of time and busyness during work" and "Resistance." However, the aspect "Workshop was not practical enough" emerged considerably less at I3 (42% at I1, 30% at I2 and 7% at I3). This suggests the usefulness of the workshop for practice increased during the project.

DISCUSSION AND CONCLUDING REMARKS

This chapter presents the outcomes of the 'quality from within' approach at six primary schools in the Netherlands. Before formulating our main conclusions in this final section, we mention an important limitation of this study: The findings reported are based on participants' self-reports. Although we believe this contributes to the ecological validity of the study, the outcomes as reported by the teachers are subjective. We addressed this by using the questionnaire data in which, for example, the actual scores on the fulfillment of the basic psychological needs were self-reported, but the *changes* in these scores over time were not. Interviewing the students about their perceptions of the teachers might have been a fruitful way of gathering more objective data.

Main Outcomes

Findings indicate that many teachers in the interviews report a number of important outcomes at various levels that remain consistent over a longer time period. Given the relatively brief intervention period, this seems noteworthy, especially in light of the well-known limitations of educational innovation (see theoretical framework section). This is even more remarkable, as the subsample of the interview data contained a higher percentage of teachers relatively negative in the beginning. We found statistically significant increases in feelings of autonomy and in self-efficacy in coaching students and colleagues. Our study, therefore, indicates that this 'quality from within' approach is a successful model of PD.

Interestingly, the competence scale and the relatedness scale did not show significant effects. This might be because of the effect that when people become aware of what there is to know about a subject, they see what they don't know (as in the proverb "The more you know, the more you know that you don't know"). This might be the same for the feelings of competence and relatedness. Furthermore, with respect to competence, the questionnaire measures a general feeling of competence and not a specific coaching competence or other competence directly related to the project. This more specific coaching competence is measured by the self-efficacy in coaching scale, which did show an increase. A similar explanation could be applied to the fulfillment of the need for relatedness.

We found a number of interesting features regarding content, context and the participating teachers. Most remarkable is that in the first interview, 96% of the participants reported that the approach fit with the school (its development, culture, methods). This concurs with the central goal of the 'quality from within' approach, namely, to build from existing qualities and to promote 'quality from within.' The project succeeded in reaching this aim. The projects at the six schools started from the qualities and commitment that teachers and students already have and *their* ideals and concerns as the basis for learning new insights, skills and attitudes, and for developing more awareness of their own qualities. At the later interview, 25% and 36% of the participants only mentioned fitting in with the school. Hence, it appears this aspect is especially relevant at the start of the project.

Multilevel Learning

Since an important principle in MLL is to promote a learning process, the findings suggest that this is indeed what happened with most participants. If we look at the 14 participants that we interviewed three times, all but one (93%) mentioned individual outcomes at three levels in at least one interview. We conclude that the principle of MLL seems to have been actualized in the schools. Based on the theoretical framework described earlier, we consider this an important explanation for the outcomes of the project.

Enhanced Feelings of Autonomy in Teachers and Students

The teachers reported that they themselves and their students experienced increased feelings of autonomy. This result is interesting given the extensive theoretical framework of the SDT (Deci & Ryan, 2000); hence, we may conclude that an increase in feelings of autonomy contributes to feelings of well-being in both teachers and their students. Feelings of autonomy are highly related to the ability to cope with stress (for an overview of studies, see Schaufeli, Maslach & Marek, 1993). Lack of personal control and freedom, on the other hand, contributes to burnout. In the Netherlands, for example, 14% of those working in education complain about burnout (CBS, 2004), the highest percentage of all organizational/institutional branches. Our results may thus show an important direction for supporting teachers in their stressful profession, and for diminishing the alarming percentages of teacher burnout.

How to Make Innovations Successful?

The analysis of the data of this study yields some interesting ideas on how to make innovations more effective.

A crucial factor in the success or failure of an innovation seems to lie in an open and active learning attitude in the teachers. By comparing the stories of enthusiastic and less enthusiastic teachers, the study showed that the learning attitude of participants directly influenced how they perceived the project and on what they learned. Van Eekelen's (2005) study of "teachers' willingness to learn" as a strong indicator of their capacity for self-directed learning concurs with what we found in our study: Teachers with an open attitude directed their own professional growth and even supported others in their learning. This raises the question of how to deal with teachers not open to learning, also because they seem to negatively influence their colleagues' learning.

Van Eekelen (2005) suggests that 'problem sensitivity' affects the first stage of the development of the willingness to learn. We recognize that the basic tenet of the 'quality from within' approach, namely, to build on existing strengths, requires these teachers have awareness, not only of their core qualities, but also of aspects of their practices that could be improved. Perhaps for reluctant teachers, a more gradual approach with more time to reflect on their daily practices and identify issues is needed.

We suspect that lack of self-confidence and fear of self-criticism may explain some of the teachers' unwillingness to learn. If so, perhaps those teachers need an even safer learning environment than the approach already tries to promote through its focus on personal strengths. It is important that teachers can feel safe to talk about their work and feel secure enough for reflecting on the deeper onion layers. This aspect is both a strong feature and a possible pitfall for those teachers who do not feel secure. Hence, an intervention could start with an opportunity to show their colleagues their strengths. We are currently experimenting with a small group assignment to share a successful experience from the previous weeks' teaching and colleagues name the core qualities of the teacher who describes the experience.

Frequently, the teacher not only feels supported, but also starts to share a concern. Safety created through emphasizing strengths supports a sensitive attitude to teacher issues and problems.

Another explanation for the absence of the willingness to learn in some teachers could be their lack of familiarity with the approach, specifically with the focus on inter-human aspects, and the language used (core qualities, flow, ideals, MLL, etc.). In order to overcome this obstacle, we believe the trainers should pay more attention to the language used and could, together with the teachers, develop a common language that everybody feels familiar with.

We also found evidence that even teachers skeptical at the beginning of the project became more open towards the 'quality from within' approach after the 3-month period. It seems they change under the influence of the change and development occurring in their team. They see that other teachers apply what they learned successfully and with interesting results, and that the culture of the school begins to change along with it.

Keeping the intervention alive through active 'developmental groups' monitoring and supporting the development within the school are critical to change and success. Such groups consist of two to five teachers and ideally contain one informal leader of the school as well as an enthusiastic and less enthusiastic teacher. This group can include the project in staff meeting discussions, daily conversations among staff and keeping it on the agenda. Specific instances include: sharing successes, discussing a 'difficult' student from the 'quality from within' view, doing small exercises with the teachers that they can do with the students as well. Also key to keeping the project alive are peer coaching in between the workshop days, modeling and highlighting of the approach by a school principal and connecting ideas from the project with other developments in school (e.g., student assessments). This directs the focus to what already exists, helps the participants make their views more explicit and uses it as the basis for further development. This supports research indicating that learning processes at the individual and the organizational level start to 'flow' much more smoothly as soon as people feel that their strengths are valued and taken seriously (cf. Day, 1999; Elliot, 1991).

On this matter, we wish to be very precise. Although the approach does not start from an *a priori* view of the change needed, it does build on expert knowledge about change, especially on notions from positive psychology and the theory of MLL. Trainers make these notions explicit during the workshop. In our experience, considerable training of the trainers is needed to make the approach effective. This is especially so as the approach radically departs from traditional models of PD; it is not a predetermined type of learning considered 'better' by experts. On the contrary, the approach equates innovation with *PD from within*, i.e., grounded in each participant's inner potential. In this view of innovation, teachers are not *being* developed in a specific direction, but *develop themselves* along self-chosen directions.

The study revealed that during this process, teachers become more aware of their own strengths and those of their colleagues and students, and more autonomous in their work. School quality stands to improve when it continuously nurtures and is nurtured by teachers' increased awareness of their inner qualities and ideals and a stronger enactment of these qualities and ideals in their work. In conclusion, it seems that the 'quality from within' approach to innovation offers a promising alternative.

NOTES

The research reported on in this chapter has been made possible thanks to external funding from Q*Primair and marCanT Foundation.

ACKNOWLEDGMENTS

The authors wish to thank all the teachers, school principals, teacher educators and trainers participating in the 'quality from within' project for their contributions to this study. Special thanks go to Janny Wolters (Q*Primair) and Mart Haitjema (chair of the school board of marCanT Foundation) for their generous support of our research. The authors are grateful to Judith Schoonenboom, Jolijn Serto and Lumine van Uden for supporting us in the data analysis.

REFERENCES

Almaas, A. H. (1986). Essence: The diamond approach to inner realization. York Beach: Samuel Weiser.
Baumeister, R., & Leary, M. R. (1995). The need to belong: Desire for interpersonal attachments as a fundamental human motivation. *Psychological Bulletin, 117*, 497–529.
Bickel, R. (2007). *Multilevel analysis for applied research: It's just regression.* New York: Guilford Press.
Borko, H. (2004). Professional development and teacher learning: Mapping the terrain. *Educational Researcher, 33*(8), 3–15.
CBS (2004). *Burnout en psychische belasting* [Burnout and physical load]. Retrieved January 5, 2011, from http://www.cbs.nl/nl-NL/menu/themas/gezondheid-welzijn/publicaties/artikelen/archief/2005/2005–1738–wm.htm
Cochran-Smith, M., & Zeichner, K. M. (Eds.). (2005). *Studying teacher education: The report of the Panel on Research and Teacher Education.* Washington, DC: American Educational Research Association.
Day, C. (1999). Developing teachers: The challenges of lifelong learning. London: Falmer Press.
Deci, E. L., & Ryan, R. M. (2000). The "what" and "why" of goal pursuits: Human needs and the self-determination of behavior. *Psychological Inquiry, 11*(4), 227–268.

Desimone, L.M. (2009). Improving impact studies of teachers' professional development: Toward better conceptualizations and measures. *Educational Researcher, 38*(3), 181–199.

Elliot, J. (1991). *Action research for educational change.* Buckingham: Open University Press.

Evelein, F. G. (2005). *Psychologische basisbehoeften van docenten in opleiding: Een onderzoek naar het verband tussen de basisbehoeftevervulling van docenten-in-opleiding, hun interpersoonlijk functioneren en de inzet van kernkwaliteiten* [Basic psychological needs of student teachers: A study on the relation between the fulfillment of basic psychological needs of student teachers, their interpersonal behavior and character strengths]. PhD thesis, Utrecht, IVLOS.

Fredrickson, B. L. (2002). Positive emotions. In C. R. Snyder & S. J. Lopez (Eds.), *Handbook of positive psychology* (pp. 120–134). Oxford: Oxford University Press.

Hamachek, D. (1999). Effective teachers: What they do, how they do it, and the importance of self-knowledge. In R. P. Lipka & T. M. Brinthaupt (Eds.), *The role of self in teacher development* (pp. 189–224). Albany: State University of New York Press.

Hargreaves, A., Lieberman, A., Fullan, M. & Hopkins, D. (Eds.). (1998). *International handbook of educational change.* Dordrecht: Kluwer.

Hodgins, H. S., Koestner, R. & Duncan, N. (1996). On the compatibility of autonomy and relatedness. *Personality and Social Psychology Bulletin, 22*(3), 227–237.

Hoekstra, A., & Korthagen, F. A. J. (in press). Teacher learning in a context of educational change: Informal learning versus systematic support. *Journal of Teacher Education.*

Holmes, M. (1998). Change and tradition in education: The loss of community. In A. Hargreaves, A. Lieberman, M. Fullan & D. Hopkins (Eds.), *International handbook of educational change* (pp. 558–575). Dordrecht: Kluwer.

Johnson, R. B., & Onwuegbuzie, A. J. (2004). Mixed method research: A research paradigm whose time has come. *Educational Researcher, 33,* 14–26.

Korthagen, F. A .J. (2004). In search of the essence of a good teacher: Towards a more holistic approach in teacher education. *Teaching and Teacher Education, 20*(1), 77–97.

Korthagen, F. A. J. (2007). The gap between research and practice revisited. *Educational Research and Evaluation, 13*(3), 303–310.

Korthagen, F. A. J., Kessels, J., Koster, B., Lagerwerf, B. & Wubbels, T. (2001). *Linking practice and theory: The pedagogy of realistic teacher education.* Mahwah, NJ: Lawrence Erlbaum Associates.

Korthagen, F. A. J., & Vasalos, A. (2005). Levels in reflection: Core reflection as a means to enhance professional development. *Teachers and Teaching: Theory and Practice, 11*(1), 47–71.

Korthagen, F. A. J., & Vasalos, A. (2008). *'Quality from within' as the key to professional development.* Paper presented at the Annual Meeting of the American Educational Research Association, New York.

Meijer, P., Korthagen, F.A.J. & Vasalos, A. (2009). Supporting presence in teacher education: The connection between the personal and professional aspects of teaching. *Teaching and Teacher Education, 25*(2), 297–308.

Ofman, D. (2000). *Core qualities: A gateway to human resources.* Schiedam: Scriptum.

Ryan, R. M. (1995). Psychological needs and the facilitation of integrative processes. *Journal of Personality, 63*(3), 397–427.

Ryan, R. M., & Deci, E. L. (2002). Overview of self-determination theory: An organismic dialectical perspective. In E. L. Deci & R. M. Ryan (Eds.), *Handbook of self-determination research* (pp. 3–33). Rochester: University of Rochester Press.

Schaufeli, W.B., Maslach, C. & Marek, T. (Eds.). (1993). *Professional burnout: Recent developments in theory and research.* Washington, DC: Taylor and Francis.

Schön, D. A. (1987). *Educating the reflective practitioner.* San Francisco, CA: Jossey-Bass.

Seligman, M. E. P., & Csikszentmihalyi, M. (2000). Positive psychology: An introduction. *American Psychologist, 55*(1), 5–14.

Strauss, A.L., & Corbin, J. (1998). *Basics of qualitative research: Techniques and procedures for developing grounded theory.* Thousand Oaks, CA: Sage Publications.

Tickle, L. (1999). Teacher self-appraisal and appraisal of self. In R. P. Lipka & T. M. Brinthaupt (Eds.), *The role of self in teacher development* (pp. 121–141). Albany: State University of New York Press.

Van Eekelen, I. M. (2005), *Teachers' will and way to learn: Studies on how teachers learn and their willingness to do so.* PhD thesis. Maastricht, Universiteit Maastricht.

8 Critical Moments as Heuristics to Transform Learning and Teacher Identity

Paulien C. Meijer and Helma W. Oolbekkink

INTRODUCTION

In examining teacher learning that matters, identity and teacher change, this chapter focuses on learning theorists like Knud Illeris (e.g., 2009) who see significant learning, expansive learning, transitional or transformative learning as the most profound type of learning. This type of learning involves personality changes. In this chapter we use the term *transformative learning*, which directly relates to identity learning and was introduced and described extensively by Mezirow (e.g., 1978, 1990, 2009). Illeris (2009) observed:

> This learning implies what could be termed personality changes . . . a break of orientation that typically occurs as the result of a crisis-like situation caused by challenges experienced as urgent and unavoidable, making it necessary to change oneself in order to get any further. Transformative learning is thus profound and extensive, it demands a lot of mental energy and when accomplished it can often be experienced physically, typically as a feeling of relief or relaxation. (p. 14)

This type of learning can be seen as a supplement to the more everyday learning described by, for example, Piaget (1952) as (cumulative) assimilative and accommodative learning. It does not happen often and, indeed, *should* not happen often, because of the energy required. In the research literature, many examples of this type of learning can be found with novice teachers (e.g., Veenman, 1984; Brock & Grady, 1997) where the relevance is acknowledged. For example, Beauchamp and Thomas (2009) wrote:

> Clearly, student teachers must undergo a shift in identity as they move through programs of teacher education and assume positions in today's challenging school contexts. In addition, further identity shifts may occur throughout a teacher's career as a result of interactions within schools and in broader communities. (p. 175)

Most research of this type of learning focuses on students or novice teachers. Some research, however, provides examples among experienced teachers who develop into experts, or who experience professional burnout and even leave the profession (e.g., Fessler & Christensen, 1992; Huberman, 1993; Troman & Woods, 2009).

In this chapter we review the literature, illustrate what this type of learning looks like for experienced teachers and develop ideas about how transformative learning might be supported so that it will lead to a source of extensive and positive professional development (PD) for this group of teachers.

ABOUT TEACHER PROFESSIONALIZATION

For many years, traditional forms of teacher professionalization started with ideas about what teachers should learn with respect to changes in curriculum or other types of national or school policies and innovations (for an overview, see Imants & van Veen, 2010). The assumption was that if teachers know what to do or change their knowledge and beliefs, they would change their practice and, by implication, impact students' learning. Clarke and Hollingsworth (2002) called this the *implicit* model of teachers' PD.

Currently, professionalization of teachers is increasingly based on research about how experienced teachers learn best. Many studies indicate that PD should begin with the teachers' own ideas, knowledge and beliefs, and that their learning should have a strong link to their teaching practice (see, e.g., Hoekstra, Beijaard, Brekelmans & Korthagen, 2007). Authentic learning, then, begins from teachers' questions (e.g., Mitchell, Reilly & Logue, 2009) and takes place in close collaboration with colleagues (e.g., Meirink, Meijer, Verloop & Bergen, 2009).

Still, in many instances, experienced teachers are expected to learn in ways that have proven less effective than expected (Mitchell et al., 2009) and that mainly entail implementing ideas developed by others, often outside the teaching community. These types of professionalization are typified by a view on learning that might be labeled assimilative or accommodative learning (Piaget, 1952; Illeris, 2009). Assimilative learning means to add a new element (knowledge, skill, etc.) linked to an existing scheme, pattern or personal theory. In accommodative learning, also called transcendent learning, (parts of) an existing scheme or theory are broken down and transformed so that the new information, situation or skill can be incorporated (cf. Illeris, 2009).

However, society expects teachers to change in ways that are not automatically covered by these types of learning. Teachers are expected to develop different roles as teachers: They are no longer primarily teaching their subject; in addition they are expected to facilitate the learning process of their students. For most teachers, this entailed a major change in how they related to their profession. Professionalization initiatives, however, focused on the development of new skills that were necessary for the new roles, but teachers felt betrayed and ignored, and many PD courses failed (cf. Lieberman & Pointer Mace, 2008). Kooy describes this situation as a "complex conundrum":

> Change and reform initiatives focus on change in learning experiences for students, but, if the current one-shot workshop model persists, reforms will stay as policy or program and effective expressions of practice will continue to elude. (2009, p. 6)

Doubts about the effects of the types of PD that focused on acquiring new knowledge and skills led to the development of other types of professionalization, at first mainly in the United States, the United Kingdom and Australia. For example, Henson (2001) wrote:

> educators and researchers are now attempting to fundamentally alter methods of teacher professional development so that teachers assume control of classroom decisions and actively assume participation in their own instructional improvement on an ongoing basis. (p. 819)

Examples of these new types of professionalization are peer coaching (e.g., Zwart, Wubbels, Bergen & Bolhuis, 2007), (collaborative) teacher research (e.g., Mitchell et al., 2009; Meijer, Meirink, Lockhorst & Oolbekkink-Marchand, 2010), book clubs/dialogic learning communities (Kooy, 2009) and courses that focus on (regaining) the passion for teaching (e.g., Day, 2004). One main characteristic of these newer types of teacher professionalization is that they include a focus on teachers' professional identity, and that learning is viewed in multiple ways, including identity learning, expansive learning, dialogical learning or transformative learning. We will elaborate on the issues of identity and transformative learning in the next two sections.

IDENTITY DEVELOPMENT IN TEACHERS

Teacher identity is an issue of growing interest regarding the increasing amount of publications in this area. The first publications on teacher identity focused mainly on the various aspects of the concept. In their review, Beijaard, Meijer and Verloop (2004) summarized the features of professional identity and found, among other things, that professional identity is an ongoing process of interpretation and reinterpretation of experiences. And much recent research also focused more on the formation and development of teacher identity (e.g., Alsup, 2006; Danielewicz, 2001; Meijer, Korthagen & Vasalos, 2009). According to Rodgers and Scott (2008), conceptions of identity share the following four basic assumptions:

- Identity is dependent upon and formed within multiple contexts.
- Identity is formed in relationship with others and involves emotions.
- Identity is shifting, unstable and multiple.
- Identity involves the construction and reconstruction of meaning through stories over time.

While experienced teachers may perceive their professional identities as stable, these theoretical notions suggest that it is an ongoing process that can involve both subtle and sudden changes in teachers' professional identity. It requires teachers to make a shift in their thinking about themselves as teachers. How these shifts occur and what is necessary for teachers to make these shifts is an interesting question. Rodgers and Scott found that most studies about teacher identity were theoretical in nature and that empirical studies were rather scarce. Meijer (in press) indicated that "one of the reasons for this might be the absence of links between literature on teacher identity and the type of learning that is required for identity shifts to occur."

In this chapter we want to focus on these changes or shifts that can be viewed as an indication of transformative learning. This kind of learning refers to identity shifts or personality changes as a reaction to what Illeris (2009) calls "crisis-like situations."

TRANSFORMATIVE LEARNING AND THE ROLE OF CRISIS

It was Mezirow who introduced the concept of transformative learning in 1978. And he and his followers found that these ideas were universal. Mezirow defined transformative learning as "the process by which we transform problematic frames of reference—sets of assumptions and expectations—to make them more inclusive, discriminating, open, reflective and emotionally able to change" (2009, p. 92). He described several "universal dimensions" of adult understanding and adult learning, some of them being of particular interest for teacher professionalization. For example, he found that adults engage in reflective discourse to assess the reasons and assumptions supporting a belief to be able to arrive at a tentative best judgment and are able to transform their frames of reference through critical reflection on assumptions, self-reflection on assumptions and dialogical reasoning when the beliefs and understandings they generate become problematic. In his review of empirical studies using transformative learning theory, Taylor (2007) concluded that this research focuses both on the fostering of transformative learning and the complex nature of critical reflection.

Looking at the process of transformative learning, one sees that *crisis* plays an eminent role in this (cf. Meijer, in press). This process seems to affect everyone, in most cultures, after major life events. A crisis can be described as a crucial or decisive point or situation; a turning point. Seeger,

Sellnow and Ulmer (1998, p. 236) described crises as "specific, unexpected, and non-routine events or series of events that [create] high levels of uncertainty and threat or perceived threat to a person's high priority goals." They view crisis as having four defining characteristics. First, that it is unexpected (i.e., a surprise); second, that it creates uncertainty; third, that it is seen as a threat to important goals; and fourth, that it involves a need for change. They argue that a crisis is a process of transformation where the old system can no longer be maintained.

Adams, Hayes and Hopson (1976) studied for many years how people deal with life changes, and in 1976 they described several features of what they called the 'transition cycle.' Transition is the way people respond to change over time (Kralik, Visentin & van Loon, 2006). People undergo transition when they need to adapt to new situations or circumstances in order to incorporate the change event into their lives. Severe changes in profession or job are such change events. Adams et al.'s transition cycle shows how a 'crisis' is related to change or a life event and, according to Williams (1999), may reflect an ancient and sophisticated mechanism for the fundamental evolutionary task of coping with change. In general, a career change or a change of role can be seen (at least at first) as a positive event, and, according to the transition cycle, an excitement phase can be expected, then a honeymoon phase, followed by a phase of inner contradictions in which people feel uncertain, have loose confidence and can become confused and depressed. Then, a few months after the change, people can feel an inner crisis. From that point on, there are basically four potential pathways, of which the upper pathway leads to new confidence and transformation. Williams (1999, p. 5) writes about this pathway as follows:

> There can be a rapid, spontaneous breakout from the crisis phase—a defining moment or catharsis that triggers this process. Once begun the restructuring or recovery process can occur within a few weeks. It liberates creativity, confidence, optimism, a search for new meanings and a Gestalt type quest for a fully integrated view of the new reality. To see a person transforming their life in the recovery phase is like watching a flower open.

The 'dangers' of a crisis are described in the three other pathways: partial recovery, extended crisis or even quitting. Based on their review, Adams et al. (1976) concluded that such transition cycles occur 10–20 times in most people's lives. If understood and supported these events can be turning points and opportunities. If not they can lead to depression, broken relationships or careers.

Sykes (1985) found that it is common for teachers between ages 37 and 45 to experience a crisis, specifically if teachers feel they have not fulfilled their professional ambitions. These crises are often accelerated by major educational reforms. Fessler and Christensen (1992) referred to such a crisis as part of the phase of *career frustration*. And Huberman (1993) discussed teachers' *reassessment* phase, characterized by self-doubt, stagnation and sometimes even disillusionment. In this phase, teachers reassess their (future) career, seek new opportunities in or outside teaching, and search for a renewed sense of commitment. Roll and Plauburg (2009) found that teachers in this phase ask the question "should I stay or should I go?" with the introduction of new educational reforms. Teachers seem to either redevelop their enthusiasm or (gradually) withdraw from teaching (Fessler & Christensen, 1992).

There are various examples in literature describing critical moments or crises teachers go through, which seem to be related to their identity as a teacher (cf. Hong, 2010). The different characteristics indicated by Rodgers and Scott (2008) can be found in the cases we describe in the following, for instance, that identity involves relationships with others and emotions, and that identity is shifting and changes over time.

Example 1: David

Van Veen, Sleegers and Van de Ven (2005) described the case of David, a secondary school teacher dealing with school reform related to his own subject: Dutch language and literature. He anticipated implementing the suggested changes because they were in line with what he was striving for as a teacher (that is, getting students to reflect, stimulating their writing, etc.), but he soon got frustrated because he felt he did not have enough time to give the students the appropriate feedback, which he felt they needed. He talked to the school board but they 'just' suggested him to be creative with the possibilities at hand, which made him feel disqualified as a professional teacher. Van Veen et al. described the teacher's response to the innovations in terms of emotions. These emotions appeared to be in conflict, both 'happiness/enthusiasm' because of the content of the innovations and 'anger/ anxiety' played an important role. These emotions referred to what was important for him as a teacher; in other words, they were related to his personal and professional identity.

David's example shows the excitement with which David started and also the phase of inner contradictions ("conflict of emotions") in which he felt uncertain, lost confidence and became frustrated. This seems to reflect an inner crisis. Van Veen et al. (2005) did not describe what happened to David after this, but it is not far-fetched to think of the dangers that lie ahead: extended crisis in terms of a burnout, or quitting, in terms of leaving the profession. The question is what might have helped him in 'choosing' the upper pathway: gaining new confidence and transformation.

Example 2: Minfang

A second example of a teacher experiencing a critical period is described in a study by Tsui (2007), who followed an English as a Foreign Language (EFL) teacher. Minfang faced the tension between accuracy and fluency in language teaching. He felt that fluency dominated his own education at the institution. After some years of teaching, he returned to the institution to finish a master's program in EFL and found that the theoretical framework of the program enabled him to theorize his personal practical knowledge. For instance, he saw that fluency and accuracy are not dichotomous. Despite the fact that he now found theoretical grounds for his personal practical knowledge, he did not feel free to use this knowledge in the classroom. He still felt he should stress fluency over accuracy. Tsui provided the following example:

> [There was] an episode in his sixth year of teaching that epitomized the conflict he had experienced. He was put in charge of preparing for the Ministry of Education's quality assurance inspection of CLT (communicative language teaching) and was appointed by the university to conduct a demonstration lesson to illustrate the principles of CLT. The pressure on him was enormous. He started to prepare the most detailed lesson he had ever planned according to the officially sanctioned methodology. The lesson was recorded in a studio and televised live in the department. The demonstration lesson, in Minfang's eyes was a disaster. The students, highly excited under the spotlight, were over-responsive. He described the lesson as unreal and the experience as traumatic. He was disgusted by his dual identity as a fake CLT practitioner and a real self (that) believed in eclecticism. He felt that CLT had been elevated as a religion in his institution rather than an approach to learning. (2007, p. 673)

This example demonstrates how Minfang felt coerced to act in a way that made him feel uncomfortable, resulting in a critical moment, in which he described himself as having a 'dual identity.' He recovered positively by reflecting on his teaching from a 'distance' while working elsewhere on his doctorate. More specifically he reflected on methodologies in teaching, and discovered no one best methodology but about the teachers' experience and a humanistic approach.

Example 3: Mrs. Albright

Milner's (2002) study concerns an English teacher (Mrs. Albright) who taught an enriched class and was criticized by some students and parents for not being "tough enough" in her teaching and grading. Mrs. Albright wanted to nurture the students, since they were freshman and just starting at a new school. The criticism shocked her, since she felt she was working very hard for these students, trying to give them what they needed. She began to question herself and her competence as a teacher.

> I was so stressed out after this, you know. You give it your all, then get crushed. I was really hurt . . . you want to nurture them . . . and at one

point I said, can I do this, you know? You question it. I was hurt, but I was also angry, too. (Milner, 2002, p. 31)

Mrs. Albright took the criticism personally, considering she worked hard and thought she was doing the right thing. She experienced sadness, anger and was hurt. By reflecting on her teaching, she began to consider what else she could do to help her students. Leaving the professional was not an option for her. She reconsidered the positive past experiences she had with her students, the positive feedback she obtained from parents and students and the feedback from her colleagues. She decided to stay as a teacher and consider the crisis as a learning moment and she gained a renewed confidence as a teacher. Milner (2002) describes this as a 'mastery experience.'

Table 8.1 summarizes the three cases. These examples show that teachers can, for various reasons such as innovations in the school and conflicting views on teaching, experience a crisis. In the cases of Minfang and Mrs. Albright, the outcomes of these crises were positive, as they resulted in new insights and renewed confidence in teaching. Conceptions of identity as previously described (Rodgers & Scott, 2008) seem to be related to these three cases. The first assumption, *identity is dependent upon and formed within multiple contexts*, is illustrated in the case of Minfang, who literally shifted contexts (from teacher education, to teaching, to a

Table 8.1   Summary of the Three Cases (Critical Moments, Circumstances, and Results)

	Critical moment	*Circumstances*	*Result of crisis*
'David,' male, teacher of Dutch language and literature	Conflict of emotions: happiness/ enthusiasm about innovation versus anger/anxiety due to circumstances innovation	Innovation, feels disqualified by school board	No explicit description in article
'Minfang,' male, EFL teacher	Conflicting views of language teaching: accuracy versus fluency in EFL teaching	Institute with dominant view of EFL as fluency	Positive: reflection on different views results in insight there is no one best methodology
'Mrs. Albright,' female, English teacher	Conflicting views on teaching: as challenging and as nurturing	Teaching in an enriched class	Positive: Reflection on her teaching, revaluing previous positive teaching experiences, and renewed confidence

master's program, to a doctorate) and found that his view on language teaching developed in these different contexts, with the demonstration lesson as a critical incident. Finally, he resolved the conflict he experienced between language teaching as accuracy versus fluency while working abroad on a doctorate.

The second assumption, *identity is formed in relationship with others and involves emotions*, is best illustrated in the case of David, who experienced conflicting emotions towards the innovations in school. Furthermore, the relation with the school board was not optimal for David. Mrs. Albright's case is also an illustration of this assumption since she experienced anger and sadness after criticism of her students and their parents.

The third assumption, *identity is shifting, unstable and multiple*, is demonstrated in all three cases since the critical periods experienced by each teacher resulted in some sort of change in the teachers related to fundamental views, revaluation of previous experience and renewed confidence in teaching.

The last assumption, *identity involves the construction and reconstruction of meaning through stories over time*, is illustrated in the case of Mrs. Albright, who was challenged to evaluate her teaching after criticism from parents and students. As a result she gave new meaning to her 'stories' with students.

Similar examples of teachers experiencing critical moments or crises are described by Kelchtermans (2009) and Troman and Woods (2009). All these examples illustrate processes that are described using different but related terms such as, critical incidents, role redefinition and professional reassessment. Also, results of a project including survey data from over 70,000 UK teachers (the VITEA project, see, e.g., Day, Sammons, Stobart, Kington & Gu, 2007) indicated that teachers with 16 to 30 years of experience are negatively impacted by external initiatives and policies that leave little space for personal interpretation.

We can link these findings to research on intensification of the teaching job that shows that multiple factors can cause teachers to experience an intensification of their job, such as educational policy, structural characteristics of the school and personal factors, and that this experience has an impact on the way teachers think about their professional self (Ballet et al., 2006). Ballet et al. described outcomes of job intensification in positive as well as more negative terms, such as self-actualization, retreatism and professional self-understanding (cf. Kelchtermans, 2009).

IMPLICATIONS FOR STIMULATING TEACHER PROFESSIONAL DEVELOPMENT

In the following we will consider possible approaches to deal with teachers in crisis. We distinguish between two kinds of situations, one in which teacher trainers (or supervisors, school principals, etc.) are confronted with crises of teachers, and the other in which teacher trainers might want to or need to encourage crises. Both kinds of situations ask for identity changes and, thus, for transformative learning.

For a teacher trainer who wants to help teachers develop as a professional when they are facing educational changes that include a change of role (such as becoming a researcher, a coach of students or of colleagues, etc.) or a change of environment (moving to another school), there are two possibilities: *supporting* transformative learning and *provoking* transformative learning.

Supporting Transformative Learning

The most important task for teacher trainers in this respect is the *support* of transformative learning of teachers who need to adapt to educational changes or have to deal with conflicting views and teaching, resulting in frustration and/or crisis. This issue has been studied more elaborately in teacher education, that is, how teacher educators deal with the so-called "practice shock" (Veenman, 1984; Brock & Grady, 1997; Danielewicz, 2001) many beginning teachers face. Although written in the context of identity development of *student* teachers, it is reasonable to expect these recommendations apply to experienced teachers as well.

Many programs for teacher education focus mainly on what teachers should learn and be able to do (e.g., Darling-Hammond & Bransford, 2005). In their chapter in the *Handbook of Research on Teacher Education*, Rodgers and Scott (2008) found only few contemporary progressive teacher education programs that advocate the support of transformative learning. Based on experiences in these programs, they recommended that teacher educators should focus on (p. 747):

- creating time and space for reflection
- creating communities of trust
- making sense of experience through stories
- asking student teachers to confront and speak back to the external forces that shape and limit who and what a teacher is, such as colleagues, pupils and parents

Experienced teachers, however, live complex lives with multiple responsibilities with little time for reflection or change. Schools, in fact, seem to prefer teachers who enact a role described by the system, rather than expect teachers to develop and enact their own vision of their role (cf. Rodgers & Scott, 2008).

Literature on adult learning provides some additional conditions that enable successful dealing with crises, which include (a) a supportive work environment—this means a culture of high respect and low control, good team morale, clear roles, life–work boundaries respected, and (b) support—briefing, practical support, life–career planning, tolerance, time off before illness, confidential counseling, freedom/recognition for new ideas (Adams et al., 1976; Illeris, 2008; Choy, 2009).

Provoking Transformative Learning

Second, teacher trainers need to *provoke* transformative learning in experienced teachers who face major change such as educational reforms. This implies that a teacher trainer should inspire resistance if necessary (Mezirow, 2009), and develop key personal competencies for effective teaching such as independence, responsibility and creativity. One way comes through creating conflict, dilemmas or critical incidents as an effective strategy (cf. Illeris, 2008) to foster critical self-reflection of assumptions needed for transformative learning. Other effective strategies include: life histories, collaborative learning, critical theory discussions and case studies. These methods, preferably used in combination (Mezirow, 2008; Cranton & King, 2003; Taylor, 2007), require personally and actively engaging in the learning experiences. Illeris stated that the aim here should be the support and encouragement of 'breakthrough' learning, before more goal-directed and constructive education can take place. This also includes accepting the defense mechanisms some teachers call on to protect themselves from identity changes. In those cases, empathetic counseling is needed (see Illeris, 2008) that involves "being sensitive, moment to moment, to the changing felt meanings which flow in this other person, to the fear or rage or tenderness or confusion or whatever that he or she is experiencing" (Rodgers, 1980). This, Rodgers notes, "means for the time being you lay aside the views and values you hold for yourself in order to enter another's world without prejudice." (p. 62).

Stimulating and Inhibiting Factors in the School

Learners need an environment in which learning in all its facets (i.e., cumulative learning, assimilative learning, accommodative learning and transformative learning, cf. Illeris, 2009) can take place, is supported and feels safe. As described by many authors (e.g., Van Veen et al., 2005; Kelchtermans, 2009), schools do not automatically provide environments that support the transformative learning required for further development of teachers' professional identity. Particularly in times of changes, schools need to create an environment for teachers in which they feel safe and supported so they can develop their identity in such a way that it provides new opportunities and a renewed enthusiasm and passion for teaching.

The PD described in the beginning of this chapter seems more suited for stimulating this type of learning. For example, initiatives in which teachers (collaboratively) engage in practitioner research encourage them to reflect critically on their own practice, change their practice and change their view of their role as teacher. Dusting (2002), a mathematics teacher investigating her own teaching practice, described that a note from a student about improvement of her mathematics classes (as part of the data collection for her action research) offended her deeply but also started a continuous process of reflection and change of practice. Facing problems in education today (e.g., teacher dropout and teacher shortages), teachers, teacher trainers and school administrators should consider the possible impact of this type of teacher learning in their schools (Geijsel & Meijers, 2005). This requires both individual and mutual efforts.

IMPLICATIONS FOR RESEARCH

In research on teacher learning, the inclusion of a transformative focus requires techniques for data collection that account for 'rocky paths' of development, instead of, for example, directly comparing two moments of data collection to demonstrate teachers' cumulative development. Taylor (2007) advocated using videos and photos to 'capture' and provoke reflection to create a more collaborative research experience for both teacher and researcher.

A growing body of research points to the importance of narratives and dialogues (e.g., Akkerman & Meijer, 2011; Beijaard et al., 2004; Kelchtermans, 2009; Kooy, 2009; Tsui, 2007) . Beijaard et al. indicated that "identity is formed and reformed by the stories we tell and which we draw upon in our communications with others" (p. 123).

Another approach worth investigating is the unique compatibility of action research and transformative learning that share similar assumptions and outcomes such as "participatory approach, emphasis on dialogue, the essentiality of a reflective process in learning, and the need for action" (Taylor, 2007, p. 188). Trent (2010) describes an attempt to combine action research and transformative learning. He investigated preservice teachers' identity development during action research in a small-scale study that showed teachers reflecting on issues related to the concept of transformative learning, for example, developing their personal perceptions about their engagement in teaching and images of teachers and teaching.

Furthermore, the context in which teachers function should be an important aspect of research on teachers' transformative learning ('landscape') (Beijaard et al., 2004; Kelchtermans, 2009). This is illustrated by the three cases discussed in this chapter, more specifically, in the context of large-scale innovation (case of David) and in the context of self-initiated shifts in own teaching practice (case of Minfang). These two contexts differ in many ways, and this might affect the type of change teachers go through.

Finally, research questions might further develop: First, research questions need to focus on situations in which the desired learning does *not* take place or, in effect, no transformation occurs. Answers to such questions might lead to a better understanding of defense mechanisms teachers use to defend their existing identity (Illeris, 2009). Such insights are needed to understand why teachers choose pathways other than the pathway of transformation and, for example, choose to leave the teaching profession and quit being a teacher. Second, research questions need to pertain more explicitly to the crises and critical moments teachers go through, how they deal with them and what helps them to become better teachers after such crises. Ideally, if understood and supported, teachers benefit from critical periods to reconstruct and (re)gain their passion for teaching.

REFERENCES

Adams, J. D., Hayes, J. & Hopson, B. (1976). *Transition: Understanding and managing personal change*. London: Martin Robertson.

Akkerman, S. F., & Meijer, P. C. (2011). A dialogical approach to conceptualizing teacher identity. *Teaching and Teacher Education, 27*(2), 308–319.

Alsup, J. (2006). *Teacher identity discourses: Negotiating personal and professional spaces*. Mahwah, NJ: Lawrence Erlbaum.

Ballet, K., & Kelchtermans, G. (2006). Beyond intensification towards a scholarship of practice: Analysing changes in teachers' work lives. *Teachers and Teaching: Theory and Practice, 12*(2), 209–229.

Beauchamp, C., & Thomas, L. (2009). Understanding teacher identity: An overview of issues in the literature and implications for teacher education. *Cambridge Journal of Education, 29*(2), 175–189.

Beijaard, D., Meijer, P. C. & Verloop, N. (2004). Reconsidering research on teachers' professional identity. *Teacher and Teacher Education, 20,* 107–128.

Brock, B.L., & Grady, M.L. (1997). *From first-year to first-rate: Principals guiding beginning teachers*. Thousand Oaks, CA: Corwin Press.

Choy, S. (2009). Transformational learning in the workplace. *Journal of Transformative Education, 7*(1), 65–84.

Clarke, D., & Hollingsworth, H. (2002) Elaborating a model of teacher professional growth. *Teaching and Teacher Education, 18*(8), 947–967.

Cranton, P., & King, K. P. (2003). Transformative learning as a professional development goal. *New Directions for Adult and Continuing Education, 98,* 31–37.

Danielewicz, J. (2001). *Teaching selves. Identity, pedagogy, and teacher education*. Albany: State University of New York Press.

Darling-Hammond, L., & Bransford, J. (Eds.). *Preparing teachers for a changing world: What teachers should learn and be able to do*. Indianapolis: Jossey-Bass.

Day, C. (2004). *A passion for teaching*. London: RoutledgeFalmer.

Day, C., Sammons, P., Stobart, G., Kington, A. & Gu, Q. (2007). *Teachers matter. Connecting lives, work and effectiveness*. New York: McGraw-Hill.

Dusting, R. (2002). Teaching for understanding: The road to enlightenment. In J. Loughran, I. Mitchell & J. Mitchell (Eds.), *Learning from teacher research* (pp. 173–195). New York: Teachers College Press.

Fessler, R., & Christensen, J. C. (1992). *The teacher career cycle: Understanding and guiding the professional development of teachers*. Boston: Allyn and Bacon.

Geijsel, F., & Meijers, F. (2005). Identity learning: The core process of educational change. *Educational Studies, 31*(4), 419–430.

Henson, R. K. (2001). The effects of participation in teacher research on teacher efficacy. *Teaching and Teacher Education, 17,* 819–836.

Hoekstra, A., Brekelmans, M., Beijaard, D. & Korthagen, F. A. J. (2007). Experienced teachers' informal learning from classroom teaching. *Teachers and Teaching: Theory and Practice, 13,* 191–208.

Hong, J.Y. (2010). Pre-service and beginning teachers' professional identity and its relation to dropping out of the profession. *Teaching and Teacher Education,* 26(8), 1530–1543.

Huberman, M. (1993). *The lives of teachers.* London: Cassell.

Illeris, K. (2008). *How we learn. Learning and non-learning in school and beyond.* London: Routledge.

Illeris, K. (2009). *Contemporary theories of learning.* London: Routledge.

Imants, J., & van Veen, K. (2010). Teacher learning as workplace learning. In E. Baker, B. MacGaw & P. L. Peterson (Eds.), *International encyclopedia of education* (3rd ed.), (pp. 503–510). Oxford: Elsevier.

Kelchtermans, G. (2009). Career stories as gateways to understanding teacher development. In M. Bayer, U. Brinkkjær, H. Plauborg & S. Rolls (Eds.), *Teachers' career trajectories and work lives* (pp. 29–48). London: Springer.

Kooy, M. (2009). Conversations and collaborations in communities of learning: Professional development that matters. In L. F. Deretchin & C. J. Craig (Eds.), *Teacher learning in small-group settings* (pp. 5–22). Lanham, MD: Rowman and Littlefield Education.

Kralik, D., Visentin, K. & van Loon, A. (2006). Transition: A literature review. *Journal of Advanced Nursing, 55*(3), 320–329.

Lieberman, A., & Pointer-Mace, D. H. (2008). Teacher learning: The key to educational reform. *Journal of Teacher Education, 59*(3), 226-234.

Meijer, P. C. (2011). The role of crisis in the development of student teachers' professional identity. In A. Lauriala, R. Rajala, H. Ruokamo & O. Ylitapio-Mäntylä (Eds.), *Navigating in Educational contexts: Identities and cultures in dialogue* (pp. 41–54). Rotterdam: Sense Publishers.

Meijer, P. C., Korthagen, F. A. J., & Vasalos, A. (2009). Supporting presence in teacher education: The connection between the personal and professional aspects of teaching. *Teaching and Teacher Education, 25,* 297–308.

Meijer, P. C., Meirink, J., Lockhorst, D. & Oolbekkink-Marchand, H. (2010). (Leren) onderzoeken door docenten in het voortgezet onderwijs [Teachers (learn to) do research in Dutch secondary education]. *Pedagogische Studiën, 87,* 232–252.

Meirink, J.A., Meijer, P.C., Verloop, N., & Bergen, T.C.M. (2009). Understanding teacher learning in secondary education: the relations of teacher activities to changed beliefs about teaching and learning. *Teaching and Teacher Education,* 25(1), 89–100.

Mezirow, J. (1978). *Education for perspective transformation: Women's re-entry programs in community colleges.* New York: Teachers College, Columbia University.

Mezirow, J. (1990). How critical reflection triggers transformative learning. In J. Mezirow (Ed.), *Fostering critical reflection in adulthood: A guide to transformative and emancipatory learning* (pp. 1–18). San Francisco: Jossey-Bass.

Mezirow, J. (2009). An overview on transformative learning. In K. Illeris (Ed.), *Contemporary theories of learning* (pp. 90–105). New York: Routledge.

Milner, H. R. (2002). A case study of an experienced English teacher's self-efficacy and persistence through "crisis" situations: Theoretical and practical considerations. *High School Journal, 86*(1), 28–35.

Mitchell, S. N., Reilly, R. C. & Logue, M. E. (2009). Benefits of collaborative action research for the beginning teacher. *Teaching and Teacher Education,* 25, 344–349.

Piaget, J. P. (1952). *The origins of intelligence in children*. New York: International Universities Press.

Rodgers, C. R. (1980). *A way of being*. Boston: Houghton Mifflin.

Rodgers, C. R., & Scott, K. H. (2008). The development of the personal self and professional identity in learning to teach. In M. Cochran-Smith, S. Feiman-Nemser, D. J. McIntyre & K. E. Demers (Eds.), *Handbook of research on teacher education* (pp. 732–755). New York: Routledge.

Rolls, S., & Plauburg, H. (2009). Teachers' career trajectories: An examination of research. In M. Bayer, U. Brinkkjær, H. Plauborg & S. Rolls (Eds.), *Teachers' career trajectories and work lives* (pp. 9–28). London: Springer.

Seeger, M. W., Sellnow, T. L. & Ulmer, R. R. (1998). Communication, organization, and crisis. *Communication Yearbook, 21*, 231–275.

Sykes, P. J. (1985). The life cycle of the teacher. In S. Ball & I. Goodson (Eds.), *Teachers' lives and careers* (pp. 27–60). London: Falmer.

Taylor, E. W. (2007). An update of transformative learning theory: A critical review of the empirical research (1999–2005). *International Journal of Lifelong Education, 26*(2), 173–191.

Trent, J. (2010). Teacher education as identity construction: Insights from action research. *Journal of Education for Teaching, 36*(2), 153–168.

Troman, G., & Woods, P. (2009). Careers under stress: Teacher adaptations at a time of intensive reform. In M. Bayer, U. Brinkkjær, H. Plauborg & S. Rolls (Eds.), *Teachers' career trajectories and work lives* (pp. 117–142). London: Springer.

Tsui, A. B. M. (2007). Complexities of identity formation: A narrative inquiry of an EFL teacher. *TESOL Quarterly, 41*(4), 657–680.

van Veen, K., Sleegers, P. & van de Ven, P. H. (2005). One teacher's identity, emotions, and commitment to change: A case study into the cognitive-affective processes of a secondary school teacher in the context of reforms. *Teaching and Teacher Education, 21*(8), 917–934.

Veenman, S. (1984). Perceived problems of beginning teachers. *Review of Educational Research, 54*(2), 143–178.

Williams, D. (1999). Human response to change. *Futures, 31*(6), 609–616.

Zwart, R. C., Wubbels, T., Bergen, T. C. M. & Bolhuis, S. (2007). Experienced teacher learning within the context of reciprocal peer coaching. *Teachers and Teaching: Theory and Practice, 13*, 165–187.

9 Writing and Professional Learning

A "Dialogic Interaction"

Graham Parr and Brenton Doecke

INTRODUCTION

People hardly get by without the clichés and other formulaic phrasing they use from day to day. Greeting someone by asking "How are you?" does not imply a request for a detailed account of his or her health. To respond to such a greeting by listing your physical ailments would be to break with social conventions (at least in Australia, where an appropriate response to this salutation would be: "Yeah, I'm okay, thanks. How are you?"). Language of this kind conceals as much as it reveals, allowing people to defer grappling with all sorts of unpalatable truths as they go about the business of their lives.

It seems that words and phrases are continually being put into currency, passed from mouth to mouth, paradoxically binding people together in a shared misrecognition of the world around them. And this misrecognition extends beyond their immediate settings, mediating their participation in the larger society. This is especially the case with the sloganeering of politicians and the big bold print of newspaper headlines that people take up in their daily conversations, as though these slogans give meaning to their lives and contemporary experiences. Sebastian Haffner recounts how his childhood was rudely interrupted by the outbreak of the First World War, when as a 7-year-old he found himself constantly hearing new words: "Ultimatum," "Mobilization," "Alliance," "Entente" (Haffner, 2002, p. 14). He recalls the language of the crowd as they cheered on those going off to the front: "Be brave!" "Stay safe and healthy!" "Come back soon!" "Smash the Serbs!" (p. 14). Has our so-called 'war on terror' been any different? In educational landscapes, can we not pose a similar question about language such as 'standards,' 'accountability,' 'learning outcomes' and 'transparency'?

Yet language, as Terry Eagleton observed, is also "a way of being among things in the world" (2007, p. 69). While language may indeed serve to shut people off from reality, it can also yield "the deepest access to it" (p. 69). Eagleton is making a claim about the value of poetry, but his account of the way poets reflexively use words, inquiring into experience by working at the interface between words and things—between 'inside' and 'outside,' 'subjectivity' and 'objectivity'—might be extended to include other writing. It might also embrace the social relationships and transactions in which people engage from day to day, such as those which constitute the institutional settings where they work, not only the world of 'things' that Eagleton invokes.

Wherever we find ourselves, and whatever linguistic resources we have at our disposal—whether writing a poem, a report about conditions in our workplace or a syllabus document mapping out the learning we anticipate our students will achieve over the next term—it is valuable to pause occasionally in order to reflexively monitor our language, interrogating the clichés and phrasing that we use in our everyday life. This does not presume that we can ever get at the 'truth,' as though an individual writer or speaker can simply clear away the jargon that others use in an effort to achieve some kind of authentic communication or—dare we say it?—a "plain language statement." Bakhtin (1984) says that truth "is not born, nor is it to be found inside the head [or the words] of an individual person." Rather, it is "born between people collectively searching for truth, in the process of dialogic interaction" (p. 110). This means resisting any notion that there can ever be a final word on any matter, as though somehow our language and ideas might be made to correspond with 'reality.' It also means cultivating a reflexive stance towards the language of "the day and hour" (Bakhtin, 1984, p. 293), even as we contribute to it by participating in a variety of social activities in a variety of settings.

In this chapter, we aim to investigate the nature and role of writing in relation to educators' professional learning. As part of this investigation, we seek to enact and in a sense capture a process of 'dialogic interaction' as we experienced it in conversations among the four of us about the role of writing in professional learning. Claire and Sidra are English teachers in secondary schools, while Graham and Brenton are English teacher educators working in university settings. Through our conversations, we have been striving to heighten our sensitivity towards the multiple ways that language mediates our relationships with ourselves and others, and how this language shapes our view of the world and the activities in which we engage, specifically our work as language educators. By enacting a process of 'dialogic interaction,' we shall try to gesture towards larger complexities than might be conveyed by definitive statements or what Schwab calls a "rhetoric of conclusions" (1964). By and large, we shall use the first-person plural (as we are doing now) and write in an analytical mode in an effort to express some of the understandings we have reached about the nature of writing and professional learning. However, we also incorporate snippets of narratives that convey our individual perspectives and interact with the analytical writing. These narratives are taken from texts each of us produced separately over recent years and in different contexts.

The interleaving narratives are not presented as best-practice models of writing that have spawned quality learning, but as part of our ongoing investigation into the nature and possibilities of writing as a form of inquiry for teachers and researchers in education. Although this narrative writing might be read as being prompted by the reflections surrounding them, it does more than simply illustrate the arguments presented in the more analytical passages. Rather than producing a seamless text in which everything folds into everything else (as in a "rhetoric of conclusions"), we work with juxtaposition and contrast, contradiction and difference, affirming the irreducibility of each of our individual voices as opposed to the universalizing pretensions that inhere within the first-person plural. In this way, we hope to prompt further reflections in the minds of our readers that point beyond this discussion, contributing to a larger conversation that will continue, even when we have put a full stop after the final sentence of this chapter.

CONFRONTING GENERALIZATIONS

What we have said thus far shows we are not arguing a case for writing *in addition to* other forms of professional learning in which educators might engage. We see writing as a *condition* for professional inquiry and learning and not a mere tool for reflecting that learning or for 'writing up' the results. As language educators, we believe language is an inescapable condition for all our work, and for our engagement with the world. Language is there, to borrow loosely from Roland Barthes (1977), like life itself. Writing—and the kind of struggle with words and meaning that writing involves (Doecke & Parr, 2005)—is a crucial means by which to inquire into the way language mediates our understanding of our work as educators, our professional identity and our relationships with each other.

Yet in a paradoxical way, we are obliged to confront the fact that writing and textual work of various kinds figure very prominently in the standards-based environment in which educators must currently operate (cf. Smith, 2005). It is unlikely that anyone would dispute the textually mediated nature of the policy environment in which teachers in both schools and universities are obliged to operate. Educators already engage in arguably an unprecedented amount of textual work—our conversations with each other over the past few months have been interrupted by the fact that Sidra and Claire have had to, for instance, write reports, mark exams, plan lessons (at one point, Sidra observed in an email that a single round of her report writing had amounted to almost 10,000 words, an observation that clearly resonated with Claire). At a schoolwide and system-wide level there is increasing emphasis on performance appraisal, involving the preparation of portfolios and other textual artifacts supposedly to demonstrate that teachers are working at a certain level of accomplishment. Any claim about the value of writing for critical inquiry must be made against a backdrop where writing is increasingly used by teachers, school administrators and bureaucrats for decidedly *uncritical* purposes, in order to demonstrate the achievement of outcomes that the system demands (cf. Parr, 2007).

The texts and textual work that typify standards-based reforms are shot through with a generalizing rhetoric involving statements about what teachers should supposedly 'know and be able to do' (to borrow a cliché from the discourse of professional standards), as though everything can be pinned down in advance and in a way that comprehends the practice of educators everywhere, regardless of the specific nature of the school communities in which they work. Such standards are sometimes presented as ideals towards which teachers might aspire without necessarily being expected to achieve them, not as benchmarks against which their performance must be judged. But even when standards take an aspirational form, they run the risk of embodying an authoritarian knowledge or discourse that brooks no challenging, as though they are literally the final word. To borrow again from Bakhtin, such discourse tends to reify into language that is:

> sharply demarcated, compact and inert. . . . it demands our unconditional allegiance. . . . Authoritative discourse [or knowledge] permits no play with the context framing it, no play with its borders, no gradual and flexible transitions, no spontaneously creative stylizing variants on it. (1981, p. 343)

The knowledge reified by so-called 'standards' sees more value in compliance than in dialogue. It does not invite inquiry into, or conversation about, the particulars of educational experience. It is not interested in the ambiguities and the inconsistencies of the social and cultural worlds that might problematize the production of that knowledge; nor is it interested in the mediating role of language in the production or reproduction (or challenging) of knowledge.[1]

Delandshere and Arens (2003) and others (e.g., Tillema & Smith, 2007; cf. Bellis, 2004; Doecke, 2005; Hay & Moss, 2005; Lyons, 1998; Piva, 2005) have charted the way 'standards' produce a rhetoric of conformity in the form of teachers' professional portfolios. The potentiality of writing in these portfolios as a vehicle for critical engagement has been undermined by the discourses of standards-based reforms, which reduce writing to simply an exercise in demonstrating professional accomplishment. Writing, therefore, is 'manufactured'; it is standardized into a generic set of texts that wrench experience out of the richly particular contexts that have given rise to it. The historical moment of professional portfolios in the United States and in Australia has quickly spawned formulae that encourage teachers to try to account for their practice by using language that has been prescribed for them, tying their descriptions and reflections about their work to a set of standards statements, as if these descriptions could then demonstrate what they 'know and are able to do.' Questions about the complexity of representing professional practice have gone begging. Rather than treating writing as a means to critically inquire into aspects of their professional practice and to make connections with individual experience, portfolios are reduced to a proliferation of generalizations. The writing begins to look the same and sound the same, and thus is emptied of meaning.

By contrast, the kind of textual work that we are envisaging is prompted by Bahktin's (1986) notion of "dialogic potential," a potential that always escapes being defined beforehand as what teachers 'should know and be able to do.' We value writing that promotes inquiry into and dialogue about the particularity and the distinctiveness of experience and practice at all levels of educational work, and that conveys a reflexive awareness of the role of language in describing and engaging with this experience.

A Grammar Lesson (Claire)

In a quiet room in the late afternoon, I sit in exam-style rows and nervously look at my colleagues around me. I'm waiting to receive the results of my test on the new grammar I was supposed to learn in our last class: adjectival clauses, intensifiers and coordinating conjunctions. This professional development workshop is designed to respond to the emphasis on grammar teaching in our new Australian Curriculum: English. The problems of the past have been identified and they will be solved . . . with grammar. This is what we need, according to the media and politicians. As English teachers we are apparently supposed to believe that all other educational issues can be swept aside while we concentrate on the curative power of grammar knowledge.

And thus my grammar class comes to order again. In a sense, I am thankful. I am apparently one of the thousands of qualified, professional and active English teachers in Australia who didn't get a 'proper' English education when I was a school student. But, as I am told, it's not our fault. It simply wasn't part of the curriculum during the 1980s and 1990s. This makes me feel better as a senior teacher participating in this workshop gives the correct answers to the test that we sat last week. We sit and listen and we smile and nod our heads as we quickly correct the errors that have been made on our own test sheets.

But my smile betrays my uncertainty. For the first time since finishing secondary school in the early 1990s, I have an overwhelming sense of dread. I am using all of the energy I can muster to appear relaxed and to try and look as though I understand everything being taught to me. It is significant that I am being taught in traditional, 'chalk and talk' pedagogy. Whatever happened to the social construction of knowledge? Some other participants seem to revel in the opportunity to ask complex questions about morphemes and lexemes. A colleague near me exclaims, "Why wasn't I taught this at school? My life would be so much easier if I knew grammar properly!" The comments that follow echo this lament. The assumption seems to be that our students will have a better experience of English when taught this grammar as per the National Curriculum guidelines. I'm not convinced.

While I acknowledge that the grammar I have been teaching through my relatively short career isn't as detailed as what I am learning in my after-school grammar workshops, I am uncomfortable. My perception of what subject English is doesn't focus on grammar in the way that many of my colleagues appear to think is desirable. I enjoy literary and textual analysis that I engage in with my whole class. I think of this kind of textual play in terms of an investigator searching for clues to an ancient mystery: the connections between language and experience. Today in my own classroom with my students, I can sense when these pivotal moments are about to take place; when my students suddenly gain an insight into something that they either hadn't really thought of before or that they didn't perceive as being of value. The confidence that they bring into the classroom and exhibit in their discussion and writing illustrates that something important and unique has happened to their perception of what makes them speakers of English. As I witness these moments I think of the way the students' feelings of accomplishment, unlike my own feelings in my after-school class, suggest that subject English plays some sort of role in their developments as people and their identity. I think of the way in which students perceive English and what it means to be an English student.

I sit and smile and wonder how my newfound knowledge of grammar will help in this. . . .

This kind of writing foregrounds the individual's experience; it never loses sight of "where an individual is," as Dorothy Smith puts it (2006, p. 3). Yet it also posits individual experience as something that necessarily eludes any attempt to pin it down. This is partly explained by the sense in which any experience is embedded within the "ongoing, never-stand-still of the social" (Smith, 2006, p. 2).

Claire's narrative begins with a sense of investigating a 'problematic' (Smith, 1987, 2005). This is Dorothy Smith's term, which she coins in contradistinction to traditional forms of research that emphasize the importance of formulating a research question and engaging in an inquiry that is concluded by reaching an 'answer' to that question (Smith, 2005; cf. Hamilton, 2005, pp. 288–289). Smith envisages inquiry quite differently, as involving, in the first instance, a refusal of what is immediately given to you. This is akin to an ethnographer's stance, in that it involves a disposition to inquire into accepted meanings, as expressed in Claire's colleagues' enthusiasm for grammar teaching. By writing her narrative she wants to create a distance between herself and the values and beliefs that appear to shape the community of practice to which she belongs. And yet it is not as though she adopts a standpoint from which she judges her colleagues' views as hopelessly mistaken. She is "not convinced"; she is "uncomfortable." She places her own self under scrutiny. Her narration involves a split between the 'I' who is doing the telling and the 'I' who smiles in agreement along with everyone else about the transformative effects of learning grammar.

Claire's writing is also an essay in thinking 'relationally' (another word that we associate with Dorothy Smith and the intellectual tradition in which she situates her work). And this extends far beyond her relationships with her colleagues and her reflections about whether her 'I' can connect with the collective identity that they apparently share. Claire's irony creates a space in which she is able to raise questions about the meaning and full implication of grammar teaching for her sense of purpose and identity as a teacher of English. Although the concrete detail of her narrative evokes a particular time and place, her story is located within a larger network of relationships that stretch beyond the here and now. We sense how this professional development (PD) session on grammar teaching is mediated by standards-based reforms, including the economic scenarios that are used to justify them. Through its rich particularity, Claire's story resists the claims about the efficacy of teaching grammar, while simultaneously prompting reflection about the social and economic determinants that have produced the here and now as she experiences it.

CONFRONTING AUTOBIOGRAPHIES

Such subjectively intense engagements with the here and now raise questions about who we are and the values and beliefs we bring to our teaching. Standards-based reforms have marginalized any sense of teaching as "a confrontation with one's own autobiography," as William Ayers puts it (1993). Thus teaching is reduced to a set of discrete skills that can be applied by an individual teacher in an ideologically neutral manner, without regard to the specific nature of the community in which that teacher is working. Teachers are supposed to 'make the difference' (cf. Hattie, 2009; Rowe, 2003)—yet another cliché that typifies standards-based reforms—but this 'difference' is conceived almost exclusively in terms of the achievement of prescribed and very narrowly defined learning outcomes. If we conceive of curriculum as a form of communication (Barnes, 1992), and of classrooms as sites where learning is negotiated, we presuppose a capacity on the part of teachers and educators to acknowledge all that their students bring to their exchanges with them. It then becomes necessary to reflect on how our values and beliefs might be shaping that conversation.

Monsieur Patrick (Brenton)

> *Murray Bridge High in the 1960s was endless rows of portables and asphalt, with weekly assemblies where our Headmaster told us to aim*

for the stars—the school motto was 'sic itur ad astra'—and not to smoke in the toilets. When we started high school, we were tested and yarded into classes ranging from 1A to 1G. Those who got into 1A stream held vague notions of going to teachers' college or university; those who landed in 1G had more limited prospects. Collectively, we somehow made sense of the world in which we found ourselves. Every morning boys and girls were bused in from nearby farming communities like Jervois and Pompoota and Mypolonga, while the kids from Tailem Bend rowdily lugged their bags on the long march from the railway station to school. For years the railway town of Tailem Bend had been promised a high school of its own, but successive governments had done nothing about it. So the Tailem Bend kids were forced to get up early every day to catch a slow train to Murray Bridge.

Our teachers were likewise creatures of this world, and it would be easy to rattle off any number of horror stories about them. Yet by and large they supported our fumbling attempts to imagine our lives differently, even as they administered a fairly nasty system of branding and culling, and I remember several of them fondly, especially my English teachers.

The one I want to tell you about was not trained as an English teacher; in fact, he did not have any formal teaching qualifications at all, something not uncommon in the 1960s. Although born in Australia, he had apparently done a degree in Music at the University of Lyons, and was employed to teach French, something he did pretty badly. However, as part of his job, Monsieur Patrick was given 2A English, a lively bunch of 15-year-olds that included me, and his approach would consist largely of reading to us any book that he was reading at the moment. He always presented whatever he read as a discovery, as something he had only just found himself.

Anyway, Monsieur Patrick would walk in, and start reading from The Catcher in the Rye, *and Holden Caulfield would be telling us about that madman stuff that happened last Christmas, and then Patrick would have us writing stories about all the crap that was happening in our own lives. I mean, it wasn't stuff I could show my parents 'cause they were quite touchy about anything like that, especially my father, and so like Holden I lived a double life, pouring out all these thoughts about myself and being a phony at home.*

Patrick brought Down and Out in Paris and London *to class and, as with* The Catcher in the Rye, *for a week Orwell's style enveloped me, as I recorded my impressions of life in Murray Bridge. The main street of Murray Bridge at eight in the morning. Only a few people about. The muffled shriek of a saw in a butcher shop. The only shops that are open are the butcher shops, etc.*

On yet another day Patrick brought along a copy of Arthur Rimbaud's prose poems, so that the following morning when I went to check my traps before going to school (I lived on a property some miles out of the town), I held the summer dawn in my arms, along with a couple of dead bunnies.

*   *   *

'Be Educated' (Sidra)

My parents (as children) and grandparents came to Australia as Jewish refugees after World War II. They came with no English, very few possessions, plenty of emotional and physical scars, but, like so many before and since, with much hope in their hearts.

Our grandparents talked to us a great deal, telling us their stories. In a way, I think they found it easier to talk about their youth, even of their experiences during the war, to us rather than to their children. Perhaps because their children were part of the story and its trauma, they felt a need to protect them through not dwelling on the past. These stories skipped a generation, so to speak.

The stories contain too much loss and pain to repeat here. I even struggle with whether I will tell them to my children. To what end? But one element drawn out from my family's experiences of dislocation that was stressed to me was: Be educated. That's what 'they' can never take away from you. My grandparents were so proud when I excelled academically. It was difficult to resist the expectation that I study Law when I got the marks. I went along with it for a couple of years until I could no longer ignore the fact that their dreams weren't my dreams. Although they respected education as a goal, they didn't seem to think much of teaching as a profession. "Better you be independent. . . ."

In so many ways, where I've come from, generationally, has shaped the person I am . . . but also the person I'm trying hard not to be. There's a push and a pull. I like to think that my family's history makes me more sensitive, empathetic and idealistic (although it also has the potential to lead to cynicism and despair). At this stage, I am not sure if or how I as a preservice teacher can channel these values into my teaching practice.

Determining the context in which I teach would help clarify things, but I'm not ready to decide on that yet. A part of me would like to teach English in a place that would make a difference. I look at today's refugee and immigrant children and see repetitions. I'd like to be able to communicate through what happens in the classroom that these young people can have a future with choices. In reality, though, I accept that there's a limit to what a teacher can do, given the inequalities of the education system and many other complicating factors. As you yourself write, Bella, putting "beliefs about social justice and equity

into practice" is fraught with complexities when the second chances on offer are themselves second rate (Illesca, 2003, pp. 9–11).

Another part of me derives much strength, orientation and joy from my heritage. For this reason, a Jewish school is a potential teaching context, also providing a space for me to express ideals and values, albeit different ones from those I've just mentioned. How to choose? The two subjects I elected to study for my teacher education course were emblematic of two sides of myself (and there are many more). I struggle with these different perspectives as I seek to write about life and identity. I empathize with Katherine Mansfield's questioning of the aphorism, "To thine own self be true."

"True to oneself!" she muses. "Which self? Which of my many— well really, that's what it looks like coming to—hundreds of selves?"

Brenton's autobiographical text here is taken from the opening of a chapter entitled "Teacher Quality: Beyond the Rhetoric" (Doecke, 2006). In that chapter he inquires critically and creatively into memories of his own schooling in response to the mantra so often chanted by politicians and still today reproduced in newspaper headlines that "teacher quality" is a "key determinant of students' outcomes and schooling." Monsieur Patrick was a teacher who certainly enhanced Brenton's awareness of life's possibilities, but whose influence on an adolescent's growing sensibility cannot be captured by crude notions of 'value adding' and 'performance appraisal.' Sidra's text, originally written for an autobiographical assignment during her preservice teacher education, is framed as part of an ongoing conversation with her lecturer at the time, Bella Illesca, whose work she refers to in the writing. She borrows the rhetoric that has come to be associated with standards-based reforms—that she might 'make a difference'—and even as she says this she is suggesting the paradoxes of such a claim.

Each text, Brenton's and Sidra's, shuttles between a distant but still very much *living* past and a discomforted present inflected by tensions and complexity. Brenton brings his contemporary professional self into contact with the sociality of the young Brenton in an English classroom in Murray Bridge High with M. Patrick reading the words and worlds of Holden Caulfield. Part of his focus on this sociality is to draw into explicit tension different language and worlds with which he was grappling then, and with which he grapples now as he writes of Rimbaud's transcendent "summer dawn in his arms" (*J'ai embrassé l'aube d'été*) along with "a couple of dead bunnies."

Sidra, writing as a preservice teacher and a mother of three children, situates her younger self as part of an ongoing conversation with her grandparents as they tell their stories of loss and pain. (She wonders whether she will pass these stories on to her own children.) And whereas she allows these stories to remain unspoken in this piece of writing, she *does* quote particular words from a different conversation with a grandparent: "Be educated" and later "Better you be independent"—presumably in response to a younger Sidra's suggestion that she'd rather teach than pursue a legal career. These few words have particular irony and resonance. They bespeak the multiple tensions and convictions that continue to inform Sidra's present and evolving self . . . or selves. For in Sidra's, as in Brenton's text, the richly dialogic sense that imbues her representation of her younger past selves lives on and speaks powerfully to a dynamic dialogic present self. It is a self whose identity gains meaning from the past, through the autobiographical glimpses, but also a self whose professional educator identity is a response to both the metaphorical and the flesh-and-blood selves of the past.

In her conception of 'memory work,' Frigga Haug (1992) sees such writing as part of a continuing inquiry into the determinants of one's 'self' (or many 'selves'), opening up a rich and more generative alternative to romantic traditions of re-creating the past. For Haug, as for Sidra and Brenton, writing is an inquiry into the past that seeks to establish dialogue between the past and the present. It is never a matter of trying to pin the past down and show "how it really was" (Haug, 1992, p. 20). The link between the past and the present is continually renegotiated and revitalized, as new dimensions of memory reveal themselves, and new questions emerge that in turn raise questions about one's sense of 'self' or identity as an actor in the present. Ricoeur (2004) writes, in *Memory, History, Forgetting*, about the Platonic aspiration to capture "[in] the present representation the absent thing" (p. 8), i.e., the past. But the past in Sidra's and Brenton's writing does not exist as a separate bounded time-space. It is not something that *happened* to them: Rather they are active participants in their pasts, a status that is reinforced by the active role of writing in the construction of the past. In this understanding of memory, and memory work, experiences are neither a prison house for nor a direct window into the soul. Sidra's conversations with her grandparents (and the stories within their stories), like Brenton's interweaving literary language and narrative fragments of life in Murray Bridge, exist as living traces in their respective interpretations and constructions of identity. Their emphasis is less on capturing or even deconstructing the past and more on constructing identity, as they interpret and "reinterpret themselves and see what benefits may be derived from doing so" (Haug, 1992, p. 20).

Writing to all of us, in the process of engaging in the conversation that that led to this chapter, Sidra comments on the 'push and pull' of her past on the present, and on what she calls "the blend of biography and practice" in her earlier writing:

> I can see that I'm still negotiating many of these questions over how to express who I am, the different parts of myself, how to channel my values and hopes into my professional practice. After 2 years of teaching English at an independent girls' school, a very positive experience in so many ways, I decided to move to a Jewish school. I guess the part of me that needed to give expression to my identity and heritage through my

teaching and through the context in which I was teaching became too strong. And yet I stand back now, having made the move, and I can see that things are not so simple.

In the more extended writing from which Brenton's and Sidra's texts were excerpted, each of them proceeds to reflect on the social justice 'perspectives' that characterize and inform so much of their professional work and their identities. While it is possible to trace the elements in their memories that help to understand this, their writing about these memories does not constitute "direct quotations from experience" (Schratz & Walker, 1995, p. 42). The writing has not begun with what we might call 'the social justice I,' and proceeded through a process of defining and illustrating that 'I,' as though in some self-righteous way to affirm a commitment to social equity. Ultimately, this social justice perspective does not translate into a neat and tidy single self 'I.' Haug would say the writing has sought to explore the particular and contradictory "worlds of experience" (1992, p. 155) and to show how these worlds continue to influence Sidra's and Brenton's ongoing professional and identity work in their different educational settings.

. . . AND CONFRONTING SITUATIONS

The kind of professional writing the four of us engage in works with more nuanced understandings of language and narrative than standards-based conceptions of professional learning. But we would hasten to stress that ours is not necessarily a new development in writing practices for educators. Writing about his own early experiences in education and about the politics of schooling in the 1980s, Harold Rosen has said it all before us. He shows how "narratives in all their diversity and multiplicity make up the fabric of our lives; they are the constitutive moments in the formation of our identities and our sense of [social] affiliations" (Doecke & Parr, 2009, p. 66). In addition to prompting us to consider our own educational experiences and biographies, Rosen advocates a more prominent role for storytelling in all forms of writing pedagogy in schools, and in teachers' professional lives. He urges "a resolute insistence on narrative and [more dialogic paradigms of] education in defiance of other priorities," as one way to challenge what he calls "rule-governed settings" (Rosen, 1985, p. 26), the sort of settings that would seem to be the goal of standards-based educational reforms. Narrative writing, as Rosen understands it, can connect with the complexity of those rule-governed settings, so that both the writing and the setting escape being classified and typified in the way that standards-based reforms presume they should be. Within those settings, educators are obliged to renew their lives each day, and narrative writing can enable them to revisit the values and beliefs they bring to their work, and to ask questions about the meaning of what is happening.

For the last 2 years in August, Graham's work as a university-based teacher educator has taken him to Johannesburg for a month at a time. Here he encountered people and settings that have continually prompted him to think about the growing pervasiveness of standards-based reforms and rule-governed settings. His role involved coordinating and mentoring a small group of Australian preservice teachers undertaking a teaching practicum in South Africa, while conducting research into these experiences. He writes elsewhere of his mixed feelings about this work: on the one hand his excitement in exploring and developing educational partnerships in different educational cultures and spaces, but also his concern whether it is possible to challenge the abiding and destructive colonial traditions of white middle-class missionaries and educators imposing their values and knowledge on communities and individuals in developing countries (cf. Parr, forthcoming).

A week into his first trip, he wrote the following to a colleague back in Melbourne.

Negotiating Boundaries in Johannesburg (Graham)

We drive onto a dusty potholed roadway leading to Mahena K–12 state school.[2] My South African colleagues have described Mahena to me as a "farm school," set up to educate the children of the surrounding farming areas. We slowly pass through rickety cyclone-wire fencing that surrounds the school, topped with the coils of that ubiquitous razor wire. I can only imagine the lifeworlds of the individual students and teachers within the school. How do they interact with each other? How do they negotiate the social relationships that constitute their school?

Later I find myself crouched, knees up to my shoulders, in a typical Grade 2 classroom chair. Moments earlier, I had appeared at the door of the classroom with one of the deputy principals of the school, and the Grade 2 teacher had responded by instructing her students to stop what they were doing, to close their books and say good morning to Dr. Parr. "Good morning, Dr. Parr," the children chorused. So much for my hopes to experience some 'everyday' teaching and learning dynamics and practices. Having completely disrupted 'normal' classroom practices, I had then sat down with a group of four children (two boys and two girls) whose tables were connected together ready for group work.

The children seem happy for me to join them; they want to read me a story. They draw a book from a nearby bookshelf of class readers. I don't want to pry too closely, but it seems many of the readers on the bookshelf are Western fairy tales. I wonder for a brief moment how (or if) these students have been able to connect the British characters, animals and countryside depicted in these stories with their own farms and their home life on the periphery of Johannesburg. But I am quickly distracted from this wondering as the children throw themselves into their reading.

The story they choose to read to me is "The Boy Who Cried Wolf." The reading proves to be a wonderful collective effort. One boy, who tells me his name is Amos, begins to read. His excitement is flecked by incipient anxiety. Soon into the story, he falters over a particular word, hesitates, but is soon prompted by his peers and is able to continue reading. The others in the group are jointly monitoring both Amos's reading (looking over his shoulder), but also my responses (casting furtive glances at me to see how I am responding). They gently offer suggestions to Amos and so maintain the flow of the narrative. Amos soon founders more seriously over a difficult phrase. A girl finally makes a decision to take over the reading in a way that seems accepted by Amos. This process continues with two subsequent readers 'taking over' in turn, until the group completes the story. Their beaming faces celebrate the journey to the end of the story.

Then they show me their workbooks. In almost all cases, boys' and girls' books are beautifully presented . . . I have joined in celebration of their collective reading of the story, but when I see these workbooks I have to confess to a feeling of deflation as I see only page after page of drills and language exercises. Not a hint of any stories they may have been reading. Not a hint of their own narratives, their own lives, their own words on the page. Wait! On one page I see a drawing. But only one. And yet the energy of these children and their 'spark' (like most children at this school) spoke of other futures and possibilities . . . perhaps.

As in the texts of Claire, Sidra and Brenton, this writing reveals some stories and keeps others hidden. It concentrates on the particularity of Graham's experience, this time in the very recent past, and yet it shuttles across space and time, between Australia and South Africa, between past and present, between the self and others. Here again is a 'push and pull' story. It is a story of the tension-ridden and contradictory worlds and values with which Graham is grappling as he seeks to make sense of his first experiences of education in South Africa with its distinctive social and cultural contexts and its history. At the same time that Graham's writing bespeaks his desire to interpret razor wire, education and social worlds of South Africa, it is also providing a language and space-time wherein he can engage with social conditions in Australia. The words 'razor wire' also evoke for him (as becomes explicit in another part of his journal) the image of detention camps and the social refugees in Australia, and where his work as an educator might sit in relation to this. It seems that governments the world over are investing significant amounts of time and money in erecting barriers between people.

But Graham's story is also one about stepping in, of moving from a familiar world into one where he self-consciously needs to interpret the signs with which he is confronted. Yes, the world over is the 'same'—the existence of razor wire and PISA testing tells us that[3]—and yet the experience of any educator beginning work in a new institution, let alone crossing oceans and cultures in the way that Graham records in his narrative, always involves a curious tension between sameness and difference. Graham is actively 'making sense' of the experience, and this active sense making is also critical to the development of his identity. He struggles to find his coordinates by engaging with the children in the reading group. Yet he is finally left with questions about the literacy practices he sees being enacted, about the hope invested in those practices and about the larger socioeconomic forces that are not visible from within this setting.

WHAT HAVE WE LEARNED?

The value of written narratives aim to unsettle the 'wisdom' that people accept without question. Terry Eagleton observed that "an image of the truth that language is not what shuts us off from reality, but what yields us the deepest access to it" (2007, p. 69). Written language, then, serves to better understand the subtle play between words and meanings that it involves.

We have been weighing up the meaning of words of our own narratives that provide a focus for scrutiny, tracing the multiple contexts in which they resonate. Ultimately, words *can* provide a means of challenging the sweeping generalizations of standards-based reforms, and of registering the impact of these reforms on the experiences of those whose everyday lives are being mediated by them. Yes, there are all sorts of 'truths' here—often invoked by words like *globalization*—yet in the first instance, we are affirming the value of individuals cultivating a receptivity to the world around, to their current situation, and raising questions about the language offered to them.

Our inquiry into the nature and role of writing in educators' professional learning has presented and critiqued the language of standards-based reforms, words that offer little more than empty clichés, formulaic phrasing and generalizations that remain at a remove from the particularities of experience they are intended to influence. As part of that inquiry, we have presented and reflected upon words of a very different character. And we have sought to show how our writing is a process of grappling with all manner of words, of investigating and being sensitive to the multiple ways in which language in all its diversity mediates our work and our learning conversations. In the end, each narrative excerpt in this chapter is less an individual set piece that represents or learns from the past and more a space for enacting a dialogue between the past and the present. Such writing does not pin down or spawn professional learning;

it constitutes a fundamental dimension of professional learning. Indeed, the value of the writing inheres not so much in the 'wisdom' or learning within the piece itself than in the role the writing might play in a dialogic conversation amongst colleagues about reflexivity, identity and professional practice.

As one of us observed as we concluded the journey of writing this chapter: "I feel I have arrived at a starting-over-again point from which I might reflect anew on the work I do now and on the work I will do in the future."

ACKNOWLEDGMENTS

The authors wish to acknowledge the two teachers, Sidra Moshinsky and Claire Tumilovics, who participated in and co-constructed the research and professional dialogue reported in this chapter.

NOTES

1. For an example of a set of professional standards that attempt to 'play with the context framing it,' and that try to conceptualize standards in a more dialogical and exploratory manner, see www.stella.org.au. These standards were developed by English teachers in Australia in an attempt to provide an alternative to standards developed only for regulatory purposes.
2. Mahena K–12 is a fictionalized name.
3. The Program for International Student Assessment (or PISA), administered by the Organization for Economic Cooperation and Development (OECD), is a major instrument of standards-based reforms. Ken Jones provides a trenchant critique of PISA's impact on European educational communities (Jones, 2010, pp.13–16). See also Van de Ven and Doecke (forthcoming) for a critique of the assumptions underpinning PISA.

REFERENCES

Ayers, W. (1993). To teach: the journey of a teacher. New York: Teachers College Press.

Bakhtin, M. (1981). *The dialogic imagination: Four essays by M. M. Bakhtin* (M. Holquist, Ed., C. Emerson & M. Holquist, Trans.). Austin: University of Texas Press.

Bakhtin, M. (1984). *Problems of Dostoevsky's poetics* (C. Emerson, Ed. & Trans.). *Theory and history of literature, 8*. Minneapolis: University of Minnesota Press.

Bakhtin, M. (1986). *Speech genres and other late essays* (C. Emerson & M. Holquist, Eds., V. McGee Trans.). Austin: University of Texas Press.

Barnes, D. (1992). *From communication to curriculum* (2nd ed.). Portsmouth, NH: Boynton/Cook.

Barthes, R. (1977). Introduction to the structuralist analysis of text. In S. Heath (Ed.), *Image-music-text* (pp. 79–124). Glasgow: Collins.

Bellis, N. (2004). Leaving the map behind: An inquiry into the VIT portfolio process. *Idiom, 40*(3), 15–20.

Delandshere, G., & Arens, S. (2003). The quality of the evidence of preservice teacher portfolios. *Journal of Teacher Education, 54*(1), 57–73.

Doecke, B. (2005). Professional standards: Maintaining a critical stance. *English in Australia, 144,* 26–34.

Doecke, B. (2006). Teacher quality: Beyond the rhetoric. In B. Doecke, M. Howie & W. Sawyer (Eds.), *'Only connect': English teaching, schooling and community* (pp. 195–208). Kent Town: AATE and Wakefield Press.

Doecke, B., & Parr, G. (2005). Writing: A common project. In B. Doecke & G. Parr (Eds.), *Writing = Learning* (pp. 1–16). Kent Town: AATE and Wakefield Press.

Doecke, B., & Parr, G. (2009). 'Crude thinking' or reclaiming our story-telling rights. Harold Rosen's essays on narrative. *Changing English, 16*(1), 63–76.

Eagleton, T. (2007). *How to write a poem.* Malden, MA: Blackwell.

Haffner, S. (2002). *Geschichte eines Deutschen. Die Erinnerungen 1914–1933.* Munich: Deutscher Taschenbuch Verlag.

Hamilton, D. (2005). Knowing practice. Editorial. *Pedagogy, Culture and Society, 13*(3), 285–289.

Hattie, J. (2009). *Visible learning: A synthesis of over 800 meta-analyses relating to achievement.* London: Routledge.

Haug, F. (1992). *Beyond female masochism: Memory-work and politics.* London: Verso.

Hay, T., & Moss, J. (2005). *Portfolios, performance and authenticity.* Frenchs Forest, NSW: Pearson Education.

Illesca, B. (2003). Speaking as 'other.' In B. Doecke, D. Homer & H. Nixon (Eds.), *English teachers at work: Narratives, counter narratives and arguments* (pp. 7–13). Kent Town: Wakefield Press.

Jones, K. (2010). The twentieth century is not yet over: Resources for the remaking of educational practice. *Changing English, 17*(1), 13–16.

Lyons, N. (Ed.). (1998). *With portfolio in hand: Validating the new teacher professionalism.* New York: Teachers College Press.

Parr, G. (2007). Writing and practitioner inquiry: Thinking relationally. *English Teaching: Practice and Critique, 6*(3), 22–47.

Parr, G. (forthcoming). *A teaching practicum in South Africa: An Australian teacher educator lives the contradictions.*

Piva, L. (2005). My professional journey. *English in Australia, 144,* 35–37.

Ricoeur, P. (2004). *Memory, history, forgetting* (K. Blamey & D. Pellauer, Trans.). Chicago: University of Chicago Press.

Rosen, H. (1985). *Stories and meanings.* Sheffield, UK: NATE.

Rowe, K. (2003). *The importance of teacher quality as a key determinant of students' experiences and outcomes of schooling* (Discussion paper prepared on behalf of the Interim Committee for a NSW Institute of Teaching). Camberwell, VIC: ACER.

Schratz, M. & Walker, R. (1995). *Research as social change: New opportunities for qualitative research.* London: Routledge.

Schwab, J. (1964). *The teaching of science as enquiry.* Cambridge, MA: Harvard University Press.

Smith, D. (1987). *The everyday world as problematic: A feminist sociology.* Boston: Northeastern University Press.

Smith, D. (2005). *Institutional ethnography: A sociology for people.* Oxford: Altamira Press.

Smith, D. (2006). *Institutional ethnography as practice*. Lanham, MD: Rowman and Littlefield.
Tilllema, H., & Smith, K. (2007). Portfolio appraisal: In search of criteria. *Teaching and Teacher Education, 23*(4), 442–456.
Van de Ven, P-H., & Doecke, B. (Eds). (forthcoming). *Literary praxis: A conversational inquiry into the teaching of literature*. Rotterdam: Sense Publishers.

10 Exploring Discursive Practices of Teacher Learning in a Cross-Institutional Professional Community in China

Issa Danjun Ying

INTRODUCTION

The past decade reveals a global trend of educational reforms (e.g., Doecke, 2004; Hargreaves & Fink, 2000; Kelchtermans, 2005) requiring teachers to play a crucial role in making educational changes. Teachers are expected to teach with evolving learning theories, update current professional literature, integrate practice with research and match changes in societal structure, values and policies (Butler, Lauscher, Jarvis-Selinger & Beckingham, 2004, p. 435). Teachers in China are no exception.

In 2001, the Ministry of Education in China issued "Fundamentals of Curriculum Reform in Basic Education" as a guideline for 18 new syllabi in 17 subjects in primary and secondary education (Zhan, 2008). This policy affected teacher education and professional development (PD). Teachers and teacher educators face great challenges given inadequate professional support; hence teachers experience resistance, feel vulnerable and suffer from pressures of accountability and professional burnout. While programs for teacher learning and PD have been provided (e.g., continuing education, in-service training and internships and informal activities), they remain the traditional expert-driven and top-down approach to teacher learning that expects teachers to passively receive information and resources and translate them into practice in schools. This deficit model views teachers as deficient and in need of fixing (e.g., by administrators, experts and researchers; see Fiszer, 2004; Gilroy & Day, 1993; Huberman & Guskey, 1995). The 'deficit model' of teacher development thrives in China, especially since the Chinese culture reflects a transmission view of knowledge and learning.

Research encouraging teachers to work collaboratively or in communities addresses issues of professional learning (Paine & Fang, 2006; Wu, 2005; Wu, Huang, Zheng, Ying & Hu, 2005; Ying, 2007). However, community learning challenges the concept of teaching as isolated and private (Little, 2006). It conflicts with Chinese cultural roots in education and adopting a Western system of education (Wu, 2006; Xu & Connelly,

2009). Hence, little research explores the dynamics of teacher learning in communities and its impact on teaching practice in China.

TATEAL AS AN EVOLVING CROSS-INSTITUTIONAL TEACHER COMMUNITY

This study focuses on professional learning in the community of Teachers and Teacher Educators in Action Learning (TATEAL) at Wuyue Teachers' College in Jiangnan. In 2001, Dr. Li, a visiting, well-known international scholar conducted workshops as part of staff development activities but opened opportunities to other institutions in the same province.

Since then, annual TEAL workshops have been held usually lasting 3 days (generally Friday evening to Sunday afternoons). The workshops encourage participants to reflect on their teaching and learning experiences through telling and writing stories. These workshops depart significantly from mainstream forms of teacher learning in China that provide course-based, project-based or certificate-based teacher training. TEAL workshops provide opportunities for sharing and engaging in reflective dialogues with each other in a safe environment. After each annual event, participants are encouraged to keep in touch via emails to share stories about teaching and information about professional learning. As a result, TEAL forms a teacher community.

In 2005, TEAL became TATEAL when some teachers working in middle schools and master's students from various colleges of education in Jiangnan province and other provinces in China joined the annual event. The research students had a minimum of 2 years of teaching experiences in schools or other educational institutions. Participants now included teacher educators, teachers, administrative leaders and research students.

As a cross-institutional teacher community, TATEAL is loosely structured and organized: no registered membership, no claimed leadership and self-funded. This fluid structure requires participants' motivation, commitment and autonomy, and simultaneously attracts participants with shared educational concerns and visions who are eager for meaningful professional learning. Shared leadership makes it more like 'teaching commons' that Huber and Hutchings (2005) describe as a space in which educators are committed to inquiry and innovation, join to exchange teaching and learning knowledge and meet the challenges of educating students for personal, professional and civic life.

Since 2005, various institutions have hosted TATEAL annual events, although Dr. Li remains the facilitator. Gradually, it has became a collaborative effort among different institutions and evolved into a teacher community with sustainable interest in teachers' professional learning across institutional boundaries.

Teacher learning in a cross-institutional community is a complex process of social participation. From a sociocultural perspective, teacher learning occurs through situated social interactions with others; language used in these social interactions creates and reflects specific social contexts (Hawkins, 2004, p. 3). Learning is contextualized, and within particular discourses. Therefore, a discourse approach to understanding how teacher learning is discursively constructed is particularly appropriate, since it examines how language-as-discourse enacts specific social activities, social identities and relationships (Gee, 2005). It 'reads' educational events or situations as contextually situated 'texts' (MacLure, 2003, p. 8) and provides a perspective to understand teacher learning as a social activity, especially in community settings.

This study aims to understand teacher learning as 'texts' produced through discursive practices. In examining TATEAL discourses and its annual activities, it explores how participants engage in social dialogues to negotiate individual and social meanings as discursive construction of teacher learning through written and spoken texts produced in the community discourses. The research intends to identify textual relations, contextual factors and power relation in text production to provide a discourse perspective on understanding teacher learning in such contexts. The concept of intertextuality, often ascribed to Bakhtin (1981), formulated by Kristeva (1986) and developed by critical discourse analysts, e.g., Fairclough (1992), becomes a tool of inquiry to 'read' and understand 'texts' of teacher learning in communities.

Little's chapter in this book, although given primarily to school-based professional communities, points to the benefits of a 'borderless' learning community. The networks represented by TATEAL include what Little calls "external ties" and a "boardless" learning community for teachers and teacher educators that allow us to examine and explore the factors that impact teacher learning and how it is constructed in this community.

TEACHER LEARNING AS DISCURSIVE PRACTICES

In recent years, the 'communities of practice' concept developed by Lave and Wenger (1991) and Wenger (1998) has influenced educational thinking since it challenges traditional teacher learning and PD in isolation. In educational research, it explores how teachers learn through active engagement in professional learning communities (e.g., Bullough Jr. & Kridel, 2003; Burbank & Kauchak, 2003; Butler et al., 2004; Huffman & Kalnin, 2003; Little, 2002). The literature presents a theory of learning for educational researchers to understand learning in informal teacher networks. However, Creese (2005, p. 55) argues that the communities of practice concept lacks a coherent theory of language-in-use. Tusting (2005) suggests that the research needs a theoretical model that enables researchers to analyze language as social practice and link it to other social elements. It is then useful to take a micro lens using a discourse approach to operationalize this focus.

Gee (2005) developed a discourse theory focused on the holistic nature of human expression and suggests that discourses include not only spoken or written language-in-use, but:

> different ways in which we humans integrate language with non-language 'stuff,' such as different ways of thinking, acting, interacting, valuing, feeling, believing, and using symbols, tools, and objects in the right places and at the right times so as to enact and recognize different identities and activities, give the material world certain meanings, distribute social goods in a certain way, make certain sorts of meaningful connections in our experience, and privilege certain symbol systems and ways of knowing over others. (p. 13)

Hence, discourses are socially oriented and incorporate multiple activities and actions, both internal and external. Foucault (1972, p. 49) suggests treating discourses as "practices that systematically form the objects of which they speak." Therefore, discourse is about the production of knowledge through language, but the discourse itself is produced by, i.e., a 'discursive practice,' of producing meaning (Hall, 2002, p. 60). The approach recognizes that language-in-use is everywhere and always situated in wider social processes (Chouliaraki & Fairclough, 1999; MacLure, 2003). This provides a textually oriented perspective to understand teacher learning as social activity in community settings (Feiman-Nemser, 1990).

Discursive practices posit language as more than "an instrument of communication or even of knowledge, but also an instrument of power" (Bourdieu, 1977, p. 660). Participants speak in community to be understood but also believed, obeyed, respected and distinguished (Bourdieu, 1977, p. 648). Therefore, linguistic relations enacted through discursive practices reveal both social and power relations existing and built in specific contexts. However, little research, especially in China, explores the relationships between language, context and power to understand teacher learning in communities.

Intertextuality as a Tool of Inquiry

A discourse approach involves methods and theories for investigating language-in-use in social contexts. Intertextuality offers a tool of inquiry for the study of meanings and uncovering what Fairclough (1995, p. 40) calls "the orders of discourse" of a social domain.

The term 'intertextuality,' coined by Kristeva (1986), originated with Bakhtin (1981, 1986) and emphasizes the dialogical properties of texts. Fairclough (2001, p. 233) suggests "that any text is explicitly or implicitly 'in dialogue with' other texts (existing or anticipated) which constitute its 'intertexts.'" Thus any text links to a chain of texts, quoting, assimilating, recontextualizing, dialoguing with, transforming or even contradicting other texts. These links, or textual relations, indicate that intertextuality is an active social process of meaning-making, and "that meaning in language results from a complex of relationships linking items within a discourse and linking current to prior instances of language" (Tannen, 2007, p. 9). Bloome, Carter, Christian, Otto and Shuart-Faris (2005, pp. 40–41) also emphasize intertextuality is socially constructed and must be "proposed, acknowledged, recognized, and have social consequence." Therefore, intertextuality is dialogic by nature and should be taken as a historical process that examines the history of language use by looking beyond "the boundaries of particular communicative events and see where the expressions used there actually come from, what their sources are, whom they speak for, and how they relate to traditions of use" (Blommaert, 2005, pp. 46–47).

Intertextuality also focuses on reflexive text–context relations since contextualization involves "an active process of negotiating in which participants reflexively examine the discourse as it is emerging, embedding assessments of its structure and significance in the speech itself" (Bauman & Briggs, 1990, p. 69). Examining contextual factors facilitates understanding of how a text dialogues and negotiates with context.

TATEAL participants produce various written and spoken texts. The social, historical and reflexive dimensions of intertextuality make clear the complex relations in the text production and meaning construction through the discursive practices of text production. Two research questions have been identified:

1. What types of relations are constructed between texts in the community discourses?
2. What factors impact on participants' text production in professional learning?

Data Collection and Data Analysis

I employed multiple research methods for data collection, including ethnographic observation during the TATEAL annual events and conversational interviews with participants to discover the stories behind teachers' reported stories in face-to-face meetings, telephone conversations, emails and/or online discussions. I also collected news reports, invitation letters and event reports.

The data were collected primarily during TATEAL annual conferences over a 4-year period (2005 to 2008). Formal and informal written and oral documents were collected. Written data included the invitation letters noting the conference themes and schedules, handouts and other documents circulated during the events, emails among participants, reflective writings during and after the annual events, written stories, transcriptions of audio recordings and online talk on MSN and blogs. Oral data included audio or video recordings, informal conversations, follow-up interviews and reflective group discussions. All plenary sessions and some group discussions were recorded. Field notes and research journals were maintained to record observation details and analytical decisions.

The data analyzed were mainly drawn from the TATEAL 2008 annual event that differed from previous ones in three aspects: (a) it became a part of a symposium on Multicultural Discourses for Language Pedagogic Reform hosted by a college in the city of Jiangnan; (b) lasted about 3 hours as the final part of the symposium rather than the usual 1 evening and 2 days; (c) the symposium increased the variety of participants. The theme, "Engaging in Professional Discourse for Teacher Development," drew 92 participants from 25 institutions. Participants included mainly teacher educators, teachers and research students from different teachers' colleges. Almost one-fourth (22%) had participated in TATEAL annual events more than once.

Data analysis included combining narrative and discourse analysis. Narratives were first constructed to explore the interpretive power, multivoices and dialogic space. Following Fairclough's (1992, 1995) model of critical discourse analysis, intertextuality was used to analyze the collected written and oral texts to examine linguistic features, textual relations, situated meanings, knowledge and power and social relations in order to identify the effects of discourses on teacher learning.

I discuss Fei's spoken and written documents collected as a cluster of texts for analysis: written stories, emails and her speech. Intertextuality, as a tool of inquiry, traced a chain of relevant texts. The cluster of texts was shaped into narratives we called, *Fei's stories*. Further analysis identified relations between these texts and the impact of contextual factors on producing these texts. Power relations between texts as well as text producers were also unfolded in the process of analysis.

Fei's Stories

Fei first heard about TATEAL conferences from her supervisor, Dr. Tian. She attended in 2005 as an MA student in Zhehua Normal University. She graduated in 2006 and returned to her previous college in a southwest province in China to teach English. She attended again in 2008. In response to the invitation, Fei wrote:

> For me, joining the event can be called a luxury action, but I will try to overcome various obstacles to realize it. So could you please tell me more detailed agenda, especially the agenda on 17 October? Because I'm afraid I have to finish the teaching task before my leaving for Jiangnan. (Excerpt 1: Fei, email, September 28, 2008)

It was always difficult for teachers to make time to attend, especially as she had to travel from one province to another. However, her trying to "overcome various obstacles" showed her eagerness to join the event. She responded eagerly and quickly to Li's message to all previous participants (the facilitator since 2001), inviting them to reflect on their TATEAL experiences:

> Within a limited time we gather, it would be desirable to be prepared with some reflections so as to optimize the quality of our dialogues, especially when we look into the future of our community. Here are some suggested questions:
>
> 1) How many times did you join the TATEAL events? In which year(s)? Why did you attend it? How did you know about it?
> 2) What do you think of your experience of TATEAL? Has TATEAL impacted on your teaching and life in your own institution? In what ways? (You can illustrate with a story.)
> 3) Would you like TATEAL as a community to continue? What would be your contributions? (Excerpt 2: Li, email, October 3, 2008)

The themes of TATEAL 2005 to 2007 prompted attendees to recall the events. Fei quickly wrote two stories in English entitled "The Courage to Speak Out a Secret Story" and "Close Your Eyes and Talk with Your Heart" (Appendix 1). It was not common for English teachers in China to communicate in English about professional activities; however, participants tended to use Chinese as the language for communication. This made Fei's reflection in English surprising.

Dr. Li opened TATEAL 2008 with an introduction and a welcome. She invited participants of previous events to speak about their experiences with respect to why they came, how they learned about TATEAL, how their thinking and practices were affected by their participation. This opened the way for a collective reflection. Fei, among others, retold, mainly in Chinese, the stories of her participation in 2005 and her changes. Some related the changes resulting from their participation.

Min made a connection with Fei's speech:

> Today, we want to talk about changes. Just now teacher [Fei] said students would be silent in class. What I want to understand is the silence. . . . From 2001 till now, I, in fact, have been very silent in aspects of research and academia. Why? Because I am a young teacher and I feel that I have not had enough training in these aspects. . . . But on the other hand, I feel what let me keep silent is because I am a female. I posit a big question mark: Does academia have a gender? Is it male or female? I seem to find that I have to hide my own gender in academia, or at least to converge towards males, analyzing it rationally with their system of logics and language. (Excerpt 4A: Min, TATEAL 2008)

Min quoted Luxun, a famous Chinese writer of the 1920s and 1930s—
"Either to die in the silence, or to explode out of the silence"—to explain her
understanding of how teachers could explode out of the silence by actively
pursuing her teacher identity. She questions students' silence in class:

> Why are students so silent? What are the reasons? Let's inquire into it
> together. For example, shall we allow students to keep silent? Could
> temporary silence be for his better explosion? Also could I possibly
> impose my ideas and values so that they dare not say anything from his
> heart? (Excerpt 4B: Min, TATEAL 2008)

Min followed Fei conducted an inquiry with different perspectives that further developed the issue of silence. This powerfully co-constructed, rather
than repeated, the knowledge.

Li asked participants to form small groups for further sharing by spending
3 to 5 quiet minutes in personal reflection. "During these few minutes, don't
interrupt each other; allow three quiet minutes. You can write down your
ideas . . . engage in an activity, a personal activity—write one sentence to represent your teaching life in the past year" (Excerpt 4D: Li, TATEAL 2008).

After TATEAL 2008, Ning, a teacher and part-time MA student in Zhehua Teachers' College, described this group activity at the beginning of her
reflection: "Actually, we were not quite sure what we were going to do at
first. Soon we were divided into groups of three or four. Dr. Li just wanted
us to feel safe. The room was quiet. . . . It made me think of Yoga" (Excerpt
4E: Ning, written reflection, 2008).

Ning's interpretation connected with her personal experience of Yoga to
help her understand the new experience. The indirect impact of Fei's speech
resonated when Ning described what other participants did (e.g., "Some
were thinking silently; some closing their eyes").

Fei's retelling and reliving of her TATEAL 2005 experiences required
her to reconstruct her understanding of past experiences, and also had an
impact on other participants' learning in the community (e.g., Min, Wei
and Ning). Both Fei and others negotiated to achieve a deeper meaning.
The written and spoken texts, as fragments of teacher learning in the community, were produced through discursive practices in this process that,
in turn, reified the moments of learning and contributed to constructing
learning in the community discourses.

Textual relations in Fei's Stories

Intertextuality provided a useful tool of inquiry to examine the various
discourse/texts produced and identify textual relations and contextual
factors to understand the discursive construction of teacher learning.
We use Fei's community learning experience as one of many episodes for
the analysis.

Figure 10.1 shows mainly two types of relations between these texts: one is downward, i.e., how one text leads to another, such as sourcing, initiating, inspiring and formatting; the other is upward, i.e., how one text responds to a prior one, such as quoting, assimilating, interpreting and transforming. These relations reveal how teacher learning occurred discursively and socially.

Downward Textual Relations

The downward relations both enable and constrain the production of upcoming texts: who can speak, what can be said and how it can be said. For example, the emails Fei received before the event initiated her written stories of experiences in TATEAL 2005, especially the one with questions (Excerpt 2) that functioned as a framework, structuring what she could write and in what way. Fei's experience, namely, what she did (said, wrote) became a source for writing stories and making meaning of her

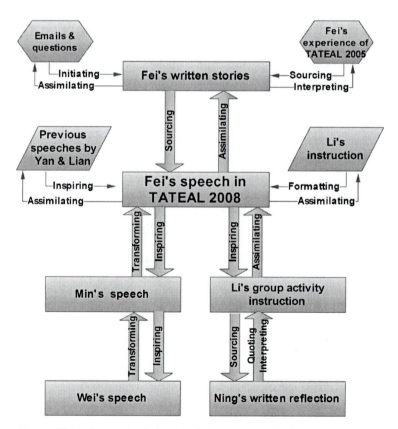

Figure 10.1   Textual relations in Fei's stories in TATEAL 2008.

experiences. A sourcing relation provides opportunities and possibilities for producing texts.

The texts in an inspiring relation with other texts are influential sources for text production, either explicitly or implicitly. For example, the speakers' speech reflected speech that came before (Bakhtin, 1981). In TATEAL 2008, previous speakers did not give clear instructions about what Fei should say, but what they said, how they said it and whether they followed Li's expectations set a genre of speech that affected and shaped Fei's speech.

> Ms Li asked us, "Close your eyes." Close eyes to think for a few minutes. I thought this was a way to let you calm down, ignoring things in the outside world. It had impact on me in my teaching practice. As a teacher, I think, in class, when you ask a question, very often the class is silent, which is very common. In the past, possibly [I] complained why students didn't want to speak, but, by participating in this community, I often reflected on myself. There should be some problems of my language that could be the reason that students would like to speak but dare not to speak. (Excerpt 5A: Fei, TATEAL 2008)

Fei's speech had an explicit impact on Min's speech (Excerpt 4A, 4B) and Li's group activity instruction. Fei's speech also inspired other participants. For example, Ning described in her written reflection what other participants did during the quiet time: "Some were thinking silently, some were closing their eyes." (Excerpt 4E)

A formatting relation shows how one text highly frames the content and structure of upcoming text(s). For example, in this situated discursive practice, Li's instruction determined who could speak, what could be said and the order of content in the speech by using the words of 'first,' 'besides,' 'afterwards' (Excerpt 3). This text set the rule of speech and was a major reason Fei's speech differed from her written stories in content and structure. The formatting relation is productive, demonstrating the high degree of power relation among texts.

Upward Textual Relations

The upward relations are responding relations, indicating how a text actively makes associations with other texts, negotiates meanings and functions as agency involving intervention and autonomy in situated practices. A quoting relation repeats what is in the previous text(s) while an interpreting relation makes sense of a previous text. For example, Ning quoted Li's instruction for organizing group work. She interpreted the meaning by relating it to her Yoga experiences.

An assimilating relation represents a dialogue between present and prior text(s) in the context of the present text. In her two written stories, Fei responded to questions posted in the email by assimilating some, but not all, and placing them in a different order. In the first paragraph, she begins addressing question 2 (Excerpt 2) by reflecting on her TATEAL experience, indicating the year of her attendance asked in question 1 (Excerpt 2). Other aspects of Question 1 remained unanswered.

> Some incidents or some people are able to carve deep prints in one's life. I suppose the two days' participation in 2005 TATEAL is such an incident. Instead of just listening to reports or speeches on any other similar occasions, here in TATEAL, I myself really took part in it. (Excerpt 5B: Excerpted from Fei's written stories, 2008)

The remaining two stories addressed in question 2 discuss the impact on her teaching and personal life. Fei practiced autonomy in her response to the questions.

Other assimilations emerged: For example, Fei's speech represented her written stories in a different context that, in effect, recontextualized the previous text. She integrated Li's instruction to restructure her stories, adding discourse markers such as 'first,' 'second' and 'third' as she spoke. Fei's assimilation of previous speeches (Yan and Lian) allowed her to add content not included in her written stories. She agreed with Yan's point, but compared Lian's talk about the difference.

Lian shared the experience of her first participation in TATEAL and claimed:

> Although it was my first time [to attend this event], I felt there was a sense of equality, and cooperation. I felt comfortable that I could say whatever I wanted to say. . . . My deepest feeling was that I was the host, the owner. I was not to attend a conference. I was not a listener. I was a participant. (Excerpt 6: Lian, TATEAL 2008)

Fei responded to Lian's speech by comparing her feeling at the beginning of TATEAL 2005 with Lian's:

> When I [first] attended this [TATEAL 2005], I was still a graduate student. I heard about it from my supervisor Mr. Tian. . . . I attended this community as a student, so maybe, unlike Ms Lian with the sense of being the host, the owner, I seemed to join it as a listener. (Excerpt 6B: Fei TATEAL 2008)

Fei's connection with Lian was a discursive practice of negotiating meaning of her experience and participant identity: What she thought about who she was in this community, and why she viewed herself in this way. What Lian said reminded her that she joined TATEAL 2005 as a passive listener first, but later engaged deeply, noting that she 'really took part in it,' not just listening.

Fei also responded to receiving TATEAL emails that connected with Yan's speech:

> Just now, Mr. Yan mentioned the importance of Ms Li's emotional support to us. I can feel the impact from attending this activity. . . . TATEAL, this community, often sent emails to notify us of the activities. For me, I am so far away from you, and can hardly keep contact with you, in fact, but it is very moving for me to receive such emails . . . It triggers my passion at least for a few days. I keep searching for something about this community, what we discussed in this community. Such an email can be as simple as giving a notice, but can also generate a lot of thinking and desire for learning. I can feel the important emotional support from the community. Hope the community can continue in the future. (Excerpt 6C: Fei, TATEAL 2008)

Fei naturally showed her emotional responses to the emails. Yan inspired these responses, not apparent in her written stories. Thus, Fei's speech was, in fact, co-constructed in the situated practices in the community by negotiating meanings and dialoguing with herself, others and the context.

A transforming relation interprets a previous text and transforms it to understand different things or situations. For example, Min responded to Fei's reflection of silent students and transformed it to understand gender issues in research and academia. Wei continued to talk about silence and explosion, but shifted it to address the demanding situation of teaching and publication.

To conclude, these textual relations, downward or upward, indicate how teacher learning happens in a weblike network in the community. Palmer (1998, p. 11) argues that "good teachers possess a capacity for connectedness. They are able to weave a complex web of connections among themselves, their subjects, and their students." Fei, like many other participants, was a weaver making connections intellectually and emotionally, and also personally and socially. Her learning became transformed and transferable by making a complex web of connections with places (such as TATEAL events venues, classroom and her home); people (herself, the facilitator, students and her husband); and activities (TATEAL activities, mistakes, dealing with students, quarrelling with her husband). Her past, present and future revealed a web with different relations, making a space for transformational learning.

Contextual Factors

The texts produced not only show how teacher learning was discursively constructed in terms of textual relations, but also indicate the contextual factors for teacher learning. Fei's texts are further examined for contextual factors (Figure 10.2) that impact text production.

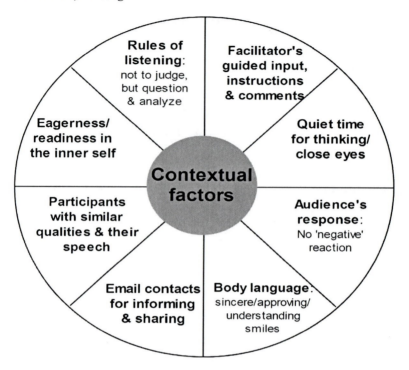

Figure 10.2   Contextual factors in Fei's text production.

Fei's written stories reveal that she deeply inquired into her experience of telling a secret story in TATEAL 2005. At the beginning, Fei interpreted her experiences as incidental, which may be true for participants who joined TATEAL only once or twice. Despite not being a regular participant, she felt she 'really took part in it,' partly due to telling a secret story. She was surprised, even shocked by her own courage to tell a secret story in public noting the story was, "an iceberg in my heart": She adds: "So the question haunted me: where did the courage come from?"

By posing this question, Fay initiates a dialogic inquiry with self and the 2005 conference context. She explores further by reflecting on her response to Dr. Li's call for reflection: "Maybe at that time I was involved too much and I touched the inner part of my soul and the story was thus brought to the table." She became aware of safety in the room: "After the other teachers' stories, there seems no negative reaction at all. Instead, sincere, approving or understanding smiles were put on every audience's face. Ms Li's comment particularly assured me of the safety to tell it." Giddens (1979, p. 57) emphasizes "monitoring of action includes the monitoring of the setting of interaction, and not just the behavior of the particular actors taken separately." All these contextual factors indicated how a safe setting of interaction was monitored collaboratively.

Fei felt that other participants shared her eagerness. In a follow-up interview by email, she explained: "They knew the purpose of storytelling, and wouldn't distort, misunderstand, or make misconnection. . . . I could probably summarize it as professional-development oriented, sincere, understanding and tolerant" (2009).

Fei's email indicates that participants seemed to have in Wenger's (1998) terms, the 'joint enterprise' of pursuing PD and 'shared repertoire.' This explains why Fei thought it safe to tell a secret story. She explained her motivation for writing stories in the follow-up interview email as: "The trust in TATEAL and the desire to 'optimize the quality of our dialogues' in the event" (2009). The phrase, 'to optimize the quality of our dialogues,' was part of a sentence in the invitation to reflect on her TATEAL experiences (Excerpt 2). This reveals her motivation of pursuing the quality of professional learning.

Fei's deep reflection led to a second story that indicated how her experiences transformed and applied to other aspects of her life, such as confronting family conflicts and the relations with her students:

> When there was a quarrel with my husband, I would say, "Let's close our eyes and comb the matter clearly." When there was silence following up a discussion topic or an open-ended question in my class, I would say, "Please close your eyes and talk with your heart, I believe you really have something to say." Most often, it really works. (Excerpt 7: Excerpted from Fei's written stories, 2008)

Writing stories enabled Fei to foster dialogues with her experience, self, others, the community and her personal and professional life. These dialogues helped Fei open a space for reflection, negotiation, interpretation, self-empowering and understanding. Such space was not limited to places and could help Fei learn beyond the boundaries of communicative events.

Fei's reattendance gave her an opportunity to reconstruct the meanings of her past experiences to extend her understanding. Her speech and discourse in the learning community were shaped by the conference context. The theme, email exchanges, Li's instruction, previous speakers' speeches and the presence of other participants were all the contextual factors for text reproduction.

In an email after the 2008 conference, Fei explained four obstacles that discouraged her from participating in the annual event at that time:

No.1 My twin babies were just ten-month old.

No.2 Every week I had to give 12 lectures, and there were many procedures in my institution for application of leave.

No.3 The cost was another problem. There was no economic support from my institution. The trip would cost me up to four thousand yuan, which was my income for one and a half's months.

No.4. I need to persuade my family members to support me. (Excerpt 8: Fei, email, 2009)

Figure 10.3   Levels of contextual factors impacting on Fei's text production and participation in TATEAL events.

The family, institutional and financial factors affected Fei's decision. Fei made the trip when she finally got family members' support, especially her mother's encouragement. In addition, one leader in her institution helped to fund the trip.

To conclude, different levels of contextual factors impact Fei's text production as teacher learning and community participation: self, community practices and social practices (Figure 10.3). Fei's eagerness, readiness and desire for a high quality of professional learning were internal factors while the community practices provided interaction settings, dialogic space and opportunities for Fei to share her stories .The three levels of contextual factors shed light on understanding how teacher learning is shaped by the community discourses.

Discursive Capability and Power Relation in Text Production

Given that not everyone is good at storytelling, there is an issue of what Giddens (1979) calls 'discursive capabilities.' Telling and retelling stories gave Fei an important opportunity to enhance her 'discursive capabilities' that enabled her to give an account of her experience and explain how she could make sense of it, which made her tacit knowledge expressible and explicit. For example, Fei was able to explain some reasons for telling a secret story in public that had been tacit knowledge in the past.

To give an account requires discursive skills and strategies. Fei's written stories and speech demonstrated her ability to articulate and interpret, and her skills to describe, sequence, elaborate, summarize and reason, and use metaphors and repetition. The guided questions in Excerpt 2 and Li's instructions in Excerpt 3 help Fei to develop her discursive capabilities that made it possible for teacher knowledge to be practiced, circulated, dialogued and co-constructed. The development of Fei's discursive capabilities indicates the important role of a professional learning community in promoting teachers' PD.

Power relations develop as discursive capabilities are enhanced. Giddens (1979, p. 209) argues that "the capability of controlling settings is one of the major prerogatives of power itself." When a text generates initiating, inspiring and formatting relations with others, it produces power. Power, as a productive force, is embodied in this textual-relation building. For example, Li's instruction set a frame for inquiry to guide participants' speech. Fei's speech inspired Li and other participants in their group activity. Downward textual relations indicated various degrees of power relations between texts: For example, an initiating relation is more powerful than a sourcing relation but less than an inspiring one, while a formatting relation indicates the most powerful productive force. The upward textual relations, on the other hand, indicate the various degrees of empowerment. Hence, an assimilating one enacts more power than a quoting one, but less than interpreting, while a transforming one demonstrates the most empowering force. Accordingly, texts in position of these high-degree textual relations become more powerful than others as a productive learning force. Fei's speech is a good example of powerful text—like a knot pulling together various powerful relations to unify and enhance its strength.

CONCLUSION

In this study, intertextuality became a tool of inquiry to understand the discursive construction of teacher learning in the community. *Fei's stories*, as one of many learning episodes in the community discourses, were narrated, analyzed and interpreted to reveal the discursive practices of teacher learning as text production in the community. The texts, written or spoken, reified learning moments in the community discourses and indicated how teacher learning discursively happened in a weblike network. Downward and upward textual relations were analyzed to reveal how texts led to others by sourcing, initiating, inspiring and formatting other texts, and how texts assumed agency by quoting, assimilating, interpreting and transforming prior texts. Contextual factors of self, community practices and social practices were identified to explore the contextual impact on teacher learning in terms of text production and community participation.

In the process of text production, participants like Fei became weavers to make discursive connections beyond the boundaries of communicative events. They incorporated their conference experiences into their professional and personal lives. Teacher learning was situated, negotiated, circulated and reconstructed in the community discourses, and thus became transformational. TATEAL provided a platform for teachers to make dialogic voices and negotiate meanings that, in turn, enhanced discursive capabilities to make tacit knowledge explicit and sustain PD and self-empowerment. This echoes what Loughran describes in another chapter in this book. He asserts that professional learning is enhanced when conditions are created to help teachers to make tacit knowledge explicit and cautions educators to be aware of the theory-practice gap and take more control of their own professional learning.

Teachers' professional autonomy and commitment to learning were crucial to their professional learning. Fei's readiness and eagerness for high-quality professional learning developed her professional autonomy. She made a choice to tell a secret story that she had never told before and to do it in an open platform, because it was a safe environment with attentive listeners. Fei made a choice to attend TATEAL 2008 in spite of the demands of heavy workload and the needs of her baby twins, and with the support from her institution. She managed to take responsibility for her own professional learning. Fei's professional efforts were not officially recognized. Ultimately, it seems teachers need to take responsibility for and be accountable for their choices for professional learning.

ACKNOWLEDGMENTS

I would like to thank Dr. Ora Kwo from the University of Hong Kong and Mr. David Johnson for their constructive comments on the draft of this chapter.

REFERENCES

Bakhtin, M. (1981). *The dialogic imagination: Four essays* (C. E. M. Holoquist, Trans.). Austin: University of Texas Press.

Bakhtin, M. (1986). *Speech genres and other late essays* (V. W. McGee, Trans.). Austin: University of Texas Press.

Bauman, R., & Briggs, C. (1990). Poetics and performances as critical perspectives on language and social life. *Annual Review of Anthropology, 19*(1), 59–88.

Blommaert, J. (2005). *Discourse: A critical introduction.* Cambridge: Cambridge University Press.

Bloome, D., Carter, S. P., Christian, B. M., Otto, S. & Shuart-Faris, N. (Eds.). (2005). *Discourse analysis & the study of classroom language & literacy events: A microethnographic perspective.* Mahwah, NJ: Lawrence Erlbaum Associates.

Bourdieu, P. (1977). The economics of linguistic exchanges. *Social Science Information, 16*(6), 645–668.

Bullough Jr., R. V., & Kridel, C. (2003). Workshops, in-service teacher education, and the eight-year study. *Teaching and Teacher Education, 19*(7), 665–679.

Burbank, M. D., & Kauchak, D. (2003). An alternative model for professional development: Investigations into effective collaboration. *Teaching and Teacher Education, 19*(5), 499–514.

Butler, D. L., Lauscher, H. N., Jarvis-Selinger, S. & Beckingham, B. (2004). Collaboration and self-regulation in teachers' professional development. *Teaching and Teacher Education, 20*(5), 435–455.

Chouliaraki, L., & Fairclough, N. (1999). *Discourse in late modernity: Rethinking critical discourse analysis.* Edinburgh: Edinburgh University Press.

Creese, A. (2005). Mediating allegations of racism in a multiethnic London school: What speech communities and communities of practice can tell us about discourse and power. In D. Barton & K. Tusting (Eds.), *Beyond communities of practice* (pp. 55–76). Cambridge: Cambridge University Press.

Doecke, B. (2004). Professional identity and educational reform: Confronting my habitual practices as a teacher educator. *Teaching and Teacher Education, 20*(2), 203–215.

Fairclough, N. (1992). *Discourse and social change.* Cambridge, UK: Polity Press.

Fairclough, N. (1995). *Critical discourse analysis: The critical study of language.* London: Longman.

Fairclough, N. (2001). The discourse of new labour: Critical discourse analysis. In M. Wetherell, S. Taylor & S. Yates (Eds.), *Discourse as data: A guide for analysis* (pp. 229–266). London: Sage/Open University Press.

Feiman-Nemser, S. (1990). Teacher education: Structural and conceptual alternatives. In W. R. Houston, M. Haberman & J. P. Sikula (Eds.), *Handbook of research on teacher education* (pp. 212–233). New York: Macmillan.

Fiszer, E. P. (2004). *How teachers learn best: An ongoing professional development model.* Lanham, Md.: Scarecrow Education.

Foucault, M. (1972). *The archaeology of knowledge.* London: Tavistock.

Gee, J. P. (2005). *An introduction to discourse analysis: Theory and method* (2nd ed.). New York: Routledge.

Giddens, A. (1979). *Central problems in social theory: Action, structure, and contradiction in social analysis.* Berkeley: University of California Press.

Gilroy, P. and Day, C. (1993) The Erosion of INSET in England and Wales: analysis and proposals for a redefinition. Journal of Education for Teaching, 19 (2), pp. 141–157.

Hall, S. (2002). The West and the rest: Discourse and power. In S. Schech & J. Haggis (Eds.), *Development: A cultural studies reader* (pp. 56–64). Oxford: Blackwell Publishers.

Hargreaves, A., & Fink, D. (2000). The three dimensions of reform. *Educational Leadership, 57*(7), 30–33.

Hawkins, M. R. (Ed.). (2004). *Language learning and teacher education: A sociocultural approach.* Clevedon: Multilingual Matters.

Huber, M. T., & Hutchings, P. (2005). *The advancement of learning.* San Francisco: Jossey-Boss.

Huberman, M., & Guskey, T. R. (1995). The diversities of professional development. In T. R. Guskey & M. Huberman (Eds.), *Professional development in education: New paradigms and practices* (pp. 269–272). New York: Teachers College Press.

Huffman, D., & Kalnin, J. (2003). Collaborative inquiry to make data-based decisions in schools. *Teaching and Teacher Education, 19*(6), 569–580.

Kelchtermans, G. (2005). Teachers' emotions in educational reforms: Self-understanding, vulnerable commitment and micropolitical literacy. *Teaching and Teacher Education, 21*(8), 995–1006.

Kristeva, J. (1986). *The Kristeva reader* (T. Moi, Ed.). New York: Columbia University Press.

Lave, J., & Wenger, E. (1991). *Situated learning, legitimate peripheral participation.* Cambridge: Cambridge University Press.

Little, J. W. (2002). Locating learning in teachers' communities of practice: Opening up problems of analysis in records of everyday work. *Teaching and Teacher Education, 18*(8), 917–946.

Little, J. W. (2006). *Professional community and professional development in the learning-centered school.* Washington, DC: National Education Association.

MacLure, M. (2003). *Discourse in educational and social research.* Buckingham: Open University.

Paine, L. W., & Fang, Y. (2006). Reform as hybrid model of teaching and teacher development in China. *International Journal of Educational Research, 45*(4–5), 279–289.

Palmer, P. J. (1998). *The courage to teach: Exploring the inner landscape of a teacher's life.* San Francisco: Jossey-Bass.

Tannen, D. (2007). *Talking voices: Repetition, dialogue, and imagery in conversational discourse* (2nd ed.). Cambridge: Cambridge University Press.

Tusting, K. (2005). Language and power in communities of practice. In D. Barton & K. Tusting (Eds.), *Beyond communities of practice* (pp. 36–54). Cambridge: Cambridge University Press.

Wenger, E. (1998). *Communities of practice: Learning, meaning and identity.* Cambridge: Cambridge University Press.

Wu, Z. (2005). *Teachers' knowing in curriculum change: A critical discourse study of language teaching.* Beijing: Foreign Language Teaching and Research Press.

Wu, Z. (2006). Understanding practitioner research as a form of life: An Eastern interpretation of exploratory practice. *Language Teaching Research, 10*(3), 331–350.

Wu, Z., Huang, A., Zheng, Z., Ying, D. & Hu, M. (2005). *Curriculum and language teacher development—the RICH educational landscape.* Hefei: Anhui Education Press.

Xu, S., & Connelly, F. M. (2009). Narrative inquiry for teacher education and development: Focus on English as a foreign language in China. *Teaching and Teacher Education, 25*(2), 219–227.

Ying, D. (2007). Teacher educators' collaborative inquiry in a context of educational innovation in China: A case study of RICH as a learning community. In T. Townsend & R. Bates (Eds.), *Handbook of teacher education: Globalization, standards and professionalism in times of change* (pp. 539–554). Dordrecht: Springer.

Zhan, S. (2008). Changes to a Chinese pre-service language teacher education program: Analysis, results and implications. *Asia-Pacific Journal of Teacher Education, 36*(1), 53–70.

Part IV

Professional Learning for Teacher Practice

11 Partnerships for Professional Renewal

The Development of a Master's Program for Teacher Professional Learning

Helen Mitchell and Alex Alexandrou

INTRODUCTION

The Organisation for Economic Co-operation and Development (OECD) report *Creating Effective Teaching and Learning Environments* (2009) recognizes the importance of recruiting well-qualified individuals to become teachers, of providing high-quality preservice programs and of ensuring ongoing and effective professional learning programs. These three key emphases are foundational and recurring ideas in national policies seeking to ensure that improved teaching results in improved pupil learning; see, for example, the McKinsey report (Barber & Mourshed, 2007) in the United States; the recent White Paper on Education in England (Department for education, 2010). The OECD report is to be welcomed for its focus on professional development (PD) through the Teaching and Learning International Study (TALIS). It is also valuable for its focus on high-quality Continuous Professional Development (CPD) programs with strong congruence to individual and institutional needs.

Reflecting the OECD agenda, current education policy in England often positions teacher professional learning as key to effectiveness schooling. Some recent policy initiatives identify the high-performing education system in Finland, in which all teachers are educated to master's level, as a model of postgraduate PD. The broad context for this chapter is just such a government initiative that aimed to improve teacher effectiveness through a CPD program at the master's level. This chapter outlines the conceptual structure and rationale for a school-based master's in Education program for teachers in primary and secondary schools in England. The program, which takes place in a large economically deprived conurbation, is coordinated by a local university in partnership with local schools. The social and economic context of the area means that many of the schools work in challenging circumstances, teaching pupils whose lives are often difficult. This school-based master's program aimed to support teachers in these challenging schools; in particular, to provide a mechanism for professional renewal that would function effectively in the context of the new public management and performativity agendas that currently dominate schooling and teacher education in England.

The chapter also includes an analysis of the findings from an external evaluation conducted over the first 18 months of the master's program. The evaluation showed that the conceptual model underpinning the program works in practice. In particular, through the development of 'new' partnership communities of practice, new knowledge could be generated through a creative disruption of existing practices in the school and university communities of practice. The evaluation also provided evidence of the positive influence of the program on the work of teachers, in improving pupil learning experiences.

Although written by only two members, this chapter articulates the views of the whole master's program teaching team. It reflects our communal views that current national education policies constrain rather than empower teachers working in schools in challenging circumstances, and sometimes fail to support a focus on the core business of learning in ways that address social inequality and result in positive learning outcomes for all pupils. But we also believe that teacher learning at the master's level has the potential to empower and militate against some of these constraints.

THE NATIONAL, LOCAL AND INSTITUTIONAL CONTEXTS FOR TEACHERS' PROFESSIONAL LEARNING

National Contexts and Constraints

The context of teacher professional learning in England has been in a state of flux for at least the past 25 years. The 1988 Education Reform Act started the move towards a 'quasi market' in education. Subsequent years of Conservative rule increasingly devolved financial and management responsibility to schools, requiring them to compete against other education providers for resources. At the same time central government tightened its control of the curriculum, pedagogy, testing, inspection and the conditions of service under which teachers work (Bates, 2005). The New Labour government's (1997 to 2010) continuation of the neoliberal policies in many ways accelerated the evolution into a competition state (Cerny & Evans, 2004).

The systems of new public management (Hood 1991) emphasized performativity and measurable outcomes, favoring the evaluation of product over process. Increasing central control of curriculum and pedagogy formalized the processes of schooling. While funding responsibility fell to schools, the funding itself was contingent on external performance criteria. Because of this, the new public management and the quasi market became, in some key ways, synonymous (Hartley, 2008).

A system of market-driven performance management impacts the professional learning of teachers in fundamental ways. Notably, the accountability of new public management constricts learning, teaching and the curriculum by reducing measures of the collective success of schools to the outcomes of standardized national tests (Sacks, 1999). Day, Sammons, Stobart, Kington and Gu (2007, p. 8) note the close monitoring of teacher and pupil performances resulting from such agendas. Consequences for teachers include implicit encouragement to comply uncritically with pedagogies such as 'teaching to the test'; challenges to their substantive identities, motivation and commitment; threats to their sense of agency and resilience; and less time to "connect with, care for and attend to the needs of individual pupils" (p. 8). Performance management has then resulted in teaching and teacher learning becoming a technical activity (Day et al.). Following Sachs (2003) and Bottery (2005), we would argue that it has also challenged previous notions of professionalism based upon trust, professional judgment and agency.

A deeper, more invasive consequence of these regimes of new public management also requires consideration. Writing about the impact of audit in the area of psychotherapy, for example, Cooper (2001, p. 357) notes that "major audit or quality assessment exercises are as much an exercise in representation as reality." In this 'virtual politics,' symbolism and policy illusion prevail over practicality of content. Furthermore, quality audits function like traditional examinations where 'accumulated learning' is tested in the space of a few hours, stimulating "the same kinds of anxieties as do school examination." Hoggett (2010) echoes this view, arguing that new public management has moved beyond functioning as a social system to decrease individual anxiety to one where politicians, regulators and managers actively collude in self-deception, creating key performance indicators and other measures that may seem coherent but are increasingly disconnected from the reality of people's lives. Besides a lack of trust or space for the negotiation of professional identity and agency, new public management leads to a 'virtual reality' that creates anxiety because it is disconnected from the realities of learning and teaching. These processes are, in our view, more intense when they occur in schools facing increasing social inequality.

The University and School Contexts

The university is a 'new' or teaching-intensive university; it was a polytechnic before 1992 when it was granted university status. Although diversifying, the university's offerings of undergraduate and graduate program qualifications are still vocational or professional courses. Situated in one of England's most deprived urban areas, the university's mission statement includes a strong commitment to supporting social justice issues and engagement with the local communities.

The School of Education within this university is the immediate setting for the development of the MA in Education program described here. It has large undergraduate enrollment in education and a major investment in preservice teacher education, as well as strong outreach relationships and partnerships with educational administrative regions (Local Authorities) that straddle the inner- and outer-city locations closest to the university. Each Local Authority has a slightly different character and different priorities. The area immediately surrounding the university, for example, has high levels of social and economic deprivation. In recent years both local and national governments have made substantial investments in this area, showing a commitment to regeneration of infrastructure, capital building, improving the skills of the local workforce and other policy measures to alleviate poverty.

Historically, this area has been a staging post for newcomers to England. For many local families, English is spoken as a second or third language. Additionally, there is often no family experience of the English education system and little history of higher education. These first-generation immigrant communities also experience high degrees of social mobility as many families move on and out of the area once they become established. However, this area also has a traditional poor and undereducated white working-class community, many of whom worked in sectors now described as 'lost industries': for example, heavy manufacturing and labor in the docks. Some schools in this local area operate amid challenges arising from 'severe socioeconomic disadvantage' for their pupils, "a high proportion of pupils with special educational needs (SEN) and meeting the needs of pupils who speak languages other than English" (Training and Development Agency [TDA], 2010). Some struggle to recruit and retain teaching staff, support pupils to achieve the minimum benchmark qualifications or manage pupil behavior to acceptable levels. Many schools also have poor building stock often unfit for purpose.

In the areas further away from the university, communities often have more wealth and stability. This wealth, however, is associated more with the start-up of small businesses, many operating as sole traders, or with individuals working in the city's financial district, than with opportunities through higher education. The schools in these areas may face fewer difficult challenges, but some still struggle to maintain the designated national levels of pupil achievement and to retain their teachers. The master's in Education program operates across all these differing geographical and socioeconomic locations.

Responding to a Government Initiative:
The First Iteration of the Master's Program

We indicated that the program described here was part of a government initiative to fund CPD programs leading to a postgraduate qualification. In 2002, the Teacher Training Agency (now TDA)[1] launched a new scheme to subsidize fees for teachers on specific programs leading to a master's or postgraduate diploma. While universities and schools were to coordinate the programs, they would be led by academic faculty at the university.

One key requirement for this national funding was that the planned programs had to have an impact on standards in schools in general and on improved pupil performance in particular. A further requirement for the participating universities was to demonstrate how their programs would achieve and measure this impact. Whilst in some ways this funding initiative marked a positive move towards engaging teachers professionally in order to achieve educational reform, the methodology of reporting impact and the bidding criteria created some tensions between instrumentality and a deeper commitment to professional learning. Notably, achievement of a postgraduate award was not directly linked to any career structure or progression for teachers.

In England, as in much of Continental Europe, the master's in Education qualifications require teachers to move beyond technical learning to critical processes of research and inquiry. Whilst the pervasive climate of anxiety and fear of failure against performativity measures can present a significant challenge to such critical learning, evidence also exists that scholarly activity focused on the core business of understanding learning and teaching can bring about professional renewal (Bird, Ding, Hanson, Leontovitsch & McCartney, 2005; Bardley-Levine, Smith & Car, 2009; Kearns, 2003; McDonald Grieve & McGinley, 2010; Mee, 2008).

In response to this national funding opportunity, the university developed a Postgraduate Professional Development (PPD) funded master's degree in 2002. In this first iteration of the MA Education program, recruitment of teachers peaked at a level that would not financially support further development. Low recruitment diminished opportunities and choice for participants, leading to a vicious circle of further under-recruitment. In particular, small group sizes limited opportunities for teachers to share practice across a wide enough range of experiences and perspectives. Given the view of teacher professional learning as a technical activity focused on achieving measurable outcomes, these adverse factors resulted in disappointing work at the master's level for some participating teachers.

As a starting point for addressing these disappointing initial outcomes and revising the program, informal discussions took place between the program leader (Helen), current and previous MA students, school-based mentors for the university's preservice programs and local head teachers and other school staff involved in PD planning. From these discussions, it became clear that whilst, superficially, the factors inhibiting participation were time and money, underlying these factors was a perception of conflict between the scholarly activity required by for study at master's level, the school's priorities and the day-to-day pressures and realities of teachers' work.

Issues superficially around time stemmed, in part, from a misconception about the relevance of master's level study for addressing national and local priorities. Studying at the master's level was seen as one more competing demand on teachers' time. Conflict regarding timescales for teacher learning and development, particularly given the national accountability frameworks and the constant stream of government initiatives requiring immediate action within schools, also arose. The longer timescales needed to address the same initiatives through a more robust and scholarly approach to teachers' professional learning were seen as a threat rather than an opportunity by a number of the school leaders.

With limited budgets for PD, school leaders were also concerned about the relationship between investment in an individual teacher's time and the impact of that investment on the development of the school. Many felt that, where teachers had engaged in previous master's programs, there had either been a poor implementation of their learning or limited influence on the quality of pupil learning beyond that individual teacher's classroom. Travel time for attending university sessions was also a concern.

Issues around money were relatively straightforward. Schools reserved their limited budgets for teachers' professional learning for initiative-led training or for creating opportunities for teachers to share practice within the school and/or with other schools. The biggest expense was the supply cover paid to release teachers to attend professional training and development courses. Even this was severely limited by teaching union cover agreements[2] that often made it too difficult to release teachers. In addition, fees for master's level study were prohibitive for many schools and teachers, even with a government subsidy in place.

It was clear that the revisions to the master's program needed to focus more explicitly on the interface between day-to-day work in schools and scholarly activity, with a very specific focus on processes that would both support teachers' individual learning and the effective 'transfer' of that learning to enhance the quality of pupil learning. To achieve this, and move beyond a merely technical engagement with professional learning, clearly required both a new program design and a revised pedagogy at the master's level.

The Conceptual and Operational Basis of the New Master's Program

Conceptualizing Master's Learning

The approach to the new program design was to start with analysis of research on, and experiences of, teacher professional learning. We considered a number of factors including: the master's level qualification descriptors provided by government and university; the imperatives of the new public management regimes for schools; and any specific issues raised in discussion with stakeholders, including, crucially, the school leaders. Following these initial planning processes, we constructed a conceptual model with the aim of maximizing knowledge, experience and expertise across a school–university partnership geared at raising the quality of pupil learning experiences.

There were strong grounds for locating the program entirely within schools, and in integrating learning opportunities with day-to-day activities. Hodkinson & Hodkinson (2005, p. 110) note that policy approaches to professional learning view it as 'acquisition,' teacher development literature views it as 'construction' and workplace learning literature views it as 'participation.' Advocating 'reflective practice" and a view of the teacher learner as a 'holistic and embedded person' (p. 113), they argue that a "combination of the construction and participation approach of teacher learning might be helpful in understanding and improving teacher learning" (p. 112).

For our model, we viewed social constructivism and participatory learning theory as grounded in the same ontology and epistemology. Ontologically, both theories premise that reality has an external validity arrived at through social consensus. Epistemologically, they both premise knowledge as socially and culturally constructed. Central to both theories are the roles of inter-subjectivity, culture and history shaping social meanings and knowledge. A key difference between these two conceptual approaches for us lay in the nature of the intersubjectivity and the extent to which learning through it involves engagement with the social world or community of practice (Lave & Wenger, 1991), and, additionally, the extent it involves close personal interactions (Vygotsky, 1978). We saw intersubjectivity in the context of social constructivism as concerned with the development of concepts through the use of tools and strategies, which afforded the learner structures to understand the world. We saw intersubjectivity in the participatory context as concerned with participation in frameworks and structures that reflected the practice of the community in which the learning was to take place.

Lave and Wenger (1991, p. 40) theorize the concept of 'legitimate peripheral participation' as providing an 'analytical perspective' upon learning as participation in communities of practice. They emphasize that legitimate peripheral participation "is not itself an educational form, much less a pedagogical strategy or technique" (p. 40). In our development of a model for our master's degree program, this concept did, however, provide a way of understanding professional learning in the workplace, in its broadest sense.

We decided that locating the new master's level program in the active workplace learning of teachers in the school community of practice would address the concerns of school leaders about the relevance and influence of that learning. At the same time, we recognized that if the frameworks and structures that define the community of practice constrained transformation, then engagement through participation alone would not be enough to bring about professional renewal. In our understanding, it was the relational view of the teacher and their learning (Lave & Wenger, 1991, p. 50) that challenged teachers' substantive identities and threatened their sense of agency and resilience.

Locating master's level learning in the active participation of teachers in the university community of practice would, we envisaged, develop participatory learning in the school community by focusing on how teachers make sense of their experiences at work. However, we theorized in the context of a master's program, the frameworks and structures of university practice were essentially constructivist. Firstly, they involved engagement with knowledge that was abstract and general, which does not sit easily with Lave and Wenger's notion of knowledge being located entirely in the community of practice (Tennant, 1977, p. 77). Secondly, assessment against predetermined learning outcomes at the master's level, as required by university regulations, meant that learning had to be made explicit in particular ways. Such assessment linked to the idea that learning is personally internalized and can be individually demonstrated.

The need to demonstrate teacher learning in particular ways underlies new public management discourses and practices in universities in England, driven by both funding and quality assurance audit mechanisms. As a planning team, we viewed assessment in the context of participatory learning as problematic, as participation "can neither be fully internalized as knowledge structures nor fully externalized as instrumental artifacts or overarching activity structures" (Lave & Wenger, 1991, p. 51). Even with a conscious focus on progressivism over performativity, the role and nature of internalization was another key difference between theories of learning as participation and learning as construction. This difference had particular relevance to our struggles to conceptualize viable and meaningful modes of assessment at the master's level.

We saw activity theory (Engeström, 1999) as describing a framework that could situate constructivism in the school community of practice, and militate against some of the influences of performativity on reflection and metacognition. It could also provide the basis for rethinking practice-based assessment at the master's level. Engeström's scheme of activity focuses on the interaction between the individual, the community and the object (conceptual or physical) that motivates the activity. This theoretical framework of activities as goal-directed actions both individual and collective (Tolman, 1999) informed our design for communities of practice. Identifying goals and the learner's or community's understanding of learning needs is key to the formation of the activity. The problem of reductionism in the context of new public management could be solved by founding a partnership between two existing communities of practice on such learning activities and goal-directed actions. Such a partnership could generate a 'new' or 'third' community of practice where participants engage with the single purpose of supporting teacher professional learning in ways that enhanced the quality of pupil learning experiences.

Lave and Wenger's concept of "continuity-displacement contradiction" (1991, p. 34) suggests that the 'new' partnership community could develop its own practices and norms of participation. All participants would, in a sense, be new to the partnership community and thereby have the potential to stimulate the generation of new knowledge through a creative disruption of existing practices in their school or university communities. In this way, learning through collective and goal-directed activity could enable the master's program to focus more centrally on the interface between day-to-day work in schools and scholarly activity. The value of locating professional learning within the school's working practices and routines—and thereby acknowledging the imperatives of the national school system—is not, then, to combine construction and participation as Hodkinson and Hodkinson advocate (2005, p. 128), but to provide a dialectic between learning as construction and learning as participation in a community of practice.

Operationalizing the Master's Program

The key features of the MA Education program, planned around this conceptual model, were that it was bespoke to every school, with the foci for learning collaboratively formulated to address the school improvement plan. Each school's program was to be integrated with the working lives of teachers and pedagogically aligned to maximize learning opportunities and the quality of engagement in the day-to-day activities of teachers in school. The program aimed to be fully inclusive of all staff at all levels, including unqualified teachers and teaching assistants, although economic realities often mean that, in practice, only qualified teachers participated. All teachers worked at the master's level, with the option either to submit work for assessed credits (the 'assessed route') or to participate without submitting assessed work (the 'nonassessed route'). Assessments were to be made through a range of artifacts, media, activities and thinking scaffolds; all modes of assessment were constructively aligned with school and master's level learning outcomes.

The partnership model operated through flat democratic structures across schools and the university. The partners developed key documentation and structures to support the emergence of a new partnership community of practice. The development process was iterative across the MA Education team and representative stakeholders. They aimed to establish broad norms of practice within the 'new' partnership community. Documentation includes a partnership agreement clearly stating the principles and aims of partnership as well as roles and responsibilities.

Two key roles enabled the partnership process to work smoothly on a day-to-day basis. Each school identified an institution link manager from their senior management team. A link university tutor[3] was also identified for each school. These two pivotal roles represented the main points of contact between school and university for operational and organizational purposes and provided a simple and clear channel of communication. Whilst linked to specific schools, a university tutor also had a role in contributing to the program in other schools where their specific knowledge and experience could support development. Institution link managers and other colleagues in schools with specific expertise contributed in similar ways.

The partnership agreement also outlined responsibilities to commit to the PD of institution link managers, and other teachers who took on roles in teaching peers and university tutors, as these roles were new in both institutional contexts. The PD of these core personnel across both schools and university was a joint enterprise, with one day each term designated as a partnership development day for addressing partnership development needs as they became identified by institution link managers, university tutors and/or participant evaluation and feedback. These semi-structured development days allowed time and space for discussions to grow or take unanticipated directions.

Our model also featured a document to ensure planning was fully collaborative across the school and university, and that planning learning activities and goal-directed action would be the partnership's foundation. This document included semi-structured areas for consideration illustrated with prompt questions to guide thinking. The document also included templates for identifying learning opportunities and practices in the school community.

Evaluating the New Master's Program

The team commissioned an independent external evaluation to cover the first 18 months of the program's operation for several reasons: firstly, to provide information that would help to monitor quality and standards at the master's level; secondly, to influence decisions made about future CPD provision at school and individual teacher levels; thirdly, to provide information that could inform curricular, pedagogic and operational development; and fourthly, to generate questions for further enquiry, ideally from collaborative research between teachers, teacher leaders and HE tutors. This 'formative evaluation design' (Verma & Mallick, 1999) aimed at capturing the participants' experiences, perceptions and beliefs, as we specifically sought to gain insight in the dynamics of the individual and communal learning processes.

The evaluation focused on the first cohort of schools in the program: six primary schools, two federated[4] and two secondary schools. All aspects of the work followed clear ethical guidelines provided by the university's ethics committee. We collected background information in the form of a documentary archive of all program-related materials during the relevant time frame, including curriculum and planning proformas and resources, minutes of meetings, quality assurance reports, university validation documents and external examiner reports and all communications with schools.

We interviewed all university-based members of the MA Education team; each person also produced personal reflective journals on a termly[5] basis. The evaluator observed regular MA Education team meetings throughout the 2008–2009 academic year. He also attended a partnership development day to observe the interactions between the MA Education team and partners from schools, and how the various stakeholders aimed to develop and strengthen the program. These participatory approaches ensured that the evaluator had a rich contextual understanding, access to practice-based views and observations focusing on the multiple relationships involved in the partnership.

All participating teachers and institution link managers completed a questionnaire to: ascertain their learning, understand how this learning was influencing classroom practice, illuminate the ways the program was or was not working and developing within each school and describe the workings of the partnership from the perspective of school colleagues. Questionnaire responses informed more detailed questions for semi-structured interview sessions to explore the emerging issues in greater detail. There was a 100% return on the questionnaires.

The research design also included planned interviews with each institution link manager, two teachers who opted for the assessed route and two who opted for the nonassessed route in each school. All seven institution link managers and 28 participants agreed to be interviewed. However, due to illness and moving schools, three teachers were unable to participate in the final phase of the evaluation and in the final event, 25 (89%) of the teachers selected were interviewed.

THE FINDINGS OF THE EVALUATION

The Partnership Community of Practice

Overall, the outcome of the evaluation was encouraging. The conceptual model seemed to have translated into practice effectively with the 'new' partnership community of practice created within each school developing effective teacher learning. This learning in turn seemed to be supporting teachers to develop less technical approaches to practice. It also seemed to enable them to better connect with, care for and attend to the needs of individual pupils (Day et al., 2007). The intuitive approach of the university-based team to developing pedagogic practices, informed by teacher experiences, also proved effective.

Responses from institution link managers showed that their role, outlined in the partnership agreement, was carried out as planned and further developed in appropriate ways by those colleagues. All institution link managers described their contribution to module planning, operational facilitation and communication across the partnership.

I helped plan the module very closely with the tutor and every 4 weeks we reviewed the course and made whatever changes were appropriate. We had regular planning meetings and obviously found this very productive and beneficial to the school. The module was tied into the Ofsted[6] key issues that the school had to improve upon.

I managed the materials, timings and timetable of the module within the school and gave and offered feedback from the staff at the planning meetings which was very useful.

I am responsible for the continuing professional development (CPD) of the staff and the progress and attainment of the pupils and they are inextricably linked. . . . I map out the needs of the staff and the staff meetings, based on school self-evaluation, with the [university] link tutor, and I identify who delivers which part of the skills, training and research aspects of each individual module . . . All the CPD undertaken is linked to pupil attainment, pupil wellbeing and the staff's well-being.

University tutors' journal entries concerning planning focused on the collaborative nature of the activity. However, whilst institution link managers were more positive about the extent of their involvement and collaboration, university tutors felt that different levels of engagement, particularly from colleagues in secondary schools, emerged. Probing the data further, the emerging norms of what constitutes collaborative planning in the 'new' partnership communities of practice seemed to consist of a progression of components:

A. identifying module focus, content, aims and outcomes in relation to school-based needs analysis
B. identifying opportunities for work-based learning time and scheduling these into timetables and calendars
C. identifying goal-directed activities appropriate to A
D. identifying details of university tutor seminars for those opting to submit work for master's credit in relation to A, B and C
E. conceptualizing the learning in B, C and D (constructivist/participatory)
F. engaging with ideas from literature and findings from research
G. exploring the ideological status of the learning in B, C and D (technical/scholarly)

The difference between university tutors' perceptions and those of some institution link managers lay in how they defined this progression in terms of what was undertaken collaboratively and what was pursued more singularly within the university community of practice. To a large extent, levels of engagement were constrained by time and a number of competing demands on institution link managers related to their wider roles within their schools.

The dominance of performativity regimes within those school contexts clearly influenced what counted as priority activities for these colleagues.

Institution link managers also had a key motivational role both within their senior leadership teams and with teaching colleagues. But the evaluation showed different levels of involvement in the senior leadership team involved in the MA program between primary and secondary schools. The majority of primary schools included senior leaders or teachers with specific expertise and the institution link manager in the planning meetings. The secondary schools had only the link manager responsible for CPD as part of a broader portfolio. Consequently, senior leaders in secondary school were less likely to be involved in the delivery and support of participating teachers. Institution link managers not supported by a wider planning team also had a more singular responsibility for developing and understanding a shared repertoire of resources (Wenger, 1998) from the partnership community to be 'disseminated' to the wider school community of practice.

> Because it was my idea to go for this I am seen as the creative force behind it by the senior leadership team and staff. So it means all the creative input for creating and planning the module and leading and delivering the module is down to me. This has implications both for working with university and the school. On occasions if I have been on leave, I expected the tutor to work well with other members of the senior leadership team and this has not worked out. It does not feel like there is any real cover for this responsibility unlike some of my other responsibilities because it is such a new relationship and there is no precedent for it.

Despite these constraints, the evaluation data indicates that the planning of learning activities and goal-directed action clearly became the foundation of the partnership communities of practice envisaged in the conceptual model. The relationships between institution link managers, the university team as a whole and the university link tutor were central to the success. Both school and university colleagues viewed relationships as extremely positive and productive. Institution link managers described their relationships with university link tutors and the university team using terms such as 'equal,' 'pragmatic and nonjudgmental,' 'responsive,' 'respectful,' 'tuned in,' 'value aligned,' 'professional,' 'complimentary,' 'effective' and 'close.'

> The tutor is very much value aligned and in an organizational sense we work well together and help to ensure the school meets deadlines . . . The whole [university] team helps in ensuring that the program fits the needs of the school rather than the university dictating the terms. They understand and are respectful of the need for the [master's] program and the school to raise attainment and the pressures we are under.

> The tutor matches the staff ethos and culture very well. In discussions with the tutor, the tutor has picked up on issues that we would like to

solve this year very quickly and has been a solution manager in that sense. The tutor has also been friendly and flexible and there has been positive feedback from the teachers about the tutor.

A particular strength of partnership community relationships was that tensions could be recognized and resisted or accommodated, although they are not always easy to navigate.

It is a good working relationship. I particularly find the [university] team responsive and keen to see things from our point of view. However, clearly the university has a different agenda from the school's agenda and there is a tension there.

Such tensions between the schools and university could be understood as a type of 'linear repulsion' between instrumentalism and progressivism, performativity and scholarly activity, and the school and the university communities of practice. However, the evaluation suggests something both more intricate and simpler, which might be described as what Gomm and Hammersley (2001, p. 5) call a "thin model of complexity".

The following presents a straightforward picture of the main components of Gomm and Hammersley's model (2001), without the indicators of how it

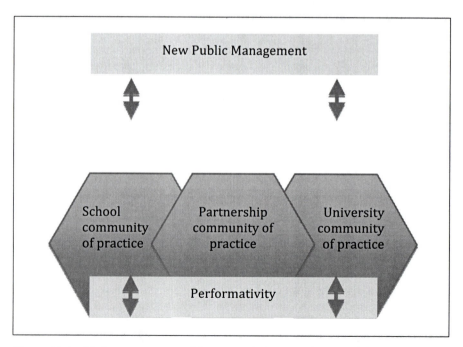

Figure 11.1   Main components of Gomm and Hammersley's model.

works as an adaptive system. The significant point here is the creation and positioning of the partnership as a new or third community of practice.

There is much literature about school–university partnerships in the UK, particularly in the context of preservice teacher education (e.g., Furlong, Barton, Miles, Whiting & Whitty, 2000; Furlong, Campbell, Howson, Lewis & McNamara, 2005; Menter, Brisard & Smith, 2006). This context conceives partnership as a bidirectional movement of interactions, practice and ideas between the school and the university. Whilst intersecting aspects of school and university aims, roles and practices may be identified (as in the center of a Venn diagram) they are constructed from the overlap between two communities of practice. Figure 11.1 depicts three communities of practice, one of which is pivotal, foundational, overarching and distinct from the other two. This 'third' community reflects neither the university perspective nor school perspective but creates its own new and unique perspective. The evaluations revealed tensions experienced by institution link managers and university tutors that were, in effect, a reaction to the constraints of new public management in each other's community of practice on conceptions of learning. The anxieties underlying performativity cultures could obscure the tensions arising from this common cause rather than from different views about professional learning and its relationship to the quality of pupil learning experiences. The partnership community became the mechanism through which these tensions could be articulated, addressed or accommodated. Over time, then, the potential for the partnership community to influence aspects of established culture and practices in both the university and school communities of practice could militate further against tensions between different performativity agendas.

Teacher Professional Learning and Its Influence at School and Classroom Level

As stated earlier, a key aspect of evaluation was to explore the program's influence on the teachers' professional learning. Institution link managers described a range of influences revealing a move towards a more 'active professionalism,' following the ideas of Sachs (2003). In particular, the evaluation showed a greater teacher engagement with, and more involvement in, decision making both at school and classroom levels.

> There are two key aspects in this module which will become embedded in practice . . . the staff identified lesson study and pupil interviews. The teachers felt that these two aspects need to become embedded, practiced and timetabled.
>
>   It has been noted that I have depoliticized the school through the CPD program . . . We understand the notion that not all of us know everything and we can pick up good elements of improving practice from the readings. In doing this we have improved our sophistication in asking questions about our practice and improving practice. This

has improved the teachers' professionalism in relation to improving the provision for the pupils and therefore their learning.

The purpose of the program was to secure much deeper thinking amongst the staff and support professional dialogue. I have seen some evidence of this and, for example, I have been in deep conversation with a colleague who has undertaken the master's and they would not have conversed like this prior to the program being initiated.

Institution link managers also commonly referred to positive changes in the ways teachers worked collaboratively to address pedagogical issues. The data also showed an emphasis on the role of literature and research in developing critical thinking, and on the development of more critical and sophisticated approaches to reflection, observation of pupil learning, peer review and lesson evaluation.

Link managers acknowledged a value for teachers not opting for assessment in having a program of interlinked development activities with a clear focus and direction. However, they varied considerably in the extent of their involvement and engagement at a deeper critical level. A number of link managers commented that, whilst increased levels of professional engagement from some teachers could begin to influence the culture and norms of the school community of practice, a danger existed of a growing divide between those who opted for the assessed route and those who did not.

A marked difference also existed between primary and secondary schools in the ways the model developed. The size and organization of secondary schools limited the opportunities for including a significant number of teachers. In one case, a secondary school focused on a specific subject department with everyone involved, and then invited other staff members to join the program if they wanted to submit work for assessment. Some whole-school staff development activities also focused on the module theme, but opportunities were very limited. In another secondary school the program only involved teachers opting to submit work for assessment.

In all cases, primary and secondary, integrating the program into the working life of the school became a crucial factor in determining the relevance and 'transferability' of teachers' professional learning, and in bringing about sustainable change in the schools. The partnership communally identified these issues as a priority focus for forthcoming partnership development days.

Participants reflected on the program experiences and any personal behavior or practice that resulted. All but one teacher opting for the assessed route felt positive change in their professional behavior and their practice. In particular, they said that they thought more about their teaching and pupil learning, and, crucially, gained the confidence to do this.

It has made me think a little more about what I am doing. It gives you a bigger picture and gives me a lot more confidence in what I am doing because I am reflecting based on the session and the conversations with my colleagues. It is important to have the opportunity to sit back to reflect and discuss. It is important to have this structured approach to reflection, when you are looking at a particular aspect of learning each term.

It does make you reflect more and if you are the sort of person who wants to change situations in the classroom you are not happy with, [then] the program allows you to do this. If I can change [pupil attitudes to learning] through educating myself through the program and understanding the motivation of pupils, or not as the case may be, [then all the better].

In the following, the teachers indicate the breadth of ways the program influenced their practice and knowledge:

In one way I am more aware of the pupils' ideas; in another sense it has got me involved more with school policy in terms of making me question it, and in another sense it has made me more patient with colleagues because we have been working within a collaborative context.

Teachers in the nonassessed program demonstrated more varied routes and a significant number did not feel that the program changed them or their practice. However, the evidence here was somewhat contradictory in that, further on in the interviews, some of these teachers cited evidence of personal change, as in the following examples:

I am still doing the same things as before. The only thing to come to light is the pupil observation, which you do anyway, but because it was a task I had to do I was more focused on it. I now understand the significance of it.

Difficult to say. The main aspect that was reinforced was the importance of the pupil interviews. It has made me want to keep up with pupil interviews. So I have realized the importance of having a specific time and place away from the classroom to undertake pupil interviews . . . which makes it a more effective and productive interview. This means you can work better with a pupil as you get to know them better.

Yet others on the nonassessed route indicated considerable learning gains, and some indicated significant changes in practice:

From the Assessment for Learning module perspective my knowledge is greater in this area. It has gone from researching this [subject] to becoming more interested in the subject, leading to greater reading and research in it, and joining a school assessment team as well.

CONCLUSION

The school-based master's program described in this chapter aimed to support teachers, often working in challenging school contexts and circumstances, to focus upon core teaching and pupil learning. In particular, the program sought to provide a mechanism for professional renewal that would function effectively, even in the contexts of the new public management and performativity agendas dominating schooling and teacher education in England. The evaluation provided some evidence that new knowledge can be stimulated and generated through a creative disruption of existing practices in the school and that with university communities of practice, a 'new' partnership community of practice can develop. Hence, we would argue that the creation and implementation of the school-based master's program to date indicate that it is a successful mechanism for helping teachers learn by focusing on the core teaching and pupil learning in challenging schools.

The Coalition Government that came into power in the UK in May 2011 has promised more professional freedom and recognition for teachers (see, for example, Department for Education, 2010; Gove, 2010). Currently, however, it seems mere rhetoric, since the development of compliance strategies and rituals of verification (Power, 1997) are set to remain the norm in schools and universities. In such bleak educational contexts, programs like the master's described here offer ways of empowering teachers and supporting their professional learning whilst also developing the quality of pupil achievement. Ultimately, our hope is that this program, unique in many ways, may continue to help individual teachers and their schools support pupils learning and militate against the constraints.

NOTES

1. The TDA is a national agency and recognized sector body responsible for the training and development of the school workforce. They work with the Department for Education to ensure high-quality teaching, a sufficient supply of suitable teachers for curriculum demands, induction and performance management experiences for teachers through support for the professional standards for teaching, induction and performance management, continuing PD for teachers and the deployment of high-quality teachers in challenging schools. The remit of the TDA is to support training and development in relation to national policy initiatives that concern schools.
2. The agreement states that teachers can only be used for a limited amount of time to cover teaching for colleagues who are absent for any reason, including PD.

3. The term 'tutor' is in regular use in teacher education in England to denote a member of academic faculty, usually on a full-time academic contract and with tenure.
4. In 2009 the Labour government published a White Paper "Your Child, Your Schools, Our Future Building a 21ˢᵗ Century Schools System." One of the aims included in the paper was to facilitate federated partnerships between successful or high-achieving schools and low-achieving schools in order to raise the attainment levels of pupils in the low-achieving school (Department for children, schools and families, 2009).
5. There are three terms in an academic school year. The program runs across three school terms rather than two semesters. One module runs for one term.
6. Ofsted is the Office for Standards in Education, Children's Services and Skills. They regulate and inspect to ensure that policy frameworks and statutory regulations relating to the achievement of "excellence in the care of children and young people, and in education and skills for learners of all ages" are met.

REFERENCES

Barber, M. & Mourshed, M. (2007) *How the World's Best-Performing School Systems Come Out on Top.* New York: McKinsey & Company.

Bates, T. (2005). Editorial. *Journal of In-Service Education, 31*(2), 229.

Bird, M., Ding, S., Hanson, A., Leontovitsch, A. & McCartney, R. (2005). There is nothing as practical as a good theory: An examination of the outcomes of a 'traditional' MA in education for educational professionals. *Journal of In-Service Education, 31*(3), 427–454.

Bottery, M. (2005). The individualization of consumption: A Trojan horse in the destruction of the public sector? *Educational Management, Administration and Leadership, 33*(3), 267–288.

Bradley-Levine, J., Smith, J. & Car, K., (2009). The role of action research in empowering teachers to change their practice. *Journal of Ethnographic and Qualitative Research, 3*, 1935–3308.

Cerny, P. G., & Evans, M. (2004). Globalisation and public policy under New Labour. *Policy Studies, 25*(1), 51–65.

Cooper, A. (2001). The state of mind we're in: Social anxiety, governance and the audit society. *Psychoanalytic Studies, 3*(3/4), 349–362.

Day, C., Sammons, P., Stobart, G., Kington, A. & Gu, Q. (2007). *Teachers matter: connecting lives, work and effectiveness.* Buckingham: Open University Press.

Department for children, schools and families (2009). *Your child, your schools, our future building a 21st century schools system.* Norwich: TSO.

Department for Education (2010). *The importance of teaching: Schools white paper.* London: Department for Education. Retrieved December 7, 2010, from http://www.education.gov.uk/b0068570/the-importance-of-teaching/

Engeström, Y. (1999). Activity theory and individual and social transformation. In Y. Engeström, R. Miettinen & R. Punamaki (Eds.), *Perspectives on activity theory* (pp. 19–38). Cambridge: Cambridge University Press.

Furlong, J., Barton, L., Miles, S., Whiting, C. & Whitty, G. (2000). *Teacher education in transition.* Buckingham: Open University Press.

Furlong, J., Campbell, A., Howson, J., Lewis, S. & McNamara, O. (2005, September). *Partnership in English initial teacher education: Changing times, changing definitions. Evidence from the TTA National Partnership Project.* Paper presented to the British Educational Research Conference, Glamorgan.

Gomm, R., & Hammersley, M. (2001, September). *Thick ethnographic description and thin models of complexity.* Paper presented at the Annual Conference of the British Educational Research Association, University of Leeds, England.

Gove, M. (2010). Speech to the National College Annual Conference. Retrieved June 17, 2010, from http://www.education.gov.uk/news/speeches/nationalcollegeannualconference

Hartley, D. (2008). Education, markets and the pedagogy of personalization. *British Journal of Educational Studies, 56*(4), 365–381.

Hodkinson, H., & Hodkinson, P. (2005). Improving schoolteachers' workplace learning. *Research Papers in Education, 20*(2), 109–131.

Hoggett, P. (2010). Government and the perverse social defense. *British Journal of Psychotherapy, 26*(2), 202–212.

Hood, C. (1991). A public management for all seasons? *Public Administration, 1,* 3–19.

Kearns, H. (2003). University accreditation of professional development in schools: Can professional development serve two master's? *Journal of In-Service Education, 29*(1), 11–29.

Lave, J., & Wenger, E. (1991). *Situated learning: Legitimate peripheral participation.* Cambridge: Cambridge University Press

MacDonald Grieve, A., & McGinley, B. P. (2010). Enhancing professionalism? Teachers' voices on continuing professional development in Scotland. *Teaching Education, 21*(2), 171–184.

Mee, A. (2008). Teachers undertaking master's level professional study: An investigation into motives and perceived outcomes. *Reflecting Education, 4*(2), 85–98.

Menter, I., Brisard, E. & Smith, I. (2006). *Covergence or divergence? Initial teacher education in Scotland and England.* Edinburgh: Dunedin Academic Press.

Organization for Economic Co-Operation and Development. (2009). Creating Effective Teaching and Learning Environments: First Results from TALIS – ISBN 978-92-64-05605-3, Teaching and Learning International Survey. Paris: OECD.

Power, M. (1997). *The audit society: Rituals of verification.* Oxford: Oxford University Press.

Sachs, J. (2003). *The activist teaching profession.* Buckingham: Open University Press.

Sacks, P. (1999). *Standardized minds: The high price of America's testing culture and what we can do to change it.* Cambridge, MA: Perseus Books.

Tennant, M. (1997). *Psychology and adult learning.* London: Routledge.

Tolman, C. (1999). Society versus context in individual development: Does theory make a difference? In Y. Engeström, R. Miettenin & R. Punamaki (Eds.), *Perspectives on activity theory* (pp. 70–106). Cambridge: Cambridge University Press.

Training and Development Agency. (2010). *Challenging schools.* Retrieved October 13, 2010, from http://www.tda.gov.uk/teacher/recruitment/challenging-schools.aspx

Verma, G. K., & Mallick, K. (1999). *Researching education: Perspectives and techniques.* London: Routledge.

Vygotsky, L. S. (1978). *Mind in society—the development of higher psychological processes.* Cambridge, MA: Harvard University Press.

Wenger, E. (1998). *Communities of practice: Learning as a social system.* Retrieved July 2, 2010, from http://www.open.ac.uk/ldc08/sites/www.open.ac.uk.ldc08/files/Learningasasocialsystem.pdf

12 Open-Ended Scientific Inquiry in a Nonformal Setting

Cognitive, Affective and Social Aspects of In-Service Elementary Teachers' Development

Stella Hadjiachilleos and Lucy Avraamidou

INTRODUCTION

This chapter describes the findings of a qualitative case study conducted with three small groups of in-service elementary teachers in Cyprus who enrolled in a specially designed module of a teachers' preparation program. This study, built on theoretical underpinnings about informal learning, investigated the impact of a specially designed, technology-enhanced, informal education module on participants' science learning. The unique aspects of the module include: (a) an outdoor setting and (b) an inquiry-based model. Research data consisted of participant observations, an evaluation test and two semi-structured interviews before and at the end of the module. Analyses of the data indicate the ways such pedagogical approaches can support teacher learning and the development of current understandings about science teaching at the elementary school. The research findings provide a readily available, concrete example of a nonformal instructional approach to in-service teachers' professional development (PD) and fill an existing gap in outdoor learning, focusing mainly on environmental concepts.

THEORETICAL UNDERPINNINGS

The study draws from theories of inquiry-based science and informal learning, "the most commonly applied term for the science learning that occurs outside the traditional, formal school realm." Such learning "is an organic, dynamic, never-ending, and holistic phenomenon of constructing personal meaning" (Dierking, Falk, Rennie, Anderson & Ellenbogen, 2003, p. 109). In 1999, the National Association for Research in Science Teaching (NARST) formed an Ad Hoc Committee in Informal Learning (Rennie et al., 2003). They described it as: (a) occurring out of school, self-motivated and involving learners' needs and interests; (b) strongly socioculturally mediated; and (c) a cumulative process involving connections and rein-forcement of a variety of learning experiences (Rennie et al., 2003).

Theoretically, the study builds on the concept that learning is socially situated within specific sociocultural contexts and bounded by individu-als' interactions. Greeno's (1996) theory of cognitive situations takes the distributed nature of cognition as a starting point and implies that thinking is situated in a particular context of intentions, social partners and tools. In this situative/pragmatist-socio-historic view, "knowledge is distributed among people and their environments, including the objects, artifacts, tools, books, and the communities of which they are a part" (pp. 16–17). Hence, in this study we view learning as a process of social participation expressed in 'communities of practice' (Lave & Wenger, 1991; Wenger, 1998). We use Wenger's (1998) definition of *participation*, which:

> refer[s] not just to local events of engagement in certain activities with certain people, but to a more encompassing process of being active participants in the *practices* of social communities and constructing *identities* in relation to these communities. (p. 4)

The nature and characteristics of such participation in the practices of the social community formed within the context of a science project is the point of interest to us and the unit of analysis of our work. We approach the orga-nization and implementation of inquiry-based science projects that build complex social interactions around meaningful learning activities. Wenger (1998, p. 272) argued that educational design should offer opportunities for engagement, which means:

1. activities requiring mutual engagement, both among students and with other people involved
2. challenges and responsibilities that call on the knowledge-ability of students yet encourage them to explore new territories
3. enough continuity for participants to develop shared practices and a long-term commitment to their enterprise and each other

We argue that engagement in informal science activities offers meaning-ful activities and opportunities to interact with others (i.e., colleagues, students, university professors, teachers, parents, friends) to explore new knowledge and experiences. Hence, we identify five main communities of practices participating and interacting in science learning to achieve spe-cific goals related to community building: teachers, university instructors, students, museum staff and parents and friends.

Constructivist theoretical perspectives view the importance of learners' prior knowledge as critical to learning. Learning is defined as a: "receptive act that involves construction of new meaning by learners within the context of their current knowledge, previous experience, and social environment"

(Bloom, Perlmutter & Burrell, 1999, p. 134). Hence, knowledge is not independent of the knower; instead, it depends on individuals' experiences and how learners construct and interpret new learning experiences outcomes (Driver, Guesne & Tiberghien, 1985). Hence, in-service teachers articulating and investigating their questions allow us to explore ways to support their development of knowledge and skills needed to design relevant curriculum materials and learn to more meaningfully and effectively teach science.

METHOD

This qualitative case study research design explores a group of in-service teachers' development in a specially designed module based on in-depth data collection involving multiple sources of information (Creswell, 1998; Merriam, 2009). We use a case study design on the assumption that this would enable us to examine the impact of certain elements of the module on in-service teachers' development and views.

The data included classroom observations, video documentation of activities both in and out of the classroom, interviews, reflective journals and various assessment measures. We co-taught the module, videotaping all sessions. One of us videotaped while the other prepared detailed field notes.

We analyzed the research data by categorizing and identifying themes using open coding (Coffey & Atkinson, 1996) and triangulating the data with other collaborating researchers. We translated the data into a narrative form for each in-service teacher group. Another member of the research group also read each narrative to construct validity (Yin, 2003). The constant comparative method and open coding (Coffey & Atkinson, 1996) allowed us to identify the main concepts emerging in the data and associated with the main research questions:

1. How does in-service teachers' reasoning progress when they are engaged in inquiry-based problem solving outside of the classroom setting?
2. Which emotions are experienced during their involvement in these kinds of inquiries and how do they affect in-service teachers' science learning and perceptions about science teaching?
3. What are in-service teachers' views about inquiry-based Science Teaching and Learning (STaL) when it takes place outside of the classroom setting?

Context and Sample

The elementary teacher education program offers three science content courses in addition to a methods course. In-service teachers can enroll in any course for PD purposes. For this study, 17 in-service teachers enrolled in a methodology course, entitled Environmental Issues. Participants formed three five to six member groups to solve an open-ended problem by conducting scientific inquiries outside of the classroom setting. We identified the female in-service teacher participants in three home groups: Group A: five teachers (Galenia, Alexis, Kyrenia, Molara and Garbina). Group B (Xevera, Zarista, Frascuela, Martina, Babette and Sabrina). Group C (Anastasia, Margarita, Andrea, Rhea, Cacia and Ardana).

The unique aspects of the module include the following: (a) Its context is defined by an outdoor setting and (b) it is inquiry-based. The course was taught during the summer over a period of 2 months during which two 3-hour classroom sessions per week were conducted. Therefore, the module was completed in 16 3-hour sessions.

Initially, in-service teachers were asked to draw a concept map of their ideas regarding the bicycle and its use in people's everyday lives. Through the concept maps, certain stereotypes regarding bicycles emerged, along with their uses and constructional features.

Subsequently, in-service teachers watched two videos on bicycles, their history and uses in various sectors such as transportation, sports and leisure. The purpose of the videos was to illustrate different kinds of bicycles and how bicycle design has changed over the years to be more effective (in terms of speed over time). The participants were then provided with the following task and were asked to design various investigations in order to collect data that would help them complete it: *Design the most efficient bicycle (maximum distance travel with the use of the least energy consumption).*

Participants went to the University Sports Center to find bicycles and additional bicycle parts (e.g., stands, wheels and tubes) as well as a variety of models (such as the mountain bike, road bike) as materials to assemble their bicycle. Using various routes and terrains available in the area, and, through guided inquiry and error, they created the bicycle that best suited their needs.

FINDINGS

Participants' Reports on Bicycle Construction

Group A. Group A defined the efficient bicycle as requiring minimum energy to travel a specific distance. They selected a group of variables that would influence their bicycle performance. The group conducted five sets of experiments, altering one variable and controlling all other variables to ensure fair testing: the surface of the road, dimensions of the tires, position of the cyclist, height of the bicycle seat and the gear. They measured the time it took the assembled bicycle to cover a distance of 50 meters. Table 12.1 presents five sets of experiments conducted by Group A.

Table 12.1 Sets of Experiments Conducted by Group A

Experimentation #	Independent variable(s)	Dependent variable	Controlled variables
1	Surface of the road	Time	Dimensions of tires Position of cyclist Position of bicycle seat Gear Distance
2	Dimensions of tires		Surface of the road Position of cyclist Position of bicycle seat Gear Distance
3	Position of cyclist		Dimensions of tires Surface of the road Position of bicycle seat Gear Distance
4	Position of bicycle seat		Dimensions of tires Surface of the road Position of cyclist Gear Distance
5	Gear		Dimensions of tires Surface of the road Position of cyclist Position of bicycle seat Distance

Group A concluded that the most efficient bicycle depends on the following characteristics:

1. The seat is at the same height as the steering wheel.
2. The tires have high pressure.
3. The surface of the road is smooth (e.g., asphalt).
4. The road is straight.
5. The gear is low.

Group B. Group B conducted three sets of experiments, focusing their attention mainly on the characteristics of the cyclist as the determining factor for efficiency of the bike. Table 12.2 presents Group B's experiments.

During the first set of experiments, two different teachers covered a specific distance while the others measured the time and it took and the

Table 12.2   Experiments Conducted by Group B

Experimentation set #	Independent variables	Dependent variables	Controlled variables
1	Cyclist (weight and height)	Time Pulse Calories	Bicycle Distance
2	Gear	CaloriesPulse	Cyclist (weight, height) Bicycle Time Surface of road Distance
3	Material of the surface of road	Pulse Calories	Cyclist (weight, height) Time Distance

calories consumed by each rider. They subsequently correlated the time and energy consumed related to their weight and height. Next, the group decided to keep the same cyclist for all measurements, the same bicycle, time and surface of the road and to only change the gear. They therefore measured the calories and pulse of the cyclist. Evidently, this group used the trial and error technique to eliminate certain variables after the first set of experiments, to end up with the variables that they would consider to have the most profound effect on bicycle performance. In the third set of experiments they examined the material of the surface of the road as a factor affecting overall bicycle efficiency.

Group B concluded that an efficient bicycle included the following:

1. The cyclist is of small height and weight.
2. The cyclist wears special clothing.
3. The bicycle frame is of a light material.
4. The wheels have to be thin.

Of the four conclusions, only the first was based on their experiments. They reached conclusions 2, 3 and 4 through their concept map and the videos they watched in class.

Group C. Group C determined that an efficient bicycle requires minimum effort and energy by the cyclist. They performed three sets of experiments, each focusing on a different factor involved in cycling—characteristics of the cyclist, bicycle and road surface—in order to determine the characteristics of the efficient bicycle. Their experiments are presented in Table 12.3.

Group C concluded that the efficiency of the bicycle is determined exclusively by its geometry and weight and that it is not relevant to other factors, such as the cyclist or the road surface.

Table 12.3 Experiments Conducted by Group C

Experimentation #	Independent variables	Dependent variables	Controlled variables
1	Cyclist clothing Cyclist height Cyclist weight Cyclist shoes	Calories Pulse	Distance Road surface Wind speed Bicycle
2	Height of bicycle seat Frame weight and geometry	Calories Pulse	Distance Road surface Wind speed Bicycle Cyclist
3	Road surface	Calories Pulse	Distance Road surface Wind speed Bicycle Cyclist Height of bicycle seat

Participants' Personal Reflective Journals

After completing the inquiry, participants created a reflective journal on their experience in inquiry-based learning in an informal setting. In the journal, each participant reflected on the methodology and their developing knowledge and emotional development.

Participants' Progression of Emotions

Table 12.4 presents the participants' progression of emotions as documented in their reflective journals.

Table 12.4 illustrates self-reports of the range of emotions experienced during the module: interest, anxiety, curiosity, confidence and joy. The in-service teachers experienced these emotions in a different order and were triggered by different parts of the module.

Interest, Enthusiasm and Curiosity

Ten out of 17 participants (Galenia, Alexis, Kyrenia, Xevera, Babette, Sabrina, Sabrina, Margarita, Andrea, Cacia) expressed positive emotions at the beginning of the module, such as interest, curiosity or enthusiasm to solve the research problem. This related to the fact that bicycles were a positive part of their childhood lives. Moreover, the informal setting generated enthusiasm as Alexis's reflective journal reveals:

Table 12.4 Participants' Progression of Emotions

Participant ID	Progression of emotions
Galenia	Enthusiasm → anxiety → fear of failure → enthusiasm → confidence
Alexis	Interest → curiosity → joy → confidence → satisfaction
Kyrenia	Enthusiasm → interest → joy
Molara	Anxiety → overwhelm → confidence
Garbina	Anxiety → interest
Xevera	Interest → anxiety → anger → confidence → joy
Zarista	Anxiety → enthusiasm → interest
Frascuela	Anxiety → interest
Martina	Anxiety → interest → surprise
Babette	Interest
Sabrina	Curiosity → interest → anxiety → joy
Sabrina	Interest → joy
Margarita	Interest → curiosity → enthusiasm
Andrea	Confidence → satisfaction
Rhea	Nostalgia → uncertainty → anxiety → confidence
Cacia	Interest → satisfaction
Ardana	Anxiety → uncertainty → calmness → satisfaction

The whole idea of this module was very interesting and original to me. First of all, the inquiry was conducted outside of the classroom setting. This made us feel that the module was a kind of game and it created a friendly and pleasant atmosphere. I believe that students that may not even be interested in class will be actively engaged and will be encouraged to more freely express their opinion when they go outside of the classroom setting. Class stops being boring. (Alexis)

Alexis was intrigued that part of the module took place outside of the classroom; it triggered her interest and enthusiasm. She also observed that an informal setting made her feel more comfortable to express ideas and, consequently, be engaged in the inquiry. We suggest, then, that a positive learning environment enhances motivation for self-development (Fallik, Eylon & Rosenfeld, 2008).

Participant Margarita entered the process enthusiastically from the beginning. Her enthusiasm, demonstrated in the following, grew out of cycling as an important part of her childhood. Revisiting those experiences in the module re-created her joy and enthusiasm.

> My experience during my engagement in the module of designing the most efficient bicycle is highly connected to a sense of "mental pleasure" during which I felt most enthusiastic to be engaged in the process, since it was based on my childhood experiences. (Margarita)

Zarista began her investigation with anxiety; she was unfamiliar with using and assembling a bicycle. She gradually overcame her misgivings after her engagement in the research:

> After the instructions were given during the introduction of the module, I was very worried because I had not used a bicycle for several years. However, when we got at the gym and then outside, anxiety turned into enthusiasm since I had the opportunity to drive a bicycle again and, at the same time, memories came back from my childhood. (Zarista)

Zarista had not used a bicycle for several years but the informal setting and actually using bicycles helped her overcome her anxiety and she felt enthusiasm and nostalgia for her childhood. This might be an indication of the fact that informal settings provide positive emotions and enable learners to connect school learning to their everyday experiences (Novak, 2002). Therefore, the informal learning might promote a sense of ownership of the newly acquired knowledge (Falk & Dierking, 1992).

Molara was initially overwhelmed by the content of the module, since she was unfamiliar with the content and (see Table 12.4) also with the methodology, but she gradually overcame her anxiety, which gave place to confidence. The following abstract is indicatory of her progression of emotions.

> Before the beginning of the class, I kept wondering what we were about to do and how we were going to do it. Always, when something is different, I feel anxiety. We were like the children when they go to watch a movie or go on a field trip or anywhere outside of the classroom. They lose control out of joy and enthusiasm even before they get to the field. So we were kind of bored in the introduction of the module and the only thing we wanted was to get outside and do our work. Therefore, our professors prepared an original introduction. They encouraged us to do the concept map and then we watched the videos—something that we all like—to calm down before the fieldwork. So when we got to the gym we were calm and confident because we had been well prepared. (Molara)

Molara stressed the importance of a well-designed module, along with the positive role of the facilitator. Concept mapping and discussion on videos are techniques more familiar to the students. Therefore, informal learning, while a more unfamiliar task, is also more intriguing and, simultaneously, more challenging. Comparing herself with her young students going on a field trip, Molara stressed her eagerness to investigate a problem in an informal setting.

Confidence

Most importantly, as evident in Table 12.4, all participants had positive responses by the end of their investigation. Five of the 17 participants (Galenia, Alexis, Molara, Xevera, Rhea) clearly felt confident that their solution was correct and based their confidence on two parameters: First, they documented their data collected during their experiments and used it to find a solution. In Rhea's reflective journal, she wrote:

> When we designed and conducted our experiments in the group, we wrote down our observations. That is when I felt so confident that my group had reached a correct solution describing the characteristics of an efficient bicycle. (Rhea)

Second, participants expressed their confidence, noting their extensive social interactions in their groups led to solutions of the research problem. Group work promoted their sense of confidence:

> I believe that I would not be able to do the assignment and fulfill the requirements for it. Also, it was the second time that we worked together as a group and I knew we would do a great work. I am really excited about what we have achieved as a group! (Galenia)

Galenia observed that through group work, she managed to fulfill the requirements for this assignment. In addition, Galenia benefited from working with the same group since she felt confident in the group dynamics and the quality of the final product.

> Working in a group was really beneficial for me because I got the opportunity to improve my social skills. I believe that this can also be achieved with elementary students. We were able to interact, to add to each other ideas, to be involved in productive dialogues and to feel free to express our ideas. After the "creative part" of assembling the most efficient bicycle, we had to work together for the written part. This brought the members of our group even closer and it made it easier for us to understand each other's way of thinking. I believe that this can be achieved among elementary students as well. (Alexis)

Alexis improved her social and communication skills and learned to understand how others think. She proposes that this interaction would be beneficial to her work as a teacher since she could implement these social skills to diagnose her students' conceptions and understanding of scientific problems in her class.

Anxiety

Some of the teachers experienced anxiety during the research. Six out of 17 participants (Molara, Garbina, Zarista, Frascuela, Martina, Ardana) experienced anxiety or uncertainty early in their involvement in the research, whereas others experienced anxiety when they had to design an experiment. On the other hand, three (Galenia, Xevera, Rhea) experienced anxiety during the module. Frascuela experienced anxiety because she was unfamiliar with how to assemble bicycle parts, although she gradually overcame that with the guidance of the facilitators:

> A week before the beginning of the module, I realized that we were actually going to construct bicycles, and I felt really nervous. I did not know how to do this and I thought that we were going to be given only parts to assemble. The day of the module, anxiety left me because the instructions were very clear and I understood that we were free to test our proposed solutions and reach our own conclusions as to what an efficient bicycle is. (Frascuela)

Frascuela points to the critical role of the facilitator to explain the instructions and support the groups during their inquiries. Participants were unaccustomed to conducting inquiry in the informal setting. Engaging in an open-ended problem-solving process in the informal settings proved challenging for some, especially with multiple possible solutions. Once they realized the degree of flexibility, however, they reduced their anxiety. Most importantly, all the teachers overcame their anxiety by the end of their investigations.

Participants' Reflections on the Methodology of the Module

Students reflected on the methodology in their reflective journals and expressed their opinions on open-ended inquiry in informal settings as a productive methodology for teaching natural sciences at the elementary level. As the data analysis indicates, students refer to three main methodological parameters:

- the informal setting as a tool for promoting science learning outcomes
- open-ended inquiry as an instructional methodology
- the role of social interactions for learning

The Informal Setting As a Tool for Promoting Science Learning Outcomes

Participants considered the problem solving as helpful for productive for science learning. Alexis, Molara, Zarista, Frascuela, Babette, Sabrina,

Margarita and Cacia connected their research with other cognitive fields or personal experiences, and, therefore, considered it productive for improving their work as educators. Frascuela's journal entry reflected the view of the group:

> Being involved was really beneficial for us, because we finally found ourselves investigating a problem and learning outside of the university building! If this method was successful with us, it can definitely be successfully implemented with elementary students. Working in the informal setting has to finally be implemented by every teacher because students come to school with knowledge they already have based on their experiences outside the classroom setting. The inquiries conducted enabled us, to construct knowledge that is meaningful to us. (Frascuela)

The participant suggested a more widespread use of the informal setting as a tool for learning since it facilitated the connection between school and everyday experience for learning (Anderson, Piscitelli, Everett & Weier, 2002). Frascuela, Babette, Sabrina and Cacia added that the informal setting enabled them to connect concepts not only with their personal experiences, but also with stereotypes they have developed:

> As a teacher, I believe that integrating content that is pleasant for the children will stimulate their interest and encourage them to participating in an inquiry. Through learning in an informal setting, I believe it is easier to help them eliminate some stereotypes, such as the bicycle being used mainly by children or immigrants. (Sabrina)

Galenia, Kyrenia, Xevera, Zarista, Frascuela, Andrea, Rhea, Cacia and Ardana stressed informal settings promote active engagement of the learners, which makes learning meaningful:

> We had the opportunity to "construct" our own solution to the problem. We became investigators and we had to create our own method for solving the problem. I believe that if elementary students can do this, their knowledge and learning will be more. (Andrea)

Andrea stressed the ownership experienced when learners have the opportunity to design and implement an investigation. The informal setting as a medium provided a learning environment that was emotionally supportive for all students. Alexis, Margarita, Rhea, Cacia and Ardana observed that working outside of the classroom setting created a friendly atmosphere among the learners that facilitated the expression of personal thoughts and opinions.

> First, the fact that the biggest time allocation took place outside of the classroom setting, gives the impression of a game and creates pleasant

atmosphere. Therefore, some students who might not participate actively in class or are indifferent for some reason are encouraged to express themselves outside of the classroom. Opinions are more easily expressed and accepted in the informal setting. I believe that even classes considered boring or overwhelming could become interesting and motivating if part of the class is conducted in informal settings. (Alexis)

Alexis suggested a more widespread use of informal settings, not only for science, but other subject areas as well. With increased student engagement, she believed that student learning would be more productive.

Open-Ended Inquiry As an Instructional Methodology

During the interviews, the teachers spoke to the effectiveness of open-ended inquiry as an instructional method in science. More specifically, Galenia, Molara, Garbina, Frascuela, Martina, Sabrina, Margarita, Andrea and Rhea suggested that the methodology enabled them to experience firsthand how to design an experiment to find a solution to an open-ended problem. They considered this methodology a tool for developing students' creativity:

We had to define an efficient bicycle in our groups before we designed the experiments. We had to select or eliminate variables from our experiments, to write down the results and come up with conclusions. We had to be creative and also had to be actively involved in the process, otherwise we would not have been able to reach a solution. Each one of us had to think "outside of the box" to reach our persona—but also well-developed solution to the problem. (Margarita)

Reaching a valid solution to the research problem required teachers' creative thinking. Andrea suggests that open-ended inquiry provides for an opportunity to develop student creativity.

We had the opportunity to be creative. We became explorers in our group and were engaged in every part of the scientific method, such as making hypotheses, designing and implementing experiments, writing down observations, and drawing conclusions based on the observations, etc. It was really practical and I believe that if a teacher is able to productively implement it in multiple subjects then students' creativity will develop. (Andrea)

Andrea proposes that this kind of methodology should be expanded beyond science education so that students will be able to use it in other subject areas.

Alexis, Kyrenia, Xevera, Frascuela and Sabrina pointed out how to reach a valid and reliable solution, a "big issue" for them. Since they were unfamiliar with this freedom, they started using the trial and error technique to eliminate some variables from their experiments.

> Finding a solution to the problem was difficult for me. During the introduction of the module, we received some information regarding the history and uses of the history of the bicycle and some information about its parts and assembly. However, it was up to us to find how we could use that information to solve the problem. We had minimum guidance as to how we would design our solution. Designing a solution was something really unfamiliar to us. In the beginning we used trial and error to see what might influence a bicycle's performance. Based on that, we selected variables and created hypotheses. For me, as a teacher, it is very difficult to implement open-ended inquiry because I might easily lose control of my students and I am not experienced enough. However, I believe in trial and error as a technique to promote students' science learning. (Xevera)

Xevera is unfamiliar with inquiry-based learning and, therefore, expressed some insecurity about implementing this methodology in her class. Kyrenia, Garbina and Cacia, on the other hand, found open-ended inquiry encouraged them towards more active participation since it motivated each group member to take part in designing and implementing a solution to the problem.

> Every one of us had to take action in the group and do something very different from what we were used to, something out of the ordinary. This is very important because we were all provided the opportunity for active participation in solving a problem. Students should always participate actively in the process of teaching and learning, and not just passively accept facts. As teachers, I believe we should implement this kind of methodology with our students. When we have the opportunity, we should give them an open-ended problem and ask them to come up with a documented solution. (Kyrenia)

Designing a solution to an open-ended problem seems to provide learners with a sense of ownership of the newly acquired knowledge.

Last, Galenia, Zarista and Ardana referred to the role of the teacher as facilitator in the process. They pointed out that the teacher's attitude and interventions during their work not only allowed them to reach a solution, but also changed the way they felt about the process by making them feel accepted and willing to participate:

> I must admit that when I heard that we would be called on designing and assembling a bicycle as a part of the requirements for this class, I was terrified! I kept thinking: "How can we possibly manage to make

a bicycle by ourselves?" "How do I know what I need to assemble a bicycle?" These thoughts caused some negative feelings to me and made me not wanting to participate. However, during the introduction, the professors were very clear. They were very encouraging and I started to relax. By the time we started to work on the project, I was not nervous at all and I even forgot that what we were doing was actually a required project! I was really excited because this was a beautiful experience that helped us acquire useful knowledge and information. The most important thing is that we learned everything by ourselves and through our own efforts! (Ardana)

Ardana stressed the role of the teacher as facilitator in the inquiry process. By providing the right guidance and emotional encouragement to students, the facilitator can actually scaffold learning and construct new knowledge. Moreover, the facilitator is vital for students to overcome their anxiety or other negative emotions that might hinder their involvement in the process.

The Role of Social Interactions for Science Learning Outcomes

Nine out of the 17 participants (Galenia, Alexis, Kyrenia, Martina, Sabrina, Sabrina, Margarita, Andrea, Ardana) highlighted the social dimension and its contribution towards meaningful learning. Alexis, Kyrenia and Sabrina found it enabled them to learn science content more accurately through the exchange of ideas. Alexis expressed that the social interactions promoted a sense of belonging in the group:

Group work brought us together. During the inquiry, the three groups came up with different solutions and this created a productive competition among the groups. After that, it was easier for each of us to understand each other's way of thinking. We felt that we belonged in a group of people sharing the same concerns. (Alexis)

Exchanging ideas in her group enabled Margarita to understand the ecological dimension of the problem and realize that the ecological crisis is also a social one since it connects to people's stereotypes. Moreover, through social interactions, inquiries can be enriched and variables affecting the outcome more easily detected. Sharing knowledge and experience promotes active participation and eliminates passively accepting knowledge:

Through group work, all members of our group had the opportunity to be actively involved in the process and produce something towards the solution of the problem. Every one had the opportunity to use our experience as teachers creatively. We interacted; shared ideas, thoughts and emotions and finally achieved our common goals. We had the opportunity to diagnose our own stereotypes, develop social skills. We had to document our ideas and develop skills to help us in our work as teachers and as citizens in general. Our personal experiences were the beginning and the end of this process. We ended up changing our thinking and learning through the evidence we collected during our inquiry. We finally realized the ecological consequences of our everyday choices. (Sabrina)

Martina noted that social interactions in the group improved her ability understand her students' initial conceptions in general since it helped her understand other people's way of thinking. Margarita found that the division of labor in the group is a catapult for developing social skills and the sense of acceptance. In addition, Ardana noted that social interactions promote decision-making.

DISCUSSION AND IMPLICATIONS

The study aimed to develop in-depth knowledge on in-service teachers' reasoning and emotions in open-ended scientific inquiry outside of the classroom setting, and the methodology's contribution to science learning and on participants' social interactions.

The three teacher groups solved the research problem, each in a distinct way since each group defined the efficiency of the bike differently (e.g., in terms of energy consumption or effort of the cyclist). However, all groups ended up identifying and controlling the variables, a vital part of scientific inquiry. Therefore, all groups designed and performed experiments that enabled them to base their conclusions on scientific evidence.

We also investigated how the teachers responded emotionally during their involvement. Analysis revealed that participants experienced both positive (e.g., interest, enthusiasm, curiosity and confidence) and negative (e.g., anxiety) emotions that affected their predisposition towards implementing inquiry-based learning in their teaching. However, most teachers responded positively to the prospect of implementing the methodology with their students since they felt it would promote more effective science learning and enable students to connect concepts they examine in class to their out-of-school, everyday experiences to develop a sense of ownership and new knowledge.

They also found ways to promote scientific content learning that may also promote skills learners can apply in other subject areas as well as their everyday lives: for instance, identifying and controlling variables, designing and conducting experiments, reaching conclusions on scientific evidence and communicating results. Moreover, the module promoted social skills among the participants, as well as creativity and a sense of ownership over the ways content is learned.

In a recent report for the National Research Council, Bell, Lewenstein, Shouse and Feder (2009) argue that across informal social settings, such as on trips to museums and zoos, in the home, in activities with friends and community projects, learners may develop awareness, interest, motivation, social competencies and practices. Much research has been conducted in the area of informal learning within the past decade; however, this research has occurred mostly within museumlike settings (Dierking et al., 2003). Nonetheless, clear evidence supports learning that happens in other 'real-world' settings (Wellinghton, 1990). Rennie (2007) points out that "out-of-school contexts are undeniable sources of learning for young people, and yet there seems to be little overlap there with what happens in school" (p. 154). This study attempts to bridge this gap in the literature as it engaged the teachers in various activities both outdoors and in a school classroom setting.

The nature of the question (i.e., *design the most efficient bicycle*) was personally meaningful and promoted the sharing of student personal experiences. Tal, Krajcik and Bluemenfeld (2006) investigated teaching practices that foster inquiry and promote student learning in urban settings and had similar findings; namely, that the real-world context (i.e., air-quality project with implications about community health) had a great value in science teaching since it promoted local and personal experiences supporting the claim that "teachers should help students compare community and cultural knowledge with school knowledge" (p. 740).

This study provides an example of an open-ended inquiry-based science module specifically designed for in-service teachers in a teacher education program. More university-based case studies are needed that use a variety of learning environments and contexts for effective PD for teachers. Future research is recommended for producing innovative university cases of specially designed modules.

The study suggests that actively involving and supporting in-service teachers' engagement in the activities allows teacher learning to matter beyond the experience itself and begin to make inroads into the classroom. From a research perspective, it is important to examine learning that happens in out-of-university settings, such as outdoors environmental studies or community-based projects, in attempting to bridge the gap between formal and informal learning.

Evidence about the success of the module in supporting in-service teachers' development exemplifies the cognitive, affective and social aspects of PD, particularly the outdoors context, the module and the use of an open-ended scientific inquiry approach. More in-depth study into such instructional innovations is warranted, for the purpose of determining appropriate pedagogies that promote meaningful PD for in-service teachers.

REFERENCES

Anderson, D., Piscitelli, B., Everett, M. & Weier, K. (2002). *The impact of multi-visit museum programs on young children's learning.* Paper presented at the National Association for Research in Science Teaching 75th Annual Meeting. New Orleans, LA.

Bell, P., Lewenstein, B., Shouse, A. & Feder, M. (2009). *Learning science in informal environments: People, places, and pursuits.* Washington, DC: National Research Council.

Bloom, L. A., Perlmutter, J. & Burrell, L. (1999). The general educator: Applying constructivism to inclusive classrooms. *Intervention in School and Clinic, 34*(3), 132–136.

Creswell, J. W. (1998). *Qualitative inquiry and research design: Choosing among five traditions.* Thousand Oaks, CA: Sage.

Dierking, L. D., Falk, J. H., Rennie, L., Anderson, D. & Ellenbogen, K. (2003). Policy statement of the 'informal science education' ad hoc committee. *Journal of Research in Science Teaching, 40*(2), 108–111.

Driver, R., Guesne, E. & Tiberghien, A. (1985). *Children's ideas in science.* Milton Keynes, UK: Open University Press.

Falk, J., & Dierking, L. (1992). *The museum experience.* Washington, DC: Whalesback Books.

Fallik, O., Eylon, B. & Rosenfeld, S. (2008). Motivating teachers to enact free-choice project- based learning in science and technology (PBLSAT): Effects of a professional development model. *Journal of Science Teacher Education, 19,* 565–591.

Greeno, J.G., Collins, A.M., & Resnick, L.B. (1996). Cognition and learning. In D. D.C Berliner and R.C. Calfee (Eds.), *Handbook of Educational Psychology* (pp. 15–46). NY, New York: Simon & Schuster Macmillan.

Lave, J., & Wenger, E. (1991). *Situated learning: Legitimate peripheral participation.* Cambridge: Cambridge University Press.

Merriam, S. B. (2009). *Qualitative research: A guide to design and implementation.* San Francisco: Jossey-Bass.

Novak, J. (2002). Meaningful learning: The essential factor for conceptual change in limited or inappropriate propositional hierarchies leading to empowerment of learners. *Science Education, 86*(4), 548–571.

Rennie, L. J. (2007). Learning science outside of school. In S. Abell & N. G. Lederman (Eds.), *Handbook of research on science education* (pp. 125–170). London: Lawrence Erlbaum.

Rennie, L., Feher, E. Dierking, L.D. and Falk, J.H. (2003). Towards an Agenda for Advanced Research on Science Learning in Out-of-School Settings. *Journal of Research in Science Teaching, 50*(2), 112–120.

Tal, T., Krajcik, J. S. & Blumenfeld, P. C. (2006). Urban schools' teachers enacting project-based science. *Journal of Research in Science Teaching, 43*(7), 722–745.

Wellinghton, J. (1990). Formal and informal learning in science: The role of the interactive science centres. *Physics Education, 25,* 247–252.

Wenger, E. (1998). *Communities of practice: Learning, meaning, and identity.* Cambridge: Cambridge University Press.

Yin, R. K. (2003). *Case study research: Design and methods.* Thousand Oaks, CA: Sage.

13 From Concept to School Practice
Professional Learning for Sustainable Change in the Primary Science Classroom

Pernilla Nilsson

INTRODUCTION

In Sweden, as in some other countries, much debate about school improvement and the raising of educational standards revolves around the issue of teachers' professional knowledge. There is no doubt that teachers play a key role in change and school improvement, but improving the quality of teaching requires much more than acquiring new tips and tricks for classroom practice.

The quality of teachers' classroom work reflects how teachers develop professionally and personally. Therefore, an understanding of teachers' professional learning not only involves the knowledge and skills that teachers should acquire but also an understanding of the context in which the teacher works and the conditions that support [or not] teachers' personal and professional growth.

A global concern about students' decreasing interest and enjoyment of science across the compulsory secondary school years continues, particularly with respect to the sharp decline in the transition from primary to secondary school (e.g., Goodrum, Hackling & Rennie, 2001; Lindahl, 2003; Schreiner, 2006). While some students enjoy science, many do not see its relevance to their life experiences and concerns. They do not realize its potential for dealing with the everyday problems they encounter in their daily lives.

A perceived lack of engagement of students with science occurs at both primary and secondary schools. The 'problem' is seen somewhat differently for primary and secondary, with concerns at the secondary level linking negative attitudes of students to the pedagogies, and at the primary level, to the lack of science content and teacher confidence with science content. It is reasonable to suggest that the way teachers present science in the classroom ultimately shapes students' attitudes towards, and learning of, science. For example, Claxton (1991) illustrated this point, citing an adolescent girl who described the difference between the sciences she experienced at primary and secondary school:

> Primary science was like being in a small plane flying over a vast open landscape like a desert. You could land anywhere to have a look around

and explore for a while. There was a sense in which it didn't seem to matter too much *where* you had landed, because it was the exploring that was important, not so much what you found. The fact that the knowledge you accumulated was patchwork, and had big 'holes' in it was not a problem. Secondary science, on the other hand, was like being on a train in carriages that had blanked-out windows. You were going in a single direction, about which you had no choice. The train stopped at every station and you had to get off, whether you liked it or were interested or not, and pay attention to what the train driver told you to enter. Then you got back on the train and went off to the next station—but because the windows were opaque you could not see the countryside in-between, so you did not know how the stations were linked or related to each other. Obviously, you were on a purposeful journey, you were going somewhere, and the train driver seemed to know where it was. Worst of all was the feeling that you were supposed to understand the direction of the journey too, even though nobody had given you a map, or let you look out of the train as it was chugging along. So there was a risk that you would come to think that it was your fault that you could not put it all together. (pp. 25–26)

This lack of a framework to give students purpose and direction to activities in school science points to a clear need for teachers (and policy makers) to stop and reflect on the direction for school science. The significant question, however, concerns how best to support teacher improvement in a situation (described earlier) calling for significant changes in pedagogy.

In Sweden, changes in school science through curriculum reform have been ongoing. In the new school science curricula (2011) the traditional dichotomy between content and process-focused primary and secondary science has given way to a more sophisticated understanding encompassing both the products and the processes of science together. As described by the girl from Claxton (1991), a broadening of thinking about the *purposes* of science in school as well as the perceptions of personal relevance for students seem to be critical factors in whether students take interest in science. Lindahl (2003) confirmed that students' interest in the sciences in most cases forms early, often in primary school, and interest drops quickly in physics, chemistry and technology in the early secondary school years. This supports the argument about rethinking science in primary schools and across the primary–secondary school transition in forming students' attitudes towards science.

I offer a metaphor: the idea of primary school science considered a 'mystery tour' where students can stop the plane wherever they want to look around for a while and be engaged as a traveler. However, a teacher's science content knowledge is critical for designing lessons for underlying science concepts and processes beyond focusing on investigation processes and "mystery tours" indicated from several studies (e.g., Harlen & Holroyd, 1997; Nilsson, 2008). In order to 'fly the plane,' primary teachers need professional learning, both of science subject knowledge and approaches to pedagogy necessary to teaching science in effective and engaging ways.

PRIMARY SCIENCE TEACHER KNOWLEDGE FOR FUTURE CHALLENGES

The last few years in Sweden, evaluations of students' scientific knowledge through TIMSS and PISA have influenced policy makers' requirements and expectations for science teaching in primary and secondary schools. Since, as research indicates, primary school teachers often lack science content knowledge and confidence in science teaching (e.g., Appleton, 2003, 2006; Harlen & Holroyd, 1997; Nilsson, 2008), much of the national discussion focuses on how to organize activities for primary teachers' professional development (PD) to bring about desired changes in (science) teaching practices.

In 1994, Sweden's national school curricula presented 5-year goals for student learning in every subject area. In 2011 the new national school curricula will present goals in science for years three and six. However, while teachers may appear to agree with the science curricula, classroom practice does not seem to correspond and, as a result, the intended curriculum is not necessarily fully implemented (Keys, 2005). Therefore, to plan learning experiences that engage and challenge pupils' science knowledge, teachers need to develop better understanding of science teaching, pupils, pupils' learning and the curriculum in ways that allow translation into meaningful practice. With these issues in mind, in 2007, the Swedish government began investing in a 3-year teacher PD program. This national response to students' decreasing interest in school science aimed to strengthen teachers' competence in science and technology in ways that might facilitate better classroom responses to students' educational needs.

To motivate teachers to bring about a sustainable change, they need to believe that the change is necessary. They also need to believe they are capable of improving their own classroom practice. Cumming (2002) suggested that there are no automatic links "between developing professional teaching standards per se, and living these out in everyday learning environments" (p. 3). Hargreaves (1994) pointed out that to produce "good teaching" requires both the capacity for teachers to change and their *desire* to change and further apply those practices. In light of these challenges, it is important to examine how science professional learning activities can support teachers' capacity and self-confidence in teaching science.

This chapter explores six Swedish primary teachers' experiences of a 5-month science professional learning course designed to develop teachers' attitudes towards, and self-confidence in, teaching science as well as develop their content knowledge and practical skills for teaching in their classrooms. The study aimed to identify *critical features* (Desimone, 2009) that influence and shape teachers' knowledge of, and attitudes towards, teaching science, and further, what may enhance their desire to develop sustainable change in their classroom practice. Throughout the literature, researchers stress that primary teachers' beliefs, attitudes and subject matter knowledge have a great impact on how they implement the science curricula in their classroom practice. Therefore, there is a need for research that provides a deeper understanding of what primary teachers consider important in facilitating changes in their beliefs, attitudes and actual school practice. Such an understanding should, therefore, provide guidance for educational leaders about how to sustain effective change in science teaching.

TEACHER KNOWLEDGE AND PROFESSIONAL LEARNING

The inherent complexity of teacher knowledge, and hence teacher learning, has been well documented in science education research literature (e.g., Berry, 2007; Loughran, Mulhall & Berry, 2006; Nilsson, 2008; Van Driel, Beijaard & Verloop, 2001). In 1986, Shulman (1986, 1987) drew attention to the knowledge required for teaching through his description of teachers' pedagogical content knowledge (PCK), which he said involved "the capacity of a teacher to transform the content knowledge he/she possesses into forms that are pedagogically powerful and yet adaptive to the variations in ability and background represented by the students" (p. 8). For developing such capacity, Nilsson (2008) stressed the importance of creating conditions for practical experiences in science teaching that are reasoned and reflected on. This chapter presents several ways of supporting primary teachers in actively participating in their professional learning of science teaching through becoming participants in a community of learners (Wenger, 1998), which involves not only acquiring the technical skills needed for teaching, but also developing a personal framework of how to value those skills and themselves as teachers.

To capture the complexity of teacher knowledge and how it develops it is helpful to reflect on how the terms professional *development* and professional *learning* are defined and applied. Loughran (2010) observed that "the replacement of one term with another is not helpful because it undermines the difference in meaning that the language is supposed to imply" (p. 200). Although in some research literature these concepts are used interchangeably, or without distinction, a difference may exist between the terms and that the difference matters. When Clark (1992) considered the phrase "professional development of teachers," he asserted that it:

> carries a great deal of negative undertones. It implies a process done to teachers; that teachers need to be forced into developing; that teachers have deficits in knowledge and skills that can be fixed by training; and that teachers are pretty much alike. (p. 75)

Hence, it could be assumed that the use of the term 'development' implies initiating a process associated with doing *to* and *for* teachers rather than *with* them; something episodic and superficial that teachers need to be forced into developing; that teachers are presumed to be passive and resistant; or, that teachers' insufficient knowledge can be "fixed" through training designed to make them do something they are being directed to learn, do and implement. Loughran (2010) calls this phenomenon a 'top-down approach,' which is about making changes formed elsewhere but that need to be implemented in classrooms.

On the other hand, professional *learning* occurs when teachers take control of their own professional knowledge development and conduct their learning in response to their perceived personal needs, issues and concerns. In considering professional learning from this perspective it suggests that such learning is directed by an initial need in the learner. The learning occurs *with* and *by* the teachers . . . not *to* or *for* the teachers and the teachers themselves have an active role in that learning process. Loughran (2006) made this clear in stating that "professional learning is not developed through simply gaining more knowledge, rather, professional learning is enhanced by one becoming more perceptive to the complexities, possibilities and nuances of teaching contexts" (p. 136). However, as teacher knowledge includes a rich blend of knowledge about subject matter, pedagogy and context and relies on the dynamic relationship between each (Nilsson, 2008), developing teachers' competence to restructure or reframe their knowledge and beliefs (i.e., professional learning) is inevitably a complex challenge.

No matter what concept is used in the research literature, it seems to be a common view that to lead to sustainable change in teachers' practice requires emphasizing teachers' social and personal growth. For example, Desimone (2009) stated that teachers experience a range of activities and interactions that may increase their knowledge and skills and improve their teaching practice as well as contribute to their personal, social and emotional growth as teachers. Harrison, Hofstein, Eylon and Simon (2008) suggested that effective PD needs to provide an opportunity for teacher reflection and learning about how new practices can be evolved or shaped from existing classroom practice. This requires teachers to reexamine what they do and how they might do it differently (Harrison et al.). Hargreaves and Fullan (1992) argued that teacher development is also a process of personal development noting that it "involves more than changing teachers' behavior . . . it also involves changing the person the teacher is" (p. 7). As such, teachers need to know their PD requirements and the impact of this on their classroom practice. In responding to the question of what we know about PD programs and their impact on teacher learning, Borko (2004) highlighted the importance of taking into account both the individual teacher learner and the context in which the learning takes place:

> For teachers, learning occurs in many different aspects of practice, including their classrooms, their school communities, and professional development courses or workshops. It can occur in a brief hallway conversation with a colleague, or after school when counselling a troubled

child. To understand teacher learning, we must study it within these multiple contexts, taking into account both the individual teacher-learners and the social systems in which they are participants. (p. 4)

Teachers are therefore challenged to justify not only to themselves, but also to their students, colleagues and others, why they bring new practices to bear in their classrooms (Harrison et al., 2008). The importance of teacher networking was further emphasized by Van Driel et al. (2001), who argued that the natural resistance to change and innovation, particularly by experienced teachers, can be reduced by learning in structures that participants from different schools collaboratively aim to achieve previously formulated objectives for a particular period of time. Hence, professional learning requires social interaction and such interactions need to be purposefully encouraged (Loughran, 2006). But then *how* do courses that focus on professional learning of science teaching actually influence teachers' attitudes and beliefs, and further, create a desire for sustainable change in teachers' classroom practice?

Desimone (2009) highlighted one way of translating the complex, interactive, formal and informal nature of teacher learning opportunities into measurable phenomena by focusing on *critical features* of the activity. Critical features are those characteristics of an activity that effectively increase teacher learning and changes in practice, and ultimately improve student learning—as opposed to simple onetime workshops or study groups. Desimone (2009) summarized five features of PD that are associated with changes in knowledge and practice: (a) *content focus* (on subject matter content and how students learn that content); (b) *active learning* (opportunities for teachers to engage in active learning, interactive feedback and discussions); (c) *coherence* (the extent of teacher learning consistent with teacher knowledge and beliefs, the consistency of what is taught in PD of science policies and programs); (d) *duration* (including both span over time and the numbers of hours spent in the activity) and support activities that are spread over a semester and include 20 hours or more of contact time; and (e) *collective participation* (teachers from the same school, grade and department). In proposing a basic model to be used in all empirical causal studies of PD, Desimone (2009, p. 185) focuses on the interactive relationships between the critical features of PD, teacher knowledge and beliefs; classroom practice; and student outcomes (see also Figure 1.1 in van Veen, Zwart & Meirink, this volume). This model allows testing of both a theory of teacher change (e.g., that PD alters teacher knowledge, beliefs or practice) and a theory of instruction (e.g., that changed practice influences student achievement). Again, it is clear that there is an imprecise use of language around these issues whereby PD and professional learning are not always differentiated. As professional learning is personal and appropriately shaped and directed by individuals (Loughran, 2010), teachers themselves must be committed to changing their own practice. Teachers' professional learning requires opportunities for teachers to engage as learners and to further reflect on how the process of framing and reframing practice might result in a personal understanding that can be translated in their own context. To make progress in understanding critical features of teachers' professional learning and subsequent change in practice points to an urgent need to unpack teacher learning from the individual teacher's point of view, experiences, needs and concerns. Hence, I contend a pressing need to identify critical features (drawn from some aspects of the literature noted earlier) for professional learning *with* teachers that might help to make it more effective than PD (with a top-down approach *for* teachers) in genuinely responding to and serving teachers' learning needs. With this background, the results of the study reported in this chapter are helpful in providing a framework for responding to primary teachers' needs and concerns in ways that might better inform those responsible for professional learning to work toward sustainable change in teachers' actions.

COURSE CONTEXT AND PARTICIPANTS

Borko (2004) found that PD programs including an explicit focus on experiences that engage teachers as learners in activities such as conducting scientific experiments are particularly effective. Therefore, the professional learning program described in this section was specifically designed to both increase primary teachers' knowledge of specific domains of science and also help them reflect on how such ideas can be developed and integrated into their own classroom practice. The design of the program further supported the characteristics of PD that Desimone (2009) described as critical to increasing teacher knowledge and skills and improving their practice. These characteristics included: (a) focus on the science subject matter content and how students learn that content; (b) opportunities for teachers to engage in active learning through having and giving interactive feedback to lectures and seminars; (c) teacher learning consistent with teachers' knowledge and beliefs and that the program was aligned with, and directly related to, the national school science curricula; (d) the course of sufficient duration lasting over a 5-month period; and, finally, (e) emphasis on collective participation with the group of teachers all working in primary school and further, at least two teachers from the same school encouraged to participate.

The goals of the course were to:

1. Expose primary teachers to central ideas in the domain of science and encourage them to try scientific activities and to further implement them effectively in their own primary school classrooms.
2. Improve primary teachers' attitudes and confidence towards science and science teaching.

3. Provide primary teachers with a network of colleagues with whom they could refer to and discuss future activities.
4. Facilitate meetings where teachers could discuss and reflect on their documented teaching practice.

One main issue in the program involved stimulating participant primary teachers to implement the course ideas into their own practice and encouraging them to explore issues that emerged while developing their own pedagogical understandings. The teachers were encouraged to share their knowledge and experiences with other participants to build on each other's learning experiences. The course facilitator developed new activities corresponding to teachers' needs and designed the seminars using an inquiry approach.

The professional learning course was conducted as 15 whole-day sessions during one school semester (5 months), with periods between the sessions where the teachers could explore, develop and further reflect on how the course activities developed in their own classrooms. Most course activities were conducted in a Science Learning Center at the university. Normally, the Science Learning Center offers teaching and learning for pupils aged 4 to 11 who attend the center to experience science lessons in addition to their regular schooling. In addition, the Science Learning Center is a context for in-service and preservice teachers' professional learning activities in which the lessons normally build on problem-based scientific inquiries and experiments.

Six primary teachers, three males and three females, participated in the course. All teaching students aged 6 to 11, their teaching experience ranged from 8 to 25 years; however, they had limited experience teaching *science*. They chose the course out of interest in learning more about science and science teaching. As such, the teachers as a group were motivated to learn but, more importantly, were newcomers to the community of science teaching. Before the course, the participants were (through emails) asked to reflect on why they had chosen the course, their expectations of the course and whether or not they could identify their specific learning needs for teaching science in a primary school context. These ideas were then discussed by the course facilitator (who was a former primary science teacher) and the author of this chapter in order to design a course that met and challenged the primary teachers' expectations and learning needs. As all teachers stressed their need for subject matter knowledge, the course was planned to present science content through lectures and workshops by faculty content "experts." The teachers, however, stressed the need to connect the science content to their practice; they did not want science content knowledge alone. Hence, to support this connection, the course instructor selected central science concepts to build on with the teachers in the Science Learning Center. As such, the course instructor aimed to support the teachers in bridging the science content and primary school practice in meaningful ways by conducting activities designed to stimulate the teachers' questioning and reasoning and to act as a critical friend for the teachers.

The course facilitator invited the teachers to actively engage in the course. He listened carefully to the needs of the teachers through discussions and evaluations. It seemed the participating teachers and instructor mutually taught and learned, again emphasizing the reciprocal nature of their professional relationships. Drawing upon ideas from sociocultural theory, the instructor and participating primary teachers created a community of practice (Wenger, 1998) in which the teachers came together to share, challenge and create ideas about their Science Teaching and Learning (STaL). As such the course was conducted *with* the teachers rather than simply doing science *to* them.

Data collection consisted of semi-structured interviews with the six primary teachers. Every teacher was interviewed one time and each interview lasted for about 45 minutes. In the interviews the teachers were asked questions such as their reasons for choosing the course; their perception of its aims; how involved they felt in the course; how it had influenced (or not) their attitudes and everyday teaching of science; which activities they considered as meaningful and why; and their identification of the course's strengths and weaknesses. Thus, the interviews gathered evidence of critical features in the course that the teachers stressed as important to their professional learning and thus changes in their science teaching practice. All six interviews were audio recorded, transcribed and later analyzed using content analysis in which transcripts were read iteratively and reflexively in greater depth to identify emerging themes of critical features. The aim of the content analysis was to identify and further analyze transcriptions within the data that appeared to be central in the primary teachers' experiences. The content analysis involved coding, categorizing (relating meaningful categories into which words, phrases and sentences can be placed), comparing categories and making links between them and finally drawing conclusions from the text data (Cohen, Manion & Morrison, 2007). In the following sections, indicative quotes and pseudonyms for the teachers have been used (Mary, Ann, Paul, Tom, Jane, Jim).

CRITICAL FEATURES FOR DEVELOPING TEACHERS' PROFESSIONAL LEARNING

In the analysis of the interviews, three main categories of critical features emerged: (a) *engagement, attitudes and shared vision of the goals of the course*; (b) *being a community of learners*; and (c) *the meaningfulness of subject matter knowledge*. These three features are explored in detail in the following.

Engagement, Attitudes and Shared Vision of the Goals of the Course

As highlighted earlier, professional *learning* occurs when teachers conduct their learning in response to their perceived personal needs and when they have an active role in that learning process (*active learning*). These arguments were well supported in the interviews. There was a clear view that engagement, in terms of the way the course facilitator and the content experts showed respect for the primary teachers' ideas, desires and expectations, was important to the teachers' professional learning. Further to this, the teachers' own attitudes towards science teaching and how these attitudes changed, from a feeling of "curious insecurity" (interview, Mary) to an eagerness to try out new ideas in the classroom, were brought up as important factors.

The participants highlighted the way the professional learning program was designed. Issues such as establishing (the facilitator and the participants) a shared vision of the goals and outcomes and maintaining flexibility in planning and implementing the course ideas in the teachers' practice were raised in the interviews. The teachers also stressed the importance of the collaboration and common understanding between the participants being actively engaged in the course and of linking the science content to practical experiments and everyday phenomena. For example, Paul mentioned that he felt engaged by the way the course design stimulated him to bring science into his own classroom (*coherence*). He stated that he had come to see how he needed to change his own teaching:

> I really need to pull myself together and change my teaching practice. Too often I know that the way I work with science is too theoretical. I let the students read a book, write a lot or I show a picture. But when we do all these practical things in a course like this I realize that this is not so good. You need some practical input to be engaged, and you need to be aware of the advantages in order to start to work with your own teaching practice. But in the end you understand that what you gain in the students' engagement and learning is more than the effort you, as a teacher need to put in.

All six teachers chose the program because of their interest in learning more science and felt privileged for being accepted; this influenced their attitudes to and engagement in the activities. They all spoke about how their students enjoyed the science activities in the classroom, something that also influenced their own attitudes towards teaching science. Also, the teachers stressed the importance of having self-confidence and engagement in trying new approaches to teaching science. For example, Jane stressed how before the course, she worried a lot about the science content, but that the way the instructors tried to meet her learning needs raised her confidence. Tom stated that teaching science and technology required materials and if, as a teacher, he did not have enough self-confidence and time to collect and try these materials, he might find an excuse for avoiding the subject. Therefore, one important aspect in the course was to show how to use everyday materials in the science teaching.

> Some teachers get scared if they need to buy too much material but one of the goals in this course seemed to be that this must not always be the case. It is possible to work with science experiments without having a lot of strange materials. It is good for us to be aware of that.

In summary, the teachers felt that they gained confidence and were engaged in learning in ways designed to pursue their individual developmental goals, namely, to change their own classroom practice.

Being a Community of Learners

A main finding was that the sociocultural practice that the primary teachers and the course facilitator were engaged in throughout the course played an essential role in promoting these teachers' professional learning. In all six interviews it was continually emphasized how learning in collaboration (*collective participation*) with colleagues, and the exchange of ideas and experiences, had encouraged these teachers to critically examine and reflect on their own practice. Two of the teachers came from the same school, which was also noted as a positive feature of the program.

> I think that having a network with whom you can discuss is crucial for how you implement the ideas and how the course actually changes your school teaching practice. Then you go back to the school and you are two persons that can convince the others. Yes it is important to have this support from the colleagues. (Jane)

Ann highlighted how reflecting on her teaching experience together with her peers in the program helped her recognize her own learning needs. The way she could listen to the others' experiences inspired her and helped her reflect on how to improve her own practice. She found the collaborative learning opportunities developed a level of trust that encouraged her to influence her school organization. For example, she spoke about coming back to school with the intention of "chang[ing] the world" (interview, Ann) but that the school management (in terms of economy) did not always support these changes. As such the community of learners that the primary teachers built during the program was also a community in which they shared experiences of how to engage with their different school managements in order to promote conditions in terms of time, economy and materials needed for the type of science teaching they wanted to develop.

These teachers also highlighted how their colleagues in school were interested in, and became inspired by, their work. Therefore, it seems reasonable to suggest that the participant teachers had a catalytic effect on their colleagues, which in turn suggests the collaborative nature of learning. In summary, all teachers stressed that collegiality helped them to build their self-confidence toward activities built on scientific inquiry and problem-solving skills in their own practice in their own classrooms. They further stressed that because of the familiarity between the facilitator and the teachers in the program, they did not feel inhibited about revealing what they did not understand. Instead, they described it as an open-minded culture that stimulated them to experience the learning activities, sometimes in a way the students might experience them, and that engaged them to think about the phenomena in a way that opened them to students' questions. Jim discussed how the course tasks in his own classroom urged him and his colleagues to reorganize their teaching during the forthcoming year to include many more scientific inquiry activities. He and his colleagues had come to design an individual science learning development plan for every student in order to assess their learning and to see how their science teaching was related to the curricula. Paul described how he discussed science teaching activities with his colleagues, who responded very positively. He also described how after the program, he became responsible for science at his school and that he had initiated a "science room" in which he worked with students from all different classes.

> It is quite interesting to see how you . . . in some way change your identity as a teacher after such a course. I mean . . . all of a sudden I was the "science expert" and everyone came to ask me. I really feel that they all listen to my ideas . . . and the science room is great.

Jane talked about how the six participants in the course became familiar with each other, which was an important factor in influencing her confidence in the group. During coffee breaks and lunches they discussed aspects related to teaching and learning more informally, something she found important as a way of sharing and reflecting on each other's learning experiences. In summary, the interviews indicated that over the time of the program, the teachers came to see themselves as a community of learners with a shared goal of improving their learning and teaching of science.

The Meaningfulness of Subject Matter Knowledge

All six teachers identified developing science subject matter knowledge (*content focus*) as a major concern before the onset of the course. As noted earlier, most had limited science subject matter knowledge. Some also stressed how they felt challenged by the science content as they felt worried about not being able to explain concepts and phenomena to their students in the classroom. In the interviews, all teachers highlighted that the way the course was designed around seminars with content experts, experimental workshops in the Science Learning Center and the program facilitator, who persistently challenged the teachers to reflect on how the content could be translated to primary school practices, influenced their learning. Also, the collaboration between the science content experts and program facilitator in linking the lectures to a primary school context proved crucial to their professional learning. Hence, all six teachers noted the importance of seeing the subject matter knowledge as meaningful for their primary teaching.

> It was very good that the course facilitator participated in the science content lectures as he could give examples of several tips and tricks about how to actually do in the school context but he could also connect his workshops to the science content that the experts brought up. However, it was very nice to listen to content experts that, even though they might not teach the content in primary school, still were eager to discuss with us how to transform the content to primary students. In such way we were involved in our own learning, and also the way we always used about a week to try out the things in our own classrooms before we met again to reflect on our learning and teaching. (Jim)

They also highlighted how they came to see how easy it was to integrate science with other subjects, such as sustainable development and social sciences. For example, Ann stressed how her enthusiasm carried her through a number of challenges as she worked to integrate electricity and energy into her teaching practice in order to create a discussion about sustainable development and energy sources. For example, she used the lecture and the workshop of electricity and energy in her own classroom.

> The week after we worked with energy and electricity I tried to implement the ideas with my students. Actually, I did not know how easy it was to do it. We had a lamp, battery and cables and then we went further to build a model that produced wind energy. Now after the course I am the one that has science and technology lessons with all students in Grade 1 (6–7 years old).

The teachers had to reflect on their subject matter knowledge as well as how they managed to transform their knowledge to promote their students' understandings and, subsequently, to experiment with the experiences of colleagues to elaborate on their own practical knowledge of teaching. As such, these primary teachers' practical experiences had a central role in shaping the way the program was conducted. When trying out the program ideas in their teaching, the teachers were continuously confronted with challenging situations, such as responding to students' questions— something that they brought back to the course when reflecting on their experiences. All six teachers emphasized the point that the program made them curious and that they wanted to learn even more science. However, the amalgamation between the science content and the development of their science PCK in terms of trying out and reflecting on how the content was transformed with their primary students was stressed as crucial to these teachers' professional learning:

I really like the concept where you work through the science content in lectures and workshops, then you need to go out and try to transform it to a group of students, then you return to the course and reflect together with peers and the course facilitator and get another view of it all. How do I as a primary teacher explain this? Yes, in order to manage an explanation I need to understand this and that. This makes us able to see the course as a *learning* and not only as an occasionally contribution. Because too many times I have been on very inspiring lectures and seminars and when I return to school there is so much about assessment, curricula goals, local work plans and all that so you very easily forget what it was that inspired you. In this case we always need to come back to our initial goals and what we have learnt in the lectures as well as in the practical workshops in the science leaning centre and also on how we actually implement the ideas on the school practice. As such the course is on our own conditions. (Jane)

In summary, all teachers mentioned how they developed subject matter knowledge and self-confidence that was meaningful for them in teaching the content. They also mentioned how they were inspired to work with everyday science and scientific inquiries in their own classrooms. During the program they came to see that the better they understood the science content, the easier it became for them to make pedagogical connections in their particular teaching approaches. Hence, it might well be asserted that the teachers did not only gain more subject matter knowledge but, more importantly, they became engaged in a process of developing subject matter for teaching.

PROFESSIONAL LEARNING FOR SUSTAINABLE CHANGE

This chapter has been built around the question of what primary teachers consider as important in order to influence and shape their knowledge of, and attitudes towards, teaching science, and further, what catalyzes a desire for a sustainable change in their own classroom practice. Borko (2004) noted a lot of questions to answer requiring many different types of inquiry to generate a rich source of knowledge to develop high-quality teacher professional learning. It is reasonable to suggest then that in stimulating teachers to become more conscious of their own assumptions and decision-making (i.e., activities *with* and *by* teachers and not *to* or *for* teachers) teachers' professional learning can grow out of PD. In this chapter, one way of demonstrating how this type of professional learning can be better supported is through teachers being involved in a community of learners—engaged in a community of science teaching practice. As Wenger (1998) asserted:

engagement in practice—in its unfolding, multidimensional complexity—it is both the stage and the object, the road and the destination. What they learn is not a static subject matter but the very process of being engaged in, and participating in developing, an ongoing practice. (p. 95)

All the teachers in this project highlighted the importance of the social interactions between their peers during the program and between the science teachers and course instructor. Wenger (1998) described participation in a community of practice as a complex process that combines doing, talking, thinking, feeling and belonging. He also argued that participation involves three aspects: engagement, the exploration of new territory and commitment. With respect to engagement, the program meetings offered opportunities for teachers' professional learning because the discussions were centered on practical issues to which the teachers could relate. Hence, participation in discussion during the seminars enabled the teachers to engage with others around their science teaching practice, something that is important if teachers' beliefs and assumptions are to be challenged in meaningful ways. Also, the way the primary teachers actively engaged in planning the activities proved essential to the success of the program as it helped to prevent weaknesses that might otherwise characterize programs designed by 'experts' unconnected to everyday teaching and lacking experience in the school environment.

The results illustrate how stimulating teachers to be open-minded and express their thoughts and beliefs help them to articulate their knowledge and to think about how to personally adjust their practice. The results also highlight the important for educators to show *interest* in teachers' learning and listen carefully to the values and beliefs underpinning practice. Hargreaves (1994) stressed that professional learning for teachers also involves an ethic of practicality: "what works and what doesn't [for] this teacher in this context . . . [a] complex and potent combination of purpose, person, politics and workplace constraints" (p. 12). Hence, learning must involve for teachers both the desire and the opportunity to develop new ways of thinking about practice.

Van Driel and colleagues (2001) argued that professional learning is not simply a case of adding new information to the existing base of teacher knowledge but a developing, ongoing task in which "teachers need to restructure their knowledge and beliefs, and, on the basis of teaching experiences, integrate the new information in their practical knowledge" (p. 140). Hence, it might well be asserted that teachers need to recognize good practice within a domain of science teaching, make sense of its complexities and understand the effects and synergies of various aspects of practice as they come to find their own ways of establishing such practice. The science professional learning program at the center of the study described in this chapter aimed to both increase participant teachers' knowledge of specific domains of science and to help them reflect on how the content could be developed and implemented in their classroom practice. Clearly, professional learning requires social interaction and when such interactions are purposefully encouraged, genuine gains in professional knowledge and practice follow (Loughran, 2006).

CONCLUSION

Considerable research indicates that students find science knowledge "taught" in uninteresting ways without relevance to their daily lives, which leads to students' decreasing interest in science over the secondary school years. In the context of science teaching, the key aspect of teacher influence on student engagement is the pedagogical practices of the teacher. Given that pedagogy is the core characteristic of an effective change process, it is important that professional learning 'that matters' stresses the need for interaction between what is being learned in the PD program and the contexts in which teachers work. Therefore, features such as teachers' engagement, motivation and attitudes and also a shared vision (between participants and program organization) of the goals of the program become crucial factors. In returning back to the teenage girl's description of the sciences she experienced at primary school in comparison to that at secondary, it becomes evident that a significant challenge for primary teachers involves building science knowledge and commitment to support students to learn about science at a conceptual rather than descriptive level. When primary teachers themselves do not necessarily have such a background or commitment, making science content meaningful for teaching is critical. Desimone's (2009) idea of the interactive relationship between the *critical features* of teacher PD, teacher knowledge and beliefs; classroom practice; and student outcomes becomes an important frame to determine *what* and *how* PD programs actually extend teachers' professional learning. Hargreaves (1994) and Hall and Hord (2001) emphasized that change in professional practice requires teachers to ground new ideas in their own personal experience. However, to influence science teaching in primary classrooms, professional learning programs need to provide knowledge, examples and approaches to teacher learning that transform into, and impact on, teaching practice in effective and engaging ways.

Through the empirical data, this chapter reflects a consensus about at least some of the characteristics of PD that are critical to increasing teachers' knowledge and skills and improving their practice. The teachers were engaged in an active learning process building on a collective participation in which a content focus was strongly related to the needs of the teachers in the contexts within which they worked. The study relates to Desimone's (2009) frame in that the five core features (*content focus, active learning, coherence, duration* and *collective participation*) were all present in the empirical data. However, it could well be argued that Desimone's features should be elaborated to include more affective aspects on teacher professional learning, such as teachers'' self-confidence, attitudes, engagement and motivation, and also the factor that the science content should be meaningful for teaching in a primary school context. As Harrison et al. (2008) noted, teachers need to familiarize themselves with new ideas and also to understand the implications for themselves as teachers and for their students before they adapt them. Effective PD needs to provide an opportunity for teachers to reflect and learn about how new practices can evolve or be shaped from existing classroom practice (Harrison et al.). In addition, the capacity to reflect on personal practice paves the way to making decisions about the nature of professional learning that also improves practice (Nilsson, 2008).

Given the complexity of these issues, it seems teacher professional learning should be based on the development of teachers' personal beliefs, attitudes and self-confidence as well as their content knowledge in a "culture of continuous or ongoing professional development" (Goodrum et al., 2001, p. 174). As Loughran (2010) asserted, professional learning must involve new ways of seeing situations, testing out new approaches to teaching and learning to see from not only a teacher's but also a learner's perspective. In essence, examining the effects of professional learning 'that matters' should be analogous to identifying the quality of teachers' learning experiences, the nature of teacher change and the extent to which such change affects students' learning. Therefore, more research that links professional learning and changing in teaching practice to students' actual achievement is needed. We also need to continue the discussion of *how* PD courses actually extend teachers' science knowledge and their repertoires of action so that professional learning results. In order to highlight teacher learning that matters, it is important to focus on the processes that are involved in such learning. Although it might be difficult to define the outcomes of professional learning courses in absolute terms, the value of teachers' learning experiences should not be underestimated. To end, it is my belief that the difference in meaning between PD and professional learning should continue to be discussed. It might be one of those unfolding stories where the journey is more important than the destination.

REFERENCES

Appleton, K. (2003). How do beginning primary school teachers cope with science? Toward an understanding of science teaching practice. *Research in Science Education, 33*, 1–25.

Appleton, K. (2006). *Science pedagogical content knowledge and elementary school.* Mahwah: Lawrence Earlbaum Associates, Inc., Publishers.

Berry, A. (2007). *Tensions in teaching about teaching. Understanding practice as a teacher educator.* Dordrecht: Springer.

Borko, H. (2004). Professional development and teacher learning: Mapping the terrain. *Educational Researcher, 33*(8), 315.

Claxton, G. (1991). *Educating the enquiring mind: The challenge for school science.* London: Harvester Wheatsheaf.

Clark, C. (1992). Teachers as designers in self-directed professional development. In A. Hargreaves & M. G. Fullan (Eds.), *Understanding teacher development* (pp. 75–84). London: Teachers College Press.

Cohen, L., Manion, L. & Morrison, K. (2007). *Research methods in education* (6th ed.). London: Routledge Falmer.

Cumming, J. (2002). Working together as a profession. *Unicorn, 28*(2), 1–4.

Desimone, L. M. (2009). Improving impact studies of teachers' professional development: Toward better conceptualizations and measures. *Educational Researcher, 38*(3), 181–199.

Goodrum, D., Hackling, M. & Rennie, L. (2001). *The status and quality of teaching and learning of science in Australian schools.* Canberra, ACT: Department of Education, Training and Youth Affairs.

Hall, G.E., & Hord, S.M. (2001). *Implementing change: Patterns, principles, and potholes.* Boston: Allyn & Bacon.

Hargreaves, A. (1994). *Changing teachers, changing times: Teachers' work and culture in the post-modern world.* London: Cassell.

Hargreaves, A., & Fullan, M. G. (Eds.). (1992). *Understanding teacher development.* London: Teachers College Press.

Harlen, W., & Holroyd, C. (1997). Primary teachers' understanding of concepts of science: Impact on confidence and teaching. *International Journal of Science Education, 19,* 93–105.

Harrison, C., Hofstein, A., Eylon, B-S. & Simon, S. (2008). Evidence-based professional development of science teachers in two countries. *International Journal of Science Education, 30*(5), 577–591.

Keys, P.M. (2005). Are teachers walking the walk or just talking the talks in science education? *Teachers and Teaching: Theory and Practice, 11*(5), 499–516.

Lindahl, B. (2003). *Lust att lära naturvetenskap och teknik? En longitudinell studie om vägen till gymnasiet* [Preferences for science or technics? A longitudinal study into highschool students' attitudes]. Diss., Göteborg studies in educational sciences 196. Göteborg: Acta Universitatis Gothoburgensis.

Loughran, J. J. (2006). *Developing a pedagogy of teacher education.* London: Routledge.

Loughran, J. J. (2010). *What expert teachers do. Enhancing professional knowledge for classroom practice.* Sydney: Allen and Unwin.

Loughran, J. J., Mulhall, P. & Berry, A. (2006). *Understanding and developing science teachers' pedagogical content knowledge.* Rotterdam: Sense Publishers.

Nilsson, P. (2008). *Learning to teach and teaching to learn—primary science student teachers' complex journey from learners to teachers.* Doctoral thesis, Linköping Studies in Science and Technology Education No 19.

Schreiner, C. (2006). *Exploring a ROSE-garden: Norwegian youth's orientations towards science—seen as signs of late modern identities.* Doctoral thesis, University of Oslo.

Shulman, L. S. (1986). Those who understand: Knowledge growth in teaching. *Educational Researcher, 15*(2), 4–14.

Shulman, L. S. (1987). Knowledge and teaching: Foundations of the new reform. *Harvard Educational Review, 57*(1), 1–22.

Van Driel, J., Beijaard, D. & Verloop, N. (2001). Professional development and reform in science education: The role of teachers' practical knowledge. *Journal of Research in Science Teaching, 38*(2), 137–158.

Wenger, E. (1998). *Communities of practice: Learning, meaning and identity.* Cambridge: Cambridge University Press.

Part V

Stepping Back by Stepping In

Reviewing the Landscape

14 Stepping Back and Stepping In
Concluding Thoughts on the Landscapes of Teacher Learning that Matters

Klaas van Veen and Mary Kooy

Building a book on teacher learning that matters is like a journey on a landscape that is both familiar (in topic) and unfamiliar given the divergent and new perspectives introduced in each new chapter. Researchers on the journey share a focus on teacher learning that positively impacts the learning and achievement of students. To be sure, educational, political, cultural contexts, perspectives and research agendas vary, but both the shared focus and difference among the research and researchers create a multifarious journey for building new knowledge for teacher learning.

The journey on the landscape of teacher learning seems to be at a crossroads: Teacher learning is increasingly situated in the context of daily teaching practice indicating that the teacher as learner is taken more seriously but attention to teacher learning is more associated with the drive to improve student performance and achievement than recognizing the teacher as professional and informed decision maker. Increasing awareness that teachers are key to change and reform has added to the need for teacher learning. Yet, for the most part, teacher learning continues to be defined and enacted through traditional forms of teacher learning (e.g., top-down, "one-shot" workshops). Large-scale policy and ideologically driven professional development (PD) for teachers that ignores their learning goals and concerns have led to disappointing results in making reforms and change a reality.

The range of research represented in the volume shares a view of effective and meaningful PD. The foci are on the core of the work of teaching (the instructional triangle or the relationships between content, pedagogy and student learning), on the teacher as key and crucial for effective student learning and on the structures and cultures of the workplaces (often, not designed for teacher learning).

Each contributor brings a unique glimpse of a complex network of educational knowledge, research, processes and practices considered within their particular national educational contexts. Moreover, the provocative uniqueness of each contributor reflexively contributes to a developing and shifting dialogue about the ways teachers learn and develop professionally.

In this concluding chapter, we look back at this journey and explore critical resonances and significant themes for next steps and further directions.

What we know about teacher learning both echoes throughout this volume and points to what remains unknown, raising questions about future directions for research. Borko (2004) noted a main problem in research on teacher learning—the lack of large-scale and longitudinal studies, studies that compare different approaches to teacher learning in different settings and controlled for different features. Most are relatively small, qualitative and examine one program or intervention in a specific setting, which precludes drawing valid, reliable and generalizable conclusions. Hence a call is out for more large-scale and rigorous studies (for this recent debate, see Desimone, 2009; Raudenbush, 2005; Slavin, 2008; Wayne, Yoon, Zhu, Cronen & Garet, 2008). Other reviews of the last 15 years (cf. Kennedy, 1998; Borko, 2004; Smith & Gillespie, 2007; Borko, Jacobs & Koellner, 2010) reach a similar conclusion, and recent studies that include a more rigid or large-scale design do not seem to provide radical new insights into teacher learning (e.g., see Garet et al., 2008; Timperley, Wilson, Barrar & Fung, 2007; Yoon, Duncan, Lee, Scarloss & Shapley, 2007). The editors of this volume agree with the carefully considered conclusion that a general conceptual saturation of effective teacher learning exists (Wayne et al.) while research of more effective features of specific situations and contexts (also summarized in the chapters of van Veen, Zwart and Meirink, and Little) is called for. One implication suggests the need for more large-scale designed studies, but another implication, indeed, the focus of this volume, is to inquire into and explore the multifarious topics and themes in the simultaneously divergent and specific contexts.

The key themes emerging in the opening stage-setting chapters situate teacher learning research on a complex and diverse landscape (van Veen, Zwart and Meirink). Little's chapter shifts attention from the more macro to a micro focus in her inquiry on a learning-centered school. The emerging and merging themes include conceptual theories for teacher learning (Loughran, Craig and Wallace, and Mulholland), teacher introspections as a heuristic for personal awareness and renewal (Attema-Noordewier et al. and Meijer and Oolbekking), teacher learning in dialogical and social contexts (Parr and Doecke, Kooy and Colarusso, and Ying) and situated professional learning (Mitchell and Alexandrou, Hadjiachilleos and Avraamidou, and Nilsson).

An overview of the discussions on teacher learning in this volume indicates key issues that require research and dialogues across boundaries, perspectives and paradigms. The first key issue relates to the persistent fragmented condition of research in PD for teachers. The resulting disconnect is that teachers receive courses that are disconnected to each other, selected based on the current demands and questions, but not related to teachers' professional learning needs over a longer period of time (Borko, 2004). In other words, in most cases, no curriculum for teacher learning seems to exist. This lack of curriculum is most apparent for novice teachers, who often experience a huge difference between teacher education programs (preservice) and teaching in the school. Increasingly, induction programs are designed and implemented for beginning teachers, but often in these programs the link with the teacher educations programs is weak. For more experienced teachers, their PD is hardly connected to previous programs. It should be noted that teachers differ significantly in their PD and learning needs, which is related to the specific context they work in and many personal and professional factors (cf. Day, Sammons, Stobart, Kington & Gu, 2007). However, based on what we know about how teachers develop from beginning to experienced and expert teachers (Berliner, 2004; Day et al.; Huberman, 1993), it would be relevant to explore how a curriculum for specific professional life phases could be designed, related to teachers' individual learning concerns and local and regional policy agendas.

Exploring such a professional lifelong learning is also relevant in the light of current policy directions; for instance, European Union nation members agreed in 2008 to promote teacher education as lifelong learning: "ensuring that provision for teachers' initial education, early career support and further professional development is coordinated, coherent, adequately resourced and quality assured" (Scheerens, 2009, p. 13). The members agreed to support teachers by:

> ensuring that teachers have access to effective early career support (induction) programs at the start of their career, and adequate mentoring support throughout their careers. . . . encouraging and supporting teachers throughout their careers to review their learning needs and to acquire new knowledge, skills and competence through formal, informal and non-formal learning. (Scheerens, 2009, p. 14)

Although the European Union agreement is an important policy initiative, the teaching profession is inadequately organized for realizing the lifelong learning mandate. As noted, schools are not well designed for teachers to learn and, thus, it will be incumbent upon policy makers to initiate a process that satisfies the call for lifelong teacher learning.

This leads to another key theme for research: negotiating the structure and culture of the schools to make teacher learning an ongoing and consistent reality. If, as Bartlett (2004) states, we get the teachers we organize for, then it follows also that we get the teacher learning we organize for. Van Veen, Zwart and Meirink indicate that schools place less emphasis on teacher learning because student learning and achievement remain the primary concerns. Research on teacher learning and PD fails to address how school organization, structure and culture impact the teacher learning opportunities. School organization literature and research on learning at the workplace, however, offer rich and valuable approaches (cf. Imants & van Veen, 2010; Little, this volume; Sleegers & Leithwood, 2010; Smylie, 1995).

A school culture promoting teacher learning ideologically and practically reflects perceptions of teachers as professionals and learning as an ongoing means of building skill and expertise. Craig argued that the underlying conceptions of policy makers, school leaders and instructional leaders inform the ways teacher learning programs are developed and organized. Kooy (2006) found that teacher learning is only infrequently scripted into school culture and, consequently, creates learning communities for teachers in both off-site and on-site settings. Programs that assume teaching is complex and that teachers can develop into better teachers and learners reflect the growth model reflected in most chapters in this volume.

Key to the possibilities for teacher learning that matters is the suggestion that teachers become active agents in their own PD. This "teacher as agent of change" model addresses what we have learned but need to know much more about since the conception of teachers as agents is crucial for successful learning, innovation and change. The inextricable link between reforms and policies, on the one hand, and actualizing them in classrooms, on the other hand, requires research that explores the liminal space between (how teacher knowledge becomes teacher practice, for instance). In that context, it also begs the question of how teacher learning and knowledge itself is effectively (and socially) constructed. In such a framework, teachers are subjects of reform and change.

The concept of teacher identity and role changes in the ways teacher work is organized. In the last two decades, the nature of teacher work has exponentially expanded. The notions of collective responsibility for students and higher involvement in school policies increasingly involves teacher tasks outside of and alongside their classroom teaching responsibilities. In secondary schools in the Netherlands, for instance, teachers spend less than 50% of time in actual classroom teaching (with 25% each for preparation and school-related tasks). This leaves little time for involvement in professional learning initiatives. This points to the need for structural changes (Bartlett, 2004; van Veen, 2008) and finding ways to understand how and what structures support teaching learning in schools.

The complexities of understanding and developing a shared vision on what constitutes good teaching reaches into developing policies and practices and for sustained and ongoing professional learning. We suggest that more research investigate how the underlying conception of professional learning communities, teachers and teaching reflect and bring teachers together in intellectual communities, perceive teachers as intellectuals and researchers and teaching as intellectual activity. Since, ultimately, teaching learning matters insofar as it shapes the learning processes of students, more research into how students learn and achieve becomes critical.

In conclusion, we suggest that the landscapes described in this volume reveal, at the deepest levels, teacher learning that matters. It clearly illustrates that while challenging and complex, teacher learning deserves serious attention since, regardless of the cultural or national or educational context, its quality positively shapes and directs the learning and achievements of students. Ultimately, all educational goals point to student learning and achievement. We invite the reader to use this volume as a guide to discover new sights and to continue this journey. We imagine that researchers around the globe will create a community that reflexively engages in critical dialogue and research into the complex networks of teacher learning that matters.

REFERENCES

Bartlett, L. (2004). Expanding teacher work roles: A resource for retention or recipe for overwork? *Journal of Education Policy, 19*(5), 565–582.

Berliner, D. C. (2004). Expert teachers: Their characteristics, development and accomplishments. *Bulletin of science, technology and society, 24*(3), 200–212.

Borko, H. (2004). Professional development and teacher learning: Mapping the terrain. *Educational Researcher, 33*(8), 3–15.

Borko, H., Jacobs, J. & Koellner, K. (2010). Contemporary approaches to teacher professional development. In E. Baker, B. McGaw & P. Peterson (Eds.), *International encyclopedia of education* (3rd ed.) (pp. 548–555). Oxford: Elsevier Scientific Publishers.

Day, C., Sammons, P., Stobart, G., Kington, A. & Gu, Q. (2007). *Teachers matter: Connecting work, lives and effectiveness.* Berkshire: Open University Press, McGraw-Hill

Desimone, L. M. (2009). Improving impact studies of teachers' professional development: Toward better conceptualizations and measures. *Educational Researcher, 38*(3), 181–199.

Garet, M. S., Cronen, S., Eaton, M., Kurki, A., Ludwig, M., Jones, W., Uekawa, W., Falk, A., Bloom, H. S., Doolittle, F., Zhu, P., Sztejnberg, L., & Silverberg, M. (2008). *The impact of two professional development interventions on early reading instruction and achievement.* Washington, DC: National Center for Educational Evaluation and Regional Assistance, Institute of Education Science, U.S. Department of Education.

Huberman, M. (1993). *The lives of teachers.* London: Cassell.

Imants, J., & van Veen, K. (2010). Teacher learning as workplace learning. In E. Baker, B. McGaw & P. Peterson (Eds.), *International encyclopedia of education* (3rd ed.) (pp. 569–574). Oxford: Elsevier Scientific Publishers.

Kennedy, M. (1998). *Form and substance of in-service teacher education.* Madison: National Institute for Science Education, University of Wisconsin-Madison.

Kooy, M. (2006). *Telling stories in book clubs: Women teachers and professional development.* New York: Springer.

Raudenbush, S. W. (2005). Learning from attempts to improve schooling: The contribution of methodological diversity. *Educational Researcher, 34*(25), 25–31.

Scheerens, J. (Ed) (2009). *Teachers' professional development. Europe in international comparison. A secondary analysis based on the TALIS dataset.* Luxembourg: Office for Official Publications of the European Union.

Slavin, R. (2008). Perspectives on evidence-based research in education—What works? Issues in synthesizing educational program evaluations. *Educational Researcher, 37*(1), 5–14.

Sleegers, P., & Leithwood, K. (2010). School development for teacher learning and change. In E. Baker, B. McGaw & P. Peterson (Eds.), *International encyclopedia of education* (3rd ed.) (pp. 557–561). Oxford: Elsevier Scientific Publishers.

Smith, C., & Gillespie, M. (2007). Research on professional development and teacher change: Implications for adult basic education. *Review of Adult Learning and Literacy, 7,* 205–244.

Smylie, M. A. (1995). Teacher learning in the workplace: Implications for school reform. In T. R. Guskey & M. Huberman (Eds.), *Professional development in education: New paradigms and practices* (pp. 92–113). New York: Teachers College Press.

Timperley, H., Wilson, A., Barrar, H. & Fung, I. (2007). *Teacher professional learning and development. Best evidence synthesis iteration (BES).* Wellington: Ministry of Education.

van Veen, K. (2008). Analysing teachers' working conditions from the perspective of teachers as professionals: The case of Dutch high school teachers. In J. Ax & P. Ponte (Eds.), *Critiquing praxis: Conceptual and empirical trends in the teaching profession* (pp. 91–112). Rotterdam: Sense Publishers.

Wayne, A. J., Yoon, K. S., Zhu, P., Cronen, S. & Garet, M. S. (2008). Experimenting with teacher professional development: Motives & methods. *Educational Researcher, 37*(8), 469–479.

Yoon, K. S., Duncan, T., Lee, S. W. Y., Scarloss, B. & Shapley, K. (2007). *Reviewing the evidence on how teacher professional development affects student achievement* (Issues & Answers Report, REL 2007–No.033). Washington, DC: Department of Education, Institute of Education Sciences, National Center for Education Evaluation and Regional Assistance, Regional Educational Laboratory Southwest.

Contributors

Alex Alexandrou is currently a freelance academic working with the Sir John Cass School of Education, University of East London. He has worked in both the public and private sectors, gaining considerable experience in developing and evaluating professional development programs, notably for teachers, military and mine action personnel. Alex is currently leading the development and delivery of leadership programs for teachers as well as being part of an international academic research project investigating teacher leadership in unusual contexts. He is an associate editor of the academic journal *Professional Development in Education* and a Visiting Professor at the Toulouse Business School.

Saskia Attema-Noordewier is a teacher educator, trainer and PhD student working at VU University in the Netherlands. Her main interests are reflection, coaching and communication in a school environment. She is always looking for a setting in which learning can take place naturally and with inspiration. The central question guiding her work is: How can people work, learn and live in contact with their full potential? In addition to her work at VU University she works as a trainer and coach at the Institute of Multilevel Learning.

Lucy Avraamidou is an Assistant Professor of Science Education at the University of Nicosia. Her research is associated with theoretical and empirical explorations of what it means to teach and understand science with the use of primarily qualitative, interpretive approaches. The theoretical framework of her work draws upon epistemological aspects of science and is informed by contemporary perspectives in cognitive psychology and philosophy of science. These perspectives are applied to teacher learning and development with emphasis on the development of teachers' Pedagogical Content Knowledge for giving priority to evidence and explanation in science teaching in both formal and informal learning environments. She has participated in a number of European and local projects and has published her work in various international science education refereed journals.

Dana Colarusso's PhD thesis, *Teaching English in the Global Age: Cultural Conversations* (OISE, 2009) won the Canadian Association for Teacher Education Dissertation Award. Dana's research interests include multicultural education, social constructivist methods in education, theories of culture and the philosophy of teaching literature. She has contributed for several years as a research assistant to Dr. Mary Kooy's longitudinal study on teacher and student learning communities. In addition, she has recently acted as liaison for the implementation of the Settlement Workers in Schools program in the Durham region. Dana has published articles in the *Canadian Journal of Education* and *Multicultural Shakespeare: Translation, Appropriation, Performance.* Dana builds her professional knowledge from her 12-year Secondary English teaching career. Currently, she is a freelance educational writer and editor.

Cheryl Craig is a Professor in the Department of Curriculum and Instruction, College of Education, University of Houston, where she coordinates the Teaching and Teacher Education program area and is the Director of Elementary Education. Her research centers on the influence of school reform on teachers' knowledge developments and their communities of knowing. Craig has authored several handbook chapters and is a regular contributor to such journals as *Teaching and Teacher Education*; *Teachers and Teaching: Theory and Practice*; *Teachers College Record*; and *American Educational Research Journal.* Her book, *Narrative Inquiries of School Reform*, was published in 2003 (Information Age Publishing). Craig currently is editor of the Association of Teacher Educators' Yearbook and secretary of the International Study Association of Teachers and Teaching.

Brenton Doecke is Chair in Education and Director: Centre for Partnerships and Projects in Education at Deakin University, Melbourne. His research interests include English Curriculum and Pedagogy, Professional Identity and the impact of Standards-Based Reforms. He played a leading role, as a member of the Australian Association for the Teaching of English, in the development of the Standards for Teachers of English Language and Literacy, providing an alternative to neoliberal constructions of professional practice. His most recent publications include *Literary Praxis: A Conversational Inquiry into the Teaching of Literature*, coedited with Piet-Hein van de Ven (Rotterdam: Sense Publishers, 2011), and a coauthored book with Douglas McClenaghan, *Confronting Practice: Classroom Based Inquiries into Language and Learning* (Putney NSW: Phoenix Education, 2011).

Stella Hadjiachilleos is an instructor at the Environmental Education Unit of the Cyprus Pedagogical Institute, and also a Lecturer of Science Education at the University of Nicosia. Her research interests are related to teaching and learning science concepts in nonformal and informal settings, conceptual change in science and to the development of teachers' Pedagogical Content Knowledge. She has developed and implemented innovative environmental education programs, which have been implemented with students from all levels of education in Cyprus. Her research has been presented in international conferences and has been published in various refereed journals.

Judith Warren Little is a Professor in Policy, Organization, Measurement and Evaluation and currently dean of the Graduate School of Education of the University of California, Berkeley, U.S. Her research interests center on the organizational and occupational contexts of teaching, with special attention to teachers' collegial relationships and to the contexts, policies and practices of teachers' professional development. In pursuing these interests, she attempts to balance attention to the daily life of schools ("the search for locally situated meanings, identities and relationships") with a broader view of the larger social, institutional and policy environments in which the work of teaching resides.

John Loughran is the dean and Foundation Chair in Curriculum and Pedagogy in the Faculty of Education, Monash University. John was a science teacher for 10 years before moving into teacher education. His research has spanned both science education and the related fields of professional knowledge, reflective practice and teacher research. John was the cofounding editor of Studying Teacher Education and his recent books include: *What Expert Teachers Do* (Allen and Unwin/Routledge, 2010); *Developing a Pedagogy of Teacher Education: Understanding Teaching and Learning about Teaching* (Routledge, 2006); *Understanding and Developing Science Teachers' Pedagogical Content Knowledge* (Sense Publishers, 2006); *The International Handbook of Self-Study of Teaching and Teacher Education Practices* (Kluwer, 2004).

Mary Kooy is an Associate Professor in the Department of Curriculum, Teaching and Learning and Director of the Centre for Teacher Education and Development at the Ontario Institute for Studies in Education of the University of Toronto in Canada. Her research interests include professional learning and development for teachers. Her longitudinal research began in 2000 with novice teachers (*Telling Stories in Book Clubs: Women Teachers and Professional Development*), continued as school-based research (2006–2010). The longitudinal inquiry, now entering phase three, will explore the effects on an online professional community distributed across Canada. Dr. Kooy teaches courses in graduate programs in professional learning communities, teacher induction and curriculum innovation.

Fred Korthagen is a Professor of Education at Utrecht University in the Netherlands, specializing in teacher education. His primary fields of interest are the professional development of teachers and teacher educators, and the pedagogy of teacher education. He has published many articles and books on these issues. Most known is his 2001 book *Linking Practice and Theory: The Pedagogy of Realistic Teacher Education*. He has been a keynote speaker at many international conferences. Twice, in 2000 and in 2006, Fred Korthagen received the Exemplary Research in Teaching and Teacher Education Award from the division Teaching and Teacher Education of the AERA. In 2009, he received the Distinguished Research Award from the Association of Teacher Educators in the United States. Fred Korthagen is not only involved in research, but he also works as a senior trainer and consultant in schools at all educational levels, in the Netherlands and in many other countries. He is one of the developers of the new approach to the professional development of teachers and school principals called *multilevel learning*, which has drawn international attention.

Paulien C. Meijer is head of the research department and Associate Professor in the research program "Teacher learning and expertise throughout the professional career" at Utrecht University (the Netherlands), Department of Education. Her research interests are teacher learning (both beginning and experienced teachers), teacher education, specifically with a focus on identity development and processes of transformative learning. She publishes preferably with colleagues from various research institutes in order to combine different research experiences and traditions. She supervises a range of PhD students in her area of interest. Her teaching experiences are in secondary education, teacher education, in the research master Educational Sciences and in the PhD program of the Dutch research school for Educational Research.

Jacobiene Meirink is an Assistant Professor at ICLON, Leiden University Graduate School of Teaching. She also works at the national Dutch teacher learning center. Her research interests are teacher professional development, teacher collaboration and teacher workplace learning.

Helen Mitchell is currently director of Continuing Professional Development at the Sir John Cass School of education, University of East London. She manages and teaches on MA Education, Master's in Teaching and Learning, and the MA Learning and Teaching in Higher Education programs, and manages partnerships associated with the MA Education school-based provision. Helen moved from teaching in primary schools in East London to teach science and music on the primary PGCE program and to lead mentor training. Her research interests include understanding the relationship between teacher development and the quality of pupil learning experiences and in developing methodologies to support this. She has been involved in developing a London-wide mentor training framework and has training and experience in coaching.

Judith Mulholland is Head of School of Education of the Australian Catholic University. She joined the staff at McAuley College in 1990 just before the college became part of Australian Catholic University. She had previously been a sessional science education lecturer at MtGravatt BCAE, a secondary science teacher in the UK and a biological sciences lecturer at QIT. She has been Bachelor of Education (Primary) course coordinator (1996–2001), and is currently Head of School of Education In Queensland. In 2008, she received an ALTC (Carrick) citation for her work in preservice teacher education and primary school science.

Pernilla Nilsson is an Associate Professor in Science Education and a teacher educator (mainly primary science) and researcher at Halmstad University in Sweden. She is also the chair of the Swedish national association of research in science education. For 9 years she has been responsible for the primary and secondary science teacher education program. In 2002 she also initiated the work with building up a science learning center at the university, which has since then been the context for her research as well as teaching practices for preservice and in-service teacher education. Her research interests concern primary teachers' and primary science student teachers' professional development such as the development of Pedagogical Content Knowledge and factors that influence that development.

Helma W. Oolbekkink is Assistant Professor at Radboud University Nijmegen (the Netherlands), department of Teacher Education. She teaches preservice teachers in the language department and gives in-service training and supervision to experienced teachers on research skills. Her research interests are in the area of professional development of teachers, more specifically through collaborative learning and practitioner research.

Graham Parr is a senior lecturer in the Faculty of Education, Monash University, Australia. His research interests include teacher professional learning, English and literature teaching, professional identity and educational work. As a secondary teacher and now as a researcher and teacher educator he has maintained strong connections with English teacher professional associations in Australia and internationally, and has published in a range of international peer-reviewed journals, including *English in Australia, Changing English, English Teaching: Practice and Critique* and *Mentoring and Tutoring*. In 2010, he published *Inquiry-Based Professional Learning: Speaking Back to Standards-Based Reforms*, drawing on his award-winning PhD dissertation.

With Doecke he coedited *Writing = Learning* (2005), a collection of scholarly writing about the nature and role of writing in student and professional learning. In 2008, with Doecke and North, he coauthored a large-scale report into teacher professional learning for the Australian government, titled *National Mapping of Teacher Professional Learning in Australia*. He has coedited a series of three books of teachers' writing about their professional learning, *Leading Professional Learning: A Case Book of Learning* (2010), *Willing to Lead: Leading Professional Learning* (2009) and *Leading Teachers' Professional Learning: Cases of Professional Dilemmas* (2008).

Klaas van Veen is an Associate Professor at ICLON Graduate School of Teaching, Leiden University in the Netherlands, where he is involved in the teacher education program and research. Since 2007, he has been the director of the National Teacher Learning Center, which is aimed at collecting recent knowledge, insights and programs on teacher learning for everyone involved in teacher development. His research interests focus on issues central to teachers and the organization of their work: teachers' professional lives and workplace conditions, educational change, teacher learning and education.

John Wallace is a Professor at the department of curriculum, teaching and learning at OISE, University of Toronto, Canada. He is a science educator whose scholarly publications include over 130 books and monographs, book chapters and refereed journal articles. His most recent coedited books are *Dilemmas of Science Teaching: Perspectives on Problems of Practice* (RoutledgeFalmer, 2002); *Leadership and Professional Development: New Possibilities for Enhancing Teacher Learning* (Routledge-Falmer, 2003); and *Contemporary Qualitative Research: Exemplars for Science and Mathematics Educators* (Springer, 2007). He is involved in several research projects in the field of teacher learning (including studies into teacher knowledge, teacher leadership and case methods in teacher education) and curriculum integration.

Issa Danjun Ying is a Senior Research Assistant in the Hong Kong Institute of Education, working on a research project that promotes autonomy by employing pedagogical strategies in various teacher education courses. As teacher educator, her research interests are primarily in the areas of teacher development, teacher identity, professional learning community and teacher learner autonomy. She is also keen on discourse analysis, narrative inquiry and action research. Since 1997, she has been working on a curriculum innovation called RICH (an acronym of Research-based learning, Integrated curriculum, Cooperative learning and Humanistic outcomes) as one of its initiators in Zhejiang Normal University, China. Since 2001, she has been actively involved in building a cross-institutional teacher community under the theme Teachers and Teacher Educators in Action Learning (TATEAL), initiated by Hangzhou Teachers' College, China. She was awarded a master's degree at the University of Central Lancashire (UK) in 2000 and a PhD degree at the University of Hong Kong in 2010.

Rosanne Zwart is an Assistant Professor at VU University in the Netherlands. Her primary fields of interest are various aspects of the professional development of teachers and teacher educators: teacher learning through reciprocal peer coaching and the knowledge development of teacher educators through (self-study) research. She also works at the National Dutch Teacher Learning Center at Leiden University.

Index